Proletarian Lives

Based on multi-year ethnographic fieldwork on the Unemployed Workers' Movement in Argentina (also known as the piqueteros), *Proletarian Lives* provides a case study of how workers affected by job loss protect their traditional forms of life by engaging in progressive grassroots mobilization. Using life-history interviews and participant observation, the book analyzes why some activists develop a strong attachment to the movement despite initial reluctance and frequent ideological differences. Marcos Pérez argues that a key appeal of participation is the opportunity to engage in age and gender-specific practices associated with a respectable blue-collar lifestyle threatened by long-term socioeconomic decline. Through their daily involvement in the movement, older participants reconstruct the routines they associate with a golden past in which factory jobs were plentiful, younger activists develop the kind of habits they were raised to see as valuable, and all members protect communal activities undermined by the expansion of poverty and violence.

Marcos E. Pérez is Assistant Professor of Sociology at Washington and Lee University. His research has appeared in the *Latin American Research Review*, Qualitative Sociology, Mobilization, *Latin American Perspectives, Conflicto Social, Sociedad*, and *Argumentos*.

T0384754

Cambridge Studies in Contentious Politics

General Editor

David S. Meyer *University of California, Irvine*

Editors

Mark Beissinger *Princeton University*
Donatella della Porta *Scuola Normale Superiore*
Jack A. Goldstone *George Mason University*
Michael Hanagan *Vassar College*
Holly J. McCammon *Vanderbilt University*
Doug McAdam *Stanford University and Center for Advanced Study
in the Behavioral Sciences*
Sarah Soule *Stanford University*
Suzanne Staggenborg *University of Pittsburgh*
Sidney Tarrow *Cornell University*
Charles Tilly (d. 2008) *Columbia University*
Elisabeth J. Wood *Yale University*
Deborah Yashar *Princeton University*

Continued after the index

Proletarian Lives

Routines, Identity, and Culture in Contentious Politics

MARCOS E. PÉREZ

Washington and Lee University

Shaftesbury Road, Cambridge CB2 8EA, United Kingdom

One Liberty Plaza, 20th Floor, New York, NY 10006, USA

477 Williamstown Road, Port Melbourne, VIC 3207, Australia

314–321, 3rd Floor, Plot 3, Splendor Forum, Jasola District Centre, New Delhi – 110025, India

103 Penang Road, #05–06/07, Visioncrest Commercial, Singapore 238467

Cambridge University Press is part of Cambridge University Press & Assessment, a department of the University of Cambridge.

We share the University's mission to contribute to society through the pursuit of education, learning and research at the highest international levels of excellence.

www.cambridge.org
Information on this title: www.cambridge.org/9781009015936

DOI: 10.1017/9781009030779

First published 2022
First paperback edition 2023

A catalogue record for this publication is available from the British Library

ISBN   978-1-316-51664-5   Hardback
ISBN   978-1-009-01593-6   Paperback

To Lindsey

Contents

Figures

Acknowledgments

A large number of people made this book possible. To all of them, my infinite thanks.

My first acknowledgment goes to the men and women in the Unemployed Workers' Movement, who shared with me their experiences, memories, and struggles. Even though I cannot reveal the real name of any respondent, each one of them was exceedingly generous with me.

Sara Doskow at Cambridge University Press played an essential role in the project. She first met with me when this book was little more than a prospectus and over time offered personal encouragement and critical ideas. Along with Cameron Daddis, Jadyn Fauconier-Herry, and Claire Sissen, she guided me through the intricacies of the editorial process and answered all my questions as the manuscript reached completion. Two anonymous reviewers provided extremely useful feedback to an earlier version of this book.

My interest in social movements emerged during my undergraduate years at Torcuato Di Tella University. Faculty encouraged my work, helped me develop my academic career after I graduated, and invited me many times in subsequent years to present my findings and discuss my research. Catalina Smulovitz, my undergraduate thesis advisor, was essential in helping me navigate graduate school applications and continued to support me once I became a PhD student. Juan Carlos Torre suggested important ways to sharpen my research question and strengthen my argument. I also thank Enrique Peruzzotti, Ana Maria Mustapic, Rut Diamint, Carlos Gervasoni, and Javier Zelaznik for their feedback.

At the University of Texas at Austin, I benefited from an outstanding group of scholars. My advisor, Javier Auyero, taught me to be a better ethnographer, develop a compelling research question, and connect my specific interests with crucial debates in social science. He was supportive of my work in countless ways and did not hesitate to offer constructive criticism when he felt my analysis needed improvement. Gracias, Javier.

I also had a great dissertation committee, in which the skills of different scholars complemented each other. Michael Young shared his extensive knowledge of social movement theory. Bryan Roberts offered the advice accumulated over decades of work as a leading Latin Americanist. Mounira Maya Charrad encouraged me to expand my focus beyond my specific case of study. Finally, Henry Dietz reminded me of the importance of interdisciplinarity and insisted I do not forget my political science roots.

Other professors at the University of Texas at Austin offered advice in too many ways to count. I thank Sheldon Ekland-Olson, Daniel Fridman, Harel Shapira, Christine Williams, Ari Adut, Peter Ward, Gloria Gonzalez-Lopez, Leticia Marteleto, Arthur Sakamoto, Penny Green, and many more.

I was also fortunate to share my days in Austin with an incredible group of fellow students, many of whom have become lifelong friends. Adrian Popan, Yuka Minagawa, Isaac Sasson, Ori Swed, Daniel Jaster, Kristine Kilanski, Vivian Shaw, Caitlin Collins, Jacinto Cuvi, Jen Scott, Jorge Derpic, Pamela Neumann, Nino Bariola, Kate Averett, David McClendon, Katherine Sobering, Katherine Jensen, Megan Neely, Hyun Jeong Ha, Corey McZeal, Esther Sullivan, Amina Zarrugh, Maro Youssef, Viviana Salinas, Denise Gerber, Laura Spagnolo, Jessica Dunning-Lozano, Sergio Cabrera, Erika Grajeda, Claude Bonazzo, Christine Wheatley, Maricarmen Hernández, and Emily Spangenberg. Through our shared time in the Department of Sociology, the Population Research Center, the Urban Ethnography Lab, and the intramural soccer team we founded, we developed long-lasting connections.

I was privileged to follow my PhD with a great postdoctoral fellowship at Colby College. Neil Gross was a constant source of ideas and inspiration. He helped me turn my dissertation into a book project and take the theoretical side of my research in directions I had not even envisioned. I also had the immense fortune of sharing two years with a community of sociologists that further enriched my work: Cheryl Gilkes, Nicole Denier, Ian Mullins, Natalie Aviles, Christel Kesler, and Damon Maryl.

At my current academic home, the Department of Sociology and Anthropology at Washington and Lee University, I have found a group of amazing colleagues who helped me complete this book. I thank Jon Eastwood, Sascha Goluboff, Lynny Chin, Alison Bell, Don Gaylord, Krzysztof Jasiewicz, Harvey Markowitz, Michael Laughy, Sandhya Narayanan, Howard Pickett, and David Novack.

Throughout the years, numerous people have helped me develop my research and offered all kinds of logistical help and suggestions for improving the project. I thus thank Julieta Daelli, Carolina Ocar, Andres Schipani, Matías Dewey, Federico Schuster, German Pérez, Melchor Armesto, Sebastián Pereyra, Julieta Quirós, Santiago Battezzatti, Kevin Remington, Alejandro Grimson, Virginia Manzano, Marcelo Bergman, Ana Natalucci, Federico Rossi, Patricio Giusto, James Jasper, Catherine Corrigall-Brown, Jocelyn Viterna, Ziad Munson, Kenneth Andrews, and Drew Halfmann.

The administrative staff at the University of Texas at Austin, Colby College, and Washington and Lee University were incredibly helpful as the project developed. Evelyn Porter, Leslie Lima, and Peggy Herring, in particular, were extremely patient and supportive. To them, my immense thanks.

The field research leading to this book was supported by funds from the Department of Sociology and the Lozano Long Institute of Latin American Studies at the University of Texas at Austin, as well as by a Doctoral Dissertation Research Improvement Grant from the National Science Foundation (Award ID: 1406244). In addition, the Gino Germani Research Institute at the University of Buenos Aires provided substantial logistical support for my fieldwork. Two Lenfest grants from Washington and Lee University supported the final stages of manuscript writing.

I shared early findings from this project at various annual meetings of the American Sociological Association, the Society for the Study of Social Problems, the Latin American Studies Association, and the International Studies Association. I also presented in workshops at the Lozano Long Institute of Latin American Studies at the University of Texas at Austin, the Department of Political Science and International Studies at Torcuato Di Tella University, and the Center for the Study of Social Movements at the University of Notre Dame. I took part in the Twenty-First Alternative Futures and Popular Protest Conference at Manchester Metropolitan University and the First Mobilization Conference on Social Movements at San Diego State University. Each of these meetings was an opportunity to share ideas and receive useful feedback, which improved the quality of my work.

On the personal side, I have been blessed with an amazing family. To my parents, Giovanna Calligaro and Norberto Pérez, goes all my gratitude. They never ceased to believe in my potential and invest their sometimes scarce resources in my education. My siblings, Ana Laura, Mariana, Alejo, and Lisandro, also shared, in different forms, their love for me and my work. To them, my siblings-in-law, and my beautiful nephews and nieces, all my recognition.

Finally, none of this would make any sense without my wife, Lindsey Pérez, to whom this book is dedicated. Over the years, she tolerated my long working hours and extended research trips. She proofread my work and listened patiently as I tried to articulate my arguments, always suggesting improvements. Lindsey had faith in me when I doubted myself and shared my joy over achievements. All along the way, she loved me selflessly and completed me. A few years ago, we were blessed with the arrival of our beloved son, Benjamin. No me alcanzan las palabras para decirles cuanto los amo.

I

Introduction

It is a cold May afternoon, and a several-hours-long meeting of activists in the district of La Matanza has just ended. It is time to leave, but I have never been to this particular neighborhood before and I have no idea where to go. Someone explains to me how to get to the bus stop, but I must look confused, for she rapidly tells me to join Antonella,[1] who is just heading for the exact same place.

Antonella is a woman in her late sixties, with a small frame and the wrinkled face of those who have worked hard all their life. As soon as we start walking, I realize she is an enthusiastic talker, with a cheerful attitude despite a frequently tragic personal story. Born in a poor rural community in the northern province of Santiago del Estero, her mother died during her birth. Abandoned by her father soon afterwards, she was raised by an aunt and a grandmother, who, despite extreme poverty and hunger, insisted that she study. By age fourteen, however, she had to drop out of school and help her family by doing odd jobs as a domestic worker and farmhand. At twenty, she moved to the national capital of Buenos Aires seeking a better life. A relative found her a job as a live-in maid, and for five years, she cleaned, cooked, and took care of several children for a wealthy family. When she was twenty-five, she married a construction worker who had also migrated from Santiago to Buenos Aires. The couple bought a small plot in what then was a sparsely inhabited area of Greater Buenos Aires and slowly began to build their house. She quit her

---

[1] To protect the anonymity of respondents, all names of people and their organizations have been replaced with pseudonyms.

live-in job but kept working as a housecleaner until her first child was born. Afterwards, she stayed at home and raised two daughters and a son.

This quaint domestic lifestyle ended with one of the regular crises that have affected Argentina's economy over the last forty years. Antonella's husband lost his job, and the family had to rely on soup kitchens for food. To make ends meet, she left her children in the care of her twelve-year-old daughter and took a cleaning job in a fur coat factory. This would become the beginning of a new occupation: Other workers gradually taught her the trade, and she used lunch breaks to practice with the machinery. Over time, she started to moonlight for the company. Every day, she went home with pieces of coats, which she sewed together at night. For more than a decade, she dedicated herself to this occupation, first as a side job and later full-time. Eventually, she stopped: Her husband by that time had a better income as an independent contractor, the children were growing up, and she felt the need to be around to make sure they behaved and studied.

However, the family's situation took a turn for the worse again in the late 1990s with the first effects of the recession that would culminate in the 2001–2002 economic collapse of the country. Unemployment soared, and people in poor communities had increasing difficulties earning a living. Antonella's daughter told her about a grassroots organization that was recruiting people to demand jobs and subsidies for the unemployed and mentioned a small-scale textile production project that the group was creating with funds from the government. Antonella told her daughter she would gladly help her with sewing but would never attend meetings or demonstrations. Her husband had always liked to participate in these kinds of events, but she never shared his interests and was deeply skeptical of politics. As the crisis deepened, the family began to rely more and more on the organization: At different points, all her children and her husband took part in workfare programs managed by the group.

With time, however, Antonella became increasingly involved. She does not recall exactly when it happened, but as time passed, she began to enjoy attending meetings and working with other activists. By her first anniversary in the movement, she was already a neighborhood coordinator, a position she has never abandoned. Other members of her family dropped out when their economic situation improved: Her daughter graduated from vocational school and found a job as a teacher, and her husband received a pension that did not depend on the organization. However, Antonella followed another trajectory. Even though she is also retired, she continues to work in a soup kitchen, represents her neighborhood in meetings, and takes part in most demonstrations. Since she receives government-funded retiree benefits, she cannot enroll in a workfare plan. Consequently, she only obtains limited resources from the organization through informal means. Still, she devotes more hours to the group than many other participants.

Antonella is one of the millions of people affected by Argentina's remarkable transition from being one of the most egalitarian societies in Latin America to one marked by high inequality and exclusion. Despite political and economic instability, for most of the twentieth century workers in the country enjoyed low unemployment, relatively high salaries, and generous welfare policies associated with strong union membership and modest levels of informality. However, the 1970s saw the beginning of a process of deindustrialization, associated with pro-market economic policies implemented first by the 1976–1983 military dictatorship and in a much more intense form by the 1990s administration of Carlos Menem. The consequence was a substantial deterioration in the job market, which became particularly acute in 2001–2002, when a combination of external shocks and an overvalued currency led to the deepest economic crisis in the nation's history.[2] Joblessness grew from less than 3 percent in 1980 to more than 20 percent in 2002. In addition, the share of manufacturing jobs fell by half and informal labor doubled. Despite periods of economic expansion since then, these indicators remain relatively weak. Even though the unemployment rate has fallen to about 10 percent,[3] only one in eight jobs are in the manufacturing sector, and informality continues to affect one third of all workers.[4]

In other words, there is a new normal in the Argentinean economy, which has become more service-oriented. The labor market is more segmented, and well-paying positions are fewer and require extensive credentials and skills. These transformations have had an enormous impact on the daily life of working-class families. Entire communities have been excluded from the formal labor market, with devastating consequences. Young people without access to the quality education required by the jobs available, as well as middle-aged individuals who are deemed too old to be

---

[2] For more on the economic collapse of 2001–2002 and its consequences, see Lozano (2002) and Gerchunoff and Llach (2003).

[3] The unemployment rate fell to 10 percent in 2006 and averaged 8 percent between 2007 and 2019. The source for these data is the World Bank Open Data database, available at https://data.worldbank.org/ (last accessed June 17, 2020).

[4] For more information on the persistence of these indicators, see MTEYSS (2013) and CEPAL (2015).

retrained, have great difficulties finding stable occupation. The result has
been an undermining of the well-being, stability, and safety of countless
households.

Not surprisingly, Argentineans reacted to these challenges in different
ways. Antonella is among the thousands who did so by joining one of the
most prominent forms of collective action in the nation's recent history.
Faced with drastic increases in structural unemployment and informality,
community leaders in the 1990s began to establish groups of laid-off
workers in different cities, demanding access to jobs and relief programs.
Despite their diverse origins, these groups rapidly developed similar repertoires that helped them recruit members and gain influence, giving birth
to what came to be known as the Unemployed Workers' Movement, or
piqueteros. Most of these organizations structured as networks of local
groups that stage roadblocks (*piquetes* in Spanish) to demand the distribution of social assistance. If successful, they distribute part of these
resources among participants and use the rest to develop an extensive
array of social services in areas where the welfare arm of the state has
retreated.

Antonella's less-than-straightforward trajectory toward involvement
in her organization is quite common. In fact, the experiences of rank-
and-file activists in the movement pose an intriguing puzzle. Most recruits
joined, in the words of many an informant, "due to necessity": They were
in dire need of resources, and an acquaintance told them about a group
that was "signing people up" for a social program. The vast majority
initially held negative views of the piqueteros and had limited experience
in politics. Once recruited, they started attending demonstrations and
other activities, receiving foodstuffs regularly, until they obtained a state-
funded workfare plan. Since organizations usually administer these positions directly, respondents are expected to sustain their involvement in
order to continue receiving benefits. Given these circumstances, we would
expect most of them to participate for as long as they acquire resources
and to withdraw when more effective sources of income become available.
However, the subsequent behavior of many of them challenges these
expectations, as they begin to make efforts to remain involved, prioritizing
activism over family time, leisure activities, and even financial self-
interest.

The puzzle is more intriguing in that several of these participants
remain indifferent or even antagonistic to central aspects of the movement's agenda. In all of the organizations I worked with, people openly
(and frequently) expressed views that contradicted the ideology of their

group. While leaders highlight that the coexistence of varied viewpoints is a key strength of the movement, partisan and media opposition has treated this diversity as evidence of the political immaturity of participants and the manipulation of people's needs for illegitimate organizational goals.[5] However, evidence from existing surveys and ethnographic studies does not support such criticism.[6] The people I met in the piquetero movement did not seem less informed or engaged than other Argentineans. Indeed, the fact that many of them regularly voice disagreement with their organizations yet continue to make sacrifices for them suggests that the characterization of these groups as composed of a mass of malleable and apathetic members is very inaccurate.

What processes, then, lead to this level of attachment? Why do people who join reluctantly, face substantial personal obstacles to activism, and do not always agree with their organizations develop such a commitment to the movement? Based on ethnographic fieldwork spanning three and a half years, as well as in-depth interviews with 133 current and former members of nine piquetero groups, this book suggests an answer. I argue that a key appeal of participation is the opportunity to engage in practices associated with a respectable blue-collar lifestyle threatened by deindustrialization and joblessness. Through their daily involvement in the movement, older participants reconstruct the routines they associate with a golden past in which factory jobs were plentiful, younger activists develop the kind of habits they were raised to see as valuable, and all members protect communal activities undermined by the expansion of poverty and violence. For Antonella as for countless others, daily activities in a piquetero organization allow the actualization of dispositions developed in fields of life that either no longer exist or are in danger of vanishing. The movement becomes a surrogate for manual labor in a factory or domestic work at home, offering consistency and respectability in a context of marked socioeconomic decline.

The argument I propose in this book reflects a critical engagement with the literature on collective action. Views of the piqueteros as inauthentic forms of protest not only reveal long-standing prejudices in Argentinean society against popular politics but may also express a narrow scholarly

---

[5] For the evolution of media coverage of the piquetero movement, see Svampa (2005, 2008) and Gómez (2009).

[6] See Latinobarómetro (2018) for survey data showing that political apathy and skepticism are widespread among Argentineans, and Quirós (2006, 2011) and Manzano (2013) for evidence of the complex motivations of participants.

understanding of activism. Despite substantial progress in the field of social movement studies, many aspects of people's participation in contentious politics remain unclear. Even though there is a large body of literature on the factors that contribute to a person's engagement in collective action, most studies tend to focus primarily on the recruitment phase and neglect what happens afterwards. Thus, we know a great deal about the factors that make initial participation more likely, but we are less knowledgeable about the mechanisms by which people develop long-term attachment (or not) to the groups they have joined. In particular, while researchers have analyzed how ideological processes sustain activism, the role that everyday practices play in the same outcome has received far less attention. Based on the experiences of individuals in the piquetero movement, I argue that activists can be hesitant about their organization's ideology yet still develop a strong attachment to their routines within it. What people think about the movements they join certainly matters, but so does what they do while mobilized.

In addition, this book provides new insight into the wave of progressive mobilization that swept through Latin America in the past decade and a half, of which the piqueteros were an essential part. The combination since the 1980s of unprecedented democratization with drastic neoliberal reforms promoted the emergence of various experiences of collective action that successfully pushed for the recognition of new rights. Even though an extensive literature[7] has explored these instances, much of it tends to portray their struggles in terms of a novel transformation of society, downplaying their more orthodox aspects. While not denying the innovative elements of anti-neoliberal movements like the piqueteros, an exploration of the life stories of activists suggests that traditional notions of labor, family, and community play a large role in their conception of social justice.

Finally, by providing a case study of how workers affected by job loss recreate their traditional forms of life through progressive grassroots mobilization, the following pages offer insight for understanding current events in other parts of the world. In recent years, the expansion of right-wing politics throughout the globe has intensified concerns over the effects of neoliberal globalization for democratic governance. Faced with economic uncertainty and reduced prospects for social mobility, working-class voters

---

[7] For studies of this wave of mobilization, see Johnston and Almeida (2006), Almeida (2007), Stakler-Sholk, Varden, and Kuecker (2008), Roberts (2008), Delamata (2009a), Silva (2009, 2013), and Prevost, Oliva Campos, and Varden (2012).

in many countries have embraced authoritarian and xenophobic agendas.[8] However, this is only part of the story. As experiences like the piqueteros show, vulnerable populations around the world have responded to deindustrialization in various ways. The connection between growing inequality, social anxiety, and reactionary extremism is neither inevitable nor irreversible.

1.1 PERSONAL BACKGROUNDS, MOBILIZATION EXPERIENCES, AND ACTIVIST DISPOSITIONS

The processes through which a person develops attachment to a social activity are complex. While, at the aggregate level, certain features may be more common among participants in a practice, the relation between these characteristics and actual behavior at the individual level is usually weak. Consequently, to understand the appeal of a social action, we need to first explore its intrinsic rewards: What do people obtain from doing something? To use Jack Katz's terms, it is essential to analyze not only the "background" of action (the personal attributes that make a person more likely to do something) but also its "foreground" (the qualities of the act that make it attractive). In his study of different forms of crime, Katz argues for focusing on the experience of deviance itself, rather than on the characteristics of offenders. Otherwise, any attempt to explain lawbreaking based on the background conditions associated with criminality will run into three problems:

(1) whatever the validity of the hereditary, psychological and social-ecological conditions of crime, many of those in the supposedly causal categories do not commit the crime at issue, (2) many who do commit the crime do not fit the causal categories, and (3) what is most provocative, many who do fit the background categories and later commit the predicted crime go for long stretches without committing the crimes to which theory directs them. (Katz 1988: 3–4)

Nevertheless, the fact that involvement in a particular social action does not follow directly from background factors does not mean that these factors are irrelevant. Quite the contrary, the process by which an action

---

[8] There is a large literature discussing the reasons behind the expansion in recent years of right-wing politics in different countries of the world. For the case of the United States, see Frank (2004), Skocpol and Williamson (2012), and Hochschild (2016). For the United Kingdom, see Bromley-Davenport, MacLeavy, and Manley (2018), and Dorling and Tomlinson (2019). In the case of Italy, see Romei (2018) and D'Alimonte (2019). For India, see Tillin (2015) and Vaishnav (2019). For Brazil, see Gethin and Morgan (2018) and Hunter and Power (2019).

generates its own incentive varies according to the characteristics of each individual. Biographies matter because they affect the ways in which people develop an attachment to certain practices (Desmond 2007; Shapira 2013). Throughout the life course, people are exposed to various forms of relations, institutions, and norms, leading to beliefs and expectations that are particular to each person. These socialization processes influence how some people are predisposed to enjoy certain activities or see them as "natural" to them. Consequently, understanding a person's attachment to a habit entails unraveling how the practices associated with it interact with other aspects of his or her life to generate specific dispositions (Bourdieu 1977).

That being said, the positive resonance between a person's life and a particular social activity is neither automatic nor permanent. Rather, it depends on constant affirmation and ratification through interaction with other participants (Benzecry 2011; Tavory 2016). In other words, the development of a sense of enjoyment with regard to a social practice is a learning process, through which individuals gradually attach new meanings to their routines and come to appreciate what was originally either unpleasant or unremarkable to them (Becker 1963; Wacquant 2004). As Howard Becker argued in his study of marijuana users, in order to enjoy an activity, beginners need to first learn from others particular techniques and perceptions, that is, specific ways of doing and appreciating the practice:

An individual will be able to use marijuana for pleasure only when he goes through a process of learning to conceive of it as an object which can be used in this way. No one becomes a user without (1) learning to smoke the drug in a way which will produce real effects; (2) learning to recognize the effects and connect them with drug use (learning, in other words, to get high); and (3) learning to enjoy the sensations he perceives. In the course of this process he develops a disposition or motivation to use marijuana which was not and could not have been present when he began use, for it involves and depends on conceptions of the drug which could only grow out of the kind of actual experience detailed above. (Becker 1963: 76)

Two aspects of this sense of enjoyment are particularly salient for the purposes of this book. The first is the opportunity to embrace behaviors seen as virtuous. As sociologists studying culture and religion have long argued, participation in certain routines helps individuals construct a self-image of goodness by personifying desirable social roles. That is, actions not only reflect a person's sense of morality but also constitute it (see Winchester 2008; Benzecry 2011; Fridman 2016). Regular engagement in specific practices allows people to claim membership in a valued category and set moral boundaries with groups deemed as less worthy (Lamont 2000). As a result, when individuals use their involvement to embody the kind of person they want to be, they are likely to appreciate such involvement as an end in itself.

Second, a central appeal of routines lies in their intrinsic predictability, which provides a sense of order in people's daily experiences – what Anthony Giddens terms "ontological security" (Giddens 1979; also see Laing 1961). The very regularity of a habit contributes to the feeling of being in control over one's life, especially in times of crisis or in the context of socioeconomic decline (Auyero and Kilanski 2015). By engaging in the same practices repeatedly, people faced with uncertainty know what to expect of each day.

In sum, commitment to a social activity emerges out of its resonance with the cultural understandings and expectations a person has been socialized into. In particular, when routines allow the embodiment of positive models of conduct and bolster an individual's sense of command over his or her situation, they are likely to become very appealing. Respectability and consistency are particularly salient for my argument because they are among the most important things individuals lose when they become unemployed. The lack of steady occupation implies more than simply a threat to sustenance: It entails the loss of a whole set of principles that organize daily life and endow people's experiences with purpose (Bird 1966; Jahoda, Lazarfeld, and Zeisel 1977; Wilson 1996). As Pierre Bourdieu explains in *Pascalian Meditations*:

In losing their work, the unemployed have also lost the countless tokens of a socially known and recognized *function*, in other words the whole set of goals posited in advance, independently of any conscious project, in the form of demands and commitments – "important" meetings, cheques to post, invoices to draw up – and the whole forth-coming already given in the immediate present, in the form of deadlines, dates and timetables to be observed – buses to take, rates to maintain, targets to meet . . . Deprived of this objective universe of incitements and indications which orientate and stimulate action and, through it, social life, they can only experience the free time that is left to them as dead time, purposeless and meaningless [emphasis in the original]. (1997: 222)

As the coming chapters will argue, long-term involvement in the piquetero movement is motivated not only by the access to material support or the appeal of organizational ideologies. The movement also offers many people an opportunity to engage in routines providing this lost sense of personal value. For countless Argentineans excluded from the labor market, piquetero organizations grant the space and resources necessary to be the kind of person they were raised to be. You can still be a worker, even if having a well-paying, stable job is a long-gone dream. Thus, from the perspective of many of my respondents, making efforts to remain involved in a group that you joined reluctantly, with whose ideology you do not necessarily agree, and which barely provides for the sustenance of your family, makes perfect sense.

1.2 THE UNEMPLOYED WORKERS' MOVEMENT

Since the 1980s, Latin America has experienced a remarkable period of democratization. Most countries in the region managed to sustain fair elections, high levels of individual freedoms, and institutional mechanisms for the transfer of power that held even in times of civil unrest. Nevertheless, this period has also coincided with extensive neoliberal reforms that caused a retrenchment of the welfare state and an increase in structural unemployment and inequality. Hence, the last three decades combine an expansion of political liberties with the persistence of widespread economic disparities. This scenario has contributed to the development of new experiences of collective action. Faced with growing chances for dissent on the one hand, and the undermining of their means of livelihood on the other, millions of Latin Americans have organized to demand access to a decent standard of living (for an overview, see Roberts 2008; Silva 2009).

Piquetero organizations have been one of the main exponents of this wave. The first expressions of the movement took place between 1996 and 1997 during a series of uprisings in company towns in the provinces of Salta and Neuquén, where residents used roadblocks to protest the sudden leap in unemployment caused by the privatization of the national oil company. The success of these events in forcing concessions from the authorities, coupled with the government's increasing use of relief programs as a way to defuse social unrest, encouraged grassroots organizers in other parts of the country to emulate these methods of protest. Consequently, organizations of unemployed workers emerged throughout the nation, developing a flexible internal structure and an efficient repertoire of contention that allowed them to rapidly gain followers. Most of these organizations consist of networks of local groups that engage in roadblocks to demand social assistance, usually in the form of workfare programs, foodstuffs, and funding for small cooperative projects. These resources are then allocated among participants following criteria based on need and merit: Whoever has more dependents and contributes more effort to the organization is prioritized. Moreover, organizations use part of these resources to offer a vast array of social services in countless poor neighborhoods, from soup kitchens and vocational training to primary healthcare and legal advice. The possibility of obtaining material support draws people into these groups, which in turn helps them continue demonstrating.

As Chapter 3 will show in more detail, this unique combination of effective methods of protest and autonomous management of state-funded assistance has allowed piquetero groups to remain active for two decades despite ebbs and flows that follow the economic conditions in the country. Between 1996 and 2003, these organizations grew exponentially as Argentina plunged into the deepest recession in its history. The movement proved to be an efficient provider of material support for poor families, as well as an influential actor in the public sphere. After 2003, however, economic recovery, coupled with the reconstitution of the political system around a center-left national administration, forced activists to adapt to a new scenario. The result was not only an overall reduction in the movement's membership but also a process of relative organizational strengthening. The election in 2015 of a right-wing government led to a neoliberal resurgence and an increase in repression, yet mediocre economic results and the persistence of structural sources of state support generated opportunities for recruiting activists, obtaining concessions from the authorities, and developing new alliances. The important role played by much of the movement in the 2019 national elections, which led to a new change of government, shows the continued political relevance of the piqueteros.

In short, while the mobilization capacity of the movement peaked in the early 2000s and wavered afterwards, the characteristics of most organizations within it have allowed them to sustain their relevance within Argentina's popular politics (Rossi 2017; Pérez 2018). Activists have been able adapt to changes in their context while maintaining their essential work in communities throughout the country.

Furthermore, an essential aspect of the persistence of piquetero organizations has been their capacity to attract and, more importantly, retain members. When asked about their experiences shortly after joining, most respondents describe a scenario of boredom, shame, and confusion:

I am proud of being a piquetera. I used to not like it. I did not like it. I used to say, "These bums, they are here bothering everyone, when they could be working."

I have no shame now, but I used to be ashamed, I truly was. I did not want to wear the organization's clothes. When I went to events, I went hidden, and came back ashamed. (Priscila, May 19, 2014)

I used to get bored because the coordinator talked a lot. He talked and read the organization's script to you, and he explained it, and back then I did not understand anything about scripts, I did not understand anything about politics, I did not understand anything. (Tatiana, February 27, 2014)

However, activists also describe a process of progressively "getting it" and "starting to like it." In other words, respondents talk about a re-signification of their practices in the movement. Through the interplay between their personal histories and their experiences in the group, mobilization gradually became an enjoyable activity, an end in itself rather than just a means to access resources. The result is what I term "resistance to quitting," a deep-seated tendency to make efforts to remain involved:

[My first day] I went to a meeting, and I said, "You have to come here to listen to this, you have to hear these stupidities?" I used to say that. Then I began to soak in, soak in, soak in, know the people, that way until I stayed in there, and I am not leaving anymore. (Macarena, May 5, 2014)

I was one of the opponents, I was one of those who thought that the piqueteros were people who did not want to work . . . I mean, no one convinced me of anything, I got here and saw it was not that way, that is why I stayed. (Sergio, June 1, 2012)

I had an in-law who was here. And she always told me, "come with us, we need people to help with administrative stuff." So it was then that I entered, at first I did not like it, because I entered due to necessity, I needed to earn something, there were no other jobs. I entered and a year later I was already a coordinator and never left. I got in more, more, and from here, I am going to leave when I die. (Valentina, February 14, 2014)

Occasionally, this evolution is presented in ideological terms. Some participants describe a process of political socialization that changed important components of their personal opinions. For instance, Julia proudly mentions how she became a socialist after joining a piquetero organization. She highlights that the lessons learned in the movement "got in my head," ending a lifetime of political apathy:

I learned a lot from our leaders. I learned a lot about social policy and party politics. Because I used to not like politics. When my husband lived, politicians from different parties invited us to celebrations. We went, but did not pay much attention, because I did not understand anything. Now I do, now I do. (July 13, 2011)

Lucila credits leaders in her organization with convincing her to stay by exposing her to new ideas and encouraging her to study:

With politics, I used to not be involved and now it is not that I am like a luminary, but I can read interpretations, do my research. As I got involved in the organization, I began reading too. I used to not touch books, I did not read much, and yet here I got involved with reading history books, knowing who was who. (June 6, 2013)

However, other activists talk less about changes in their viewpoints. Some seem actually indifferent to their organization's ideology. For example, Jazmín claims to love her work in the movement but avoids discussing politics:

I do not understand politics, and you cannot like something that you do not understand. For me politics are super difficult, I do not understand politics much. Well, I participate in what they ask me and go, but I do not like being in politics, I do not understand it, no. (May 26, 2014)

Other activists are even antagonistic to their group's ideology. For instance, Vanesa joined the movement more than fifteen years ago. She has never left since then, but she openly holds opinions that contradict her group's main standpoints. For example, she supported the national government at the time of our interview, something that was anathema to Laura, the main leader in her organization. Between laughs, she told me:

When we go in front of the government's palace, they begin to sing against the president, and I never sing. Laura tells me "Vanesa, sing!" and I do not. That happens all the time. (February 13, 2014)

Despite having differences with their respective organizations, throughout my fieldwork, I saw Jazmín and Vanesa volunteering extra time and effort. Jazmín spends several hours a day helping with paperwork and holds the contentious position of *planillera*, the person in charge of taking attendance and making sure that participants show up for work. Her discussions with other activists do not seem to affect her enthusiasm: Quite the contrary, she is active in recruiting new members. In the case of Vanesa, her workfare plan has relatively few requirements, and in addition, she suffers from intense lower back pain brought about by decades of housecleaning work and exacerbated by a domestic accident. However, she eagerly participates in demanding tasks such as the distribution of foodstuffs, sits at the front during most meetings, and goes to demonstrations notwithstanding the strong opposition of her family.

Examples like Jazmín and Vanesa suggest that some activists' attachment to the movement takes place regardless of and not because of their political ideology. Piquetero organizations represent almost all traditions in Argentina's left-wing politics, from progressive nationalism and liberation theology to Maoism and Trotskyism. However, this has not prevented them from incorporating members with different viewpoints. In particular, the importance of Peronism as a multifaceted source of identification for working-class Argentineans (Auyero 2001; Rossi 2017), coupled with the heterogeneous legacy of grassroots experiences in their communities (Lobato and Suriano 2003; Merklen 2005; Pereyra 2008), means that a large portion of participants hold opinions that frequently diverge from the official platform of their organizations. Leaders themselves acknowledge the variety of outlooks and perspectives within their groups, and some even celebrate it as one of the movement's strengths:

In our organization we have folks from every ideology ... that is what we are. We are one big unique front, a great political and social alliance that tries to contain everyone. (Diego, June 9, 2012)

The people are very diverse in their opinions, they are not homogenized behind a common idea. Therefore, naturally the organizations that the people create for themselves are also diverse. (Humberto, July 21, 2011)

[Our organization] is not absolutely monochromatic or monotone, plus we do not require that because we want a broad organization that is based in solving people's concrete issues. (Patricio, July 21, 2011)

Nevertheless, the ideological diversity prevalent within piquetero organizations does not mean that they do not uphold certain values and norms. Quite the opposite, entering the movement entails accepting a working-class ethos associated with a whole set of expectations, an implicit contract that Julieta Quirós (2011) describes as the equation between "doing and deserving." In all the groups I observed, members are expected to participate in demonstrations and attend regular meetings. In addition, those who receive a workfare plan must fulfill the official requirements associated with it. Even though government supervision of these programs is lax (during my fieldwork, I only witnessed a visit of officials checking the work of beneficiaries once), groups in my study are relatively strict concerning attendance and punctuality. This attitude solves a key dilemma at the root of each organization: Their only way to obtain more resources to sustain themselves and their members is through negotiation with the authorities, but their bargaining power is related to their mobilization capacity. By demanding that those who receive benefits through the group make efforts to keep them (taking part in demonstrations, going to meetings, and fulfilling the daily requirements of workfare plans), organizations enhance internal discipline and guarantee the availability of people for protests. Moreover, the equation of "doing and deserving" also allows the movement to sustain a crucial attraction: an ethos of discipline and self-sufficiency. Probably the best example of this appeal is Jazmín, who, despite her avoidance of political debates, likes participating because it allows her to fulfill the social role of a responsible worker. She compares herself favorably to friends who refused offers to join the movement:

[They] do not want to come here, because they do not want to have a schedule to follow, they do not want to come to the demonstrations. There are people who do not like to do things, they do not like to get up early, come to work. I like it. (February 25, 2014)

The fact that people like Jazmín claim to be indifferent toward politics but feel strongly about the value of hard work reflects a crucial, yet frequently overlooked aspect of piquetero organizations: how they serve as refuges for the routines of a proletarian lifestyle endangered by the elimination of the kind of jobs that made it possible. The decline in industrial employment precluded the type of life that working-class Argentineans associate with virtue: a man who leaves for work early every day, a woman who raises children and makes sure they stay out of trouble, and the whole family accumulating wealth in the form of their own plot of land and a self-built house. Respondents refer to these conditions as vanishing:

These days, in a marriage the woman needs to go out to work. It is not like fifty years ago, when the man went to work and that was enough. The woman took care of children, and then children got a better education. Today women have to go out to work, kids stay with the grandmother, the grandmother until they are eleven, twelve can control them, then they go to the street corner, and do not study anymore. There, what is missing is the mother! The father works, the mother guides the kids. (Alberto, July 20, 2011)

When I was a kid, the only one who worked was my old man. And there was always an adult person in the house. Who checked your homework, controlled you, taught you a lifestyle. In the 90s many lost their jobs, or both parents had to go find work so they could feed their family. The kids were left alone, at home, from home to the street corner, from the street corner to let's see what we do. Those were three steps that were inevitable. I know a lot of kids whose fathers lost their jobs, and they ended up stealing. (Luis, June 27, 2013)

All the boys and girls, we used to get together, when we ran errands, we would gather on the corner to have a soda. Everyone worked, the fathers worked, the mothers stayed at home with the children, then it began to change ... mothers had to go out, leaving the kids alone, locked up, so the kids started taking to the streets, and getting into drugs. (Aldana, February 12, 2014)

This ideal proletarian life is embodied in the demand for "genuine work," that is, decently paid, stable blue-collar jobs associated with specific routines, tasks, and skills. Participants describe this kind of employment as the ideal way for people to sustain themselves honorably. Few express this notion as clearly as Isabel, a retiree in her 70s:

These days the government gives you a plan, that is useless, I want that they put the money from the plan into factories, so our grandchildren learn to punch a timecard, so they learn to follow a schedule, just as we learned it, and that they have a good retirement plan, a good salary. (May 6, 2014)

This proletarian ethos is certainly not exclusive to Argentina. Michèle Lamont's (2000) study of workers in France and the United States shows that a central component of how her respondents understand their place in the world is a discourse centered on the ideal of hard work and discipline. Simon Charlesworth (2000) reaches similar conclusions with regard to English workers affected by deindustrialization. As classic studies of working-class culture have shown, being a worker is much more than a source of livelihood: it grants access to a comprehensive set of ideas regarding right and wrong (Hoggart 1963; Thompson 1971), a moral code that provides a sense of meaning and self-worth. The appeal of an identity grounded in manual labor remains in place even when the material conditions that sustain it disappear, as demonstrated by studies such as Philippe Bourgois's work on drug dealers in New York (Bourgois 1996) and Loïc Wacquant's ethnography of boxers in Chicago (Wacquant 2004).

A similar phenomenon takes place in my case of study. As Federico Rossi (2017) argues, one of the main goals of piquetero organizations since their emergence has been the reconstitution of social links severed by neoliberalism. In other words, rather than the creation of new forms of social organization, the central objective of the unemployed workers' movement has been the restoration of previously existing relations between workers, employers, and the state. The focus of this book is on the micro-dynamics of these reincorporation struggles. Just as at the organization level groups in the movement seek to reincorporate segments of the population excluded by decades of pro-market reforms, at the individual level activists engage in a valued lifestyle they see as endangered. Being a member provides the resources and rationale necessary for engaging in idealized routines which confer respectability and consistency to people's daily experiences. By getting involved day after day in practices they were raised to see as wholesome (such as waking up early, following a schedule, making efforts to earn resources), some activists are able to think of themselves as moral beings in charge of their own destiny, rather than passive victims of forces beyond their control. In other words, participation offers them an opportunity to address both the material and symbolic deprivation caused by mass joblessness.

The specifics of this process vary substantially from individual to individual. Given that personal backgrounds impact how people come to appreciate certain activities as ends in themselves, participants develop attachment to their organizations differently based on their age and gender. Concerning age, the timing of deindustrialization creates a generational divide. Thus, the piquetero movement is similar to other instances of collective action in that the age of activists influence their experiences (Fillieule 2010; Corrigall-Brown 2011). Older members (usually beyond their forties) *reconstruct* the practices that they associate with a golden past in which they were breadwinners in a factory line or homemakers in their households. Industrial job opportunities were still available when these individuals became adults, but became increasingly uncommon later in their lives. In contrast, younger members (in their forties or less) *develop* the kind of habits that they see as respectable but that they never had the chance to experience. These people came of age in a context in which manufacturing labor was already in steep decline. Coupled with the lack of educational opportunities, they face a different situation than their elders: instead of being expelled from the formal job market, most of them were never included to begin with. Finally, all members regardless of age *protect* communal activities, as public life in their communities is undermined by persistent unemployment, state neglect, and rising violence.

With regard to gender, piquetero organizations frequently outperform the state in terms of providing services for women in poor neighborhoods of Argentina. However, organizations in my study also reproduce established notions of masculinity and femininity ingrained in local working-class culture. Given that the proletarian lifestyle participants seek to save from extinction is itself gendered, the experiences of male and female activists tend to be different. Just as men reconstruct routines associated with blue-collar labor, women in the movement usually reenact the type of household duties that were the counterpart of factory work. Like other organizations around the world (See Robnett 1997; Ferree and McClurg Mueller 2004; Taylor et al. 2009; Viterna 2013), piquetero groups are not isolated from their context, and consequently their daily functioning reflects cultural norms prevalent in society, including those concerning gender relations.

In summary, many people become piquetero activists because the movement allows them to sustain themselves while embracing routines associated with an increasingly uncommon working-class world, offering refuge from the personal consequences of decades of socioeconomic decline. This finding, I argue, has important implications for our understanding of collective action.

1.3 WORKING-CLASS ROUTINES AND SOCIAL MOVEMENT THEORY

Exploring how personal histories and activist routines combine to promote long-term mobilization enhances existing research on political participation in two ways. First, it allows us to interpret the post-recruitment experiences of participants not only as the reflection of background characteristics but also (and primarily) as the result of dynamic processes. Second, it illuminates the relation between ideas and practices in the development of long-term engagement in a social movement.

Concerning the first aspect, in the past fifty years scholars have developed an elaborate understanding of the factors that increase a person's likelihood of engaging in collective action. Research has shown how activism is facilitated by the absence of alternative personal obligations (McAdam 1988; Goodwin 1997; White 2010), an immersion in militant circles (Passy and Giugni 2000; Diani 2004; Corrigall-Brown 2011), emotional dynamics such as outrage, anger, and fear (Gould 2009; Jasper 2011), and the expectation of obtaining collective and individual rewards (Olson 1965; McAdam 1982; Klandermans 1997). However, the relation between these factors and individual behavior is far from straightforward, especially once people are already mobilized. Work and family duties do not always preclude sustained involvement (Nepstad 2004), networks can pull people out of particular movements (Klatch 2004; Fisher and McInerney 2012), emotional dynamics may contribute to withdrawal (Hirschman 1982; Gould 2009), and people frequently sustain commitment despite a lack of tangible results or the existence of extreme costs (Wood 2003; Nepstad 2004; Summers Effler 2010). In other words, the attributes highlighted by the literature as conducive to sustained participation are poor predictors of the actual long-term trajectories of individual activists.

In part, this limitation is related to the fact that social movement theory has historically focused more on the emergence of contention than on its sustainment and decline (Owens 2009). As a result, our understanding of the factors that influence activism is much more sophisticated with regard to recruitment than concerning later stages of participation (Nepstad 2004; Fillieule, 2010; White 2010; Corrigall-Brown 2011). However, the imperfect association between personal attributes and trajectories following recruitment also reflects the inherent complexity of political participation. The development, sustainment, and erosion of activism are processes whose outcomes are not predetermined by the background of participants (Klandermans 1997; Munson 2008), because once a person is mobilized the relation between biography and activism becomes bidirectional. That is, people's lives, networks, beliefs, and incentives not only affect contention but are affected by it as well. Involvement in collective action exposes individuals to new worldviews, connects them to diverse networks, and helps them acquire new skills, all of which can influence the life course of activists (Giugni 2007; Fillieule 2010; Corrigall-Brown 2011) and transform their sense of self (Taylor and Whittier 1992; Jasper 2011). Thus, in order to analyze activism following recruitment, it is important to discern not only which aspects of a person's life matter but also how those aspects interact with the experience of mobilization (McAdam 1988; Crossley 2003).

Embracing this approach can contribute to an expanding body of research on the post-recruitment trajectories of activists. In recent years, several studies on "activist careers" have highlighted the diversity of forms that involvement in collective action can take, not only among different people but also in different periods of the same person's life (Passy and Giugni 2000; Fillieule 2010; Corrigall-Brown 2011). I build on this literature by shifting the focus from activist trajectories to activist dispositions. In other words, the main goal of this book is not to create a more accurate or extensive categorization of activist paths, but to analyze the general mechanisms by which people come to appreciate political participation in different ways, with a particular emphasis on the role that the desire for consistency and respectability plays in the whole process.

With regard to the second aspect, over the past five decades scholars have also learned much about how ideologies and beliefs contribute to the emergence, sustainment, and decline of political participation. Studies have analyzed how individuals embrace perspectives that in turn promote involvement in collective action (Lofland and Stark 1965; Snow and Phillips 1980; Klandermans 1997; Munson 2008), and how the alignment between a movement's ideology and personal beliefs contributes to the emergence of activism (Jasper 1997; Benford and Snow 2000; Poletta and Jasper 2001). Researchers have also explored the influence that the relation between individual and organizational ideologies has on the long-term trajectories of activists (Passy and Giugni 2000; White 2010; Corrigall-Brown 2011), as well as how people's attachment to certain political views sustains participation along the life course (McAdam 1988; Andrews 1991).

Nevertheless, much of this literature has also challenged the existence of a direct relation between ideology and social movement participation, indicating that other mechanisms also play a role in the development and sustainment of activism. Not only is joining a movement the result of a contingent process whose outcome is rarely determined from the beginning by any particular set of ideas (Klandermans 1997; Munson 2008; Corrigall-Brown 2011), but also life events, resource availability, and interpersonal connections mediate between a person's beliefs and his or her political involvement (Goodwin 1997; Passy and Giugni 2000; White 2010). Moreover, evidence from case studies suggests that the experience of engaging in mobilization itself can be a key motivator aside from any moral, material, or ideological imperative (McAdam 1988; Wood 2003; Shapira 2013). In other words, the practices associated with collective action can serve as their own incentive.

The lack of a one-on-one relation between beliefs and collective action is consistent with a broader psychological and sociological literature. Research on Attitude-Behavior Consistency strongly suggests that people's actions do not always match their opinions – and even less so their stated opinions (Gross and Niman 1975; Schuman and Johnson 1976; Jerolmack and Khan 2014). Ann Swidler's work on the uses of culture indicates that the daily actions of most individuals do not reflect a cohesive set of ideas and norms. In contrast, people use cultural resources as a "toolkit," pragmatically drawing different components to construct strategies of action dealing with the diverse situations that arise in everyday life (Swidler 2001). Thus, while worldviews are certainly important variables, their explanatory power is limited due to the fact that their connection to actual individual behavior is not necessarily straightforward.

For all these reasons, the following pages argue for a more multifaceted exploration of the motivations behind people's engagement in politics. The debate on this issue has for the most part assumed that long-term involvement in collective action requires some degree of alignment between personal worldviews and organizational ideologies. Much of the disagreement relates to whether ideas precede action or vice versa. For instance, while Jim Jasper's classic study on morality and protest (1997) explores how threats to central aspects of people's beliefs can spur engagement in contention, Ziad Munson's analysis of pro-life activists contends that an individual's conversion to a cause does not always precede his or her involvement in mobilization (2008). This book does not aim to solve this crucial debate, in fact, my goal is to go beyond discussing the direction of the link between ideology and activism, arguing instead that people's practices and opinions influence and constitute each other in complex ways. Discrepancies with leaders and indifference toward central aspects of their organizations' agendas have not prevented many of my respondents from developing attachment to collective action. Consequently, without denying the importance of people's views, I suggest that ideological skepticism does not necessarily preclude long-term commitment to a social movement. That is, morality in a social movement can be expressed not just by embracing a particular standpoint but also by engaging in certain practices seen as marks of a virtuous and wholesome self.

In summary, a complete analysis of the reasons why individuals commit to a social movement needs to consider how they come to see the practices associated with it as intrinsically valuable. Understanding sustained activism entails exploring the ways in which the interaction between personal characteristics and experiences while mobilized generates dispositions that in turn sustain commitment – what Nick Crossley (2003) calls a "radical habitus." Such an approach can help us identify similarities and patterns in the mechanisms affecting mobilization experiences throughout the world.

1.4 PIQUETE AND BEYOND

As one of the most visible instances of social protest in Argentina since the 1990s and the largest movement of unemployed workers in the world, the piqueteros have attracted much scholarly interest. However, while the trajectories of organizations have been thoroughly researched (see, e.g., Svampa and Pereyra 2003; Pereyra, Pérez, and Schuster 2008; Rossi 2017), the experiences of rank-and-file activists have received far less attention. A number of scholars have produced detailed ethnographic studies on the matter, suggesting the existence of a great variety of motivations and viewpoints among members (Auyero 2003; Quirós 2011; Manzano 2013). However, these works usually focus on one event, group, or district. Remarkably, in two decades, virtually no book has systematically studied the ways in which the experience of mobilization interacts with other aspects of participants' lives across different organizations, in various locations, and over a period of several years. As a result, the richness of individual experiences within one of Latin America's biggest grassroots movements remains underexplored, and the question of why some people develop commitment while others in a similar situation do not (which is crucial for both academics and organizers) is still poorly understood.

Addressing these questions can also teach us a great deal about the relation between working-class decline, grassroots mobilization, and democratic governance at the regional and global level. First, the piquetero movement has been part of a wave of contention that strongly affected Latin America in the last several decades. The combination of political and economic liberalization promoted the emergence of diverse experiences of collective action by marginalized populations. Moreover, the "pink tide" of left-wing governments in the region in the first fifteen years of the twenty-first century generated opportunities for community leaders to gain influence and state support. Despite an extensive literature on these developments, much of it has failed to address the complex meanings that rank-and-file members attach to their participation (for exemptions, see Wolford 2010). By focusing on the experiences and views of regular activists, I show how participants in movements like the piqueteros frame their struggle not only in terms of a novel transformation of society but also as an effort to reestablish past forms of social organization (see Rossi 2017; Benclowicz 2013). This finding suggests that antineoliberal movements in Latin America may be more traditionally oriented than usually assumed.

Second, the processes causing deindustrialization and mobilization in Latin America are global in nature. Over the past four decades, the world has witnessed a dramatic expansion in technological capabilities and interconnectedness, which has been accompanied by paradigm shifts in terms of economic and political governance (see Hobsbawm 1994; Harvey 2005; Piketty 2014). While these transformations have created opportunities for economic growth and lifted millions of people from extreme poverty, they also have caused an increase in global inequality and concentration of wealth. The consequences of these changes for democracy worldwide are still unclear. In some countries, the idealization of a golden past and an ethic of individual self-sufficiency have led vulnerable segments of society to support authoritarian right-wing agendas. However, cases like the piqueteros show that attempts to return to a romanticized working-class past can also motivate participation in movements pushing for redistributive policies. By exploring how communities affected by neoliberal globalization react in diverse ways to comparable challenges, social movement scholars can contribute to addressing one of today's most important questions.

In order to do that, it is crucial to abandon the confines of our field. In recent years, a new generation of scholars has addressed the limitations of existing paradigms of individual engagement in collective action, questioning prevailing views of activism as overly rationalistic, schematic, and unidimensional (Munson 2008; Fillieule 2010; Corrigall-Brown 2011; Viterna 2013). This promising body of research can be further strengthened by engaging a broader theoretical and empirical literature. Since the mechanisms influencing people's attachment to social movements are also present in other instances of collective life, we can expand our analytical toolkit by drawing on analogies between people's practices while mobilized and other social activities (Vaughan 2004, 2014). Activists themselves rarely isolate protest and contention from other aspects of their lives (Mische 2008; Litcherman and Eliasoph 2015). Hence, we must place political participation in the context of a larger set of experiences in which people get involved. Theoretical broadening and empirical contextualization are key to the future of research on mobilization.

1.5 A NOTE ON METHODOLOGY

I collected the evidence for this book through ethnographic fieldwork over a period of three and a half years in six districts of the Buenos Aires Metropolitan Area (the Autonomous City of Buenos Aires, Lomas de Zamora, La Matanza, Florencio Varela, Lanús, and Esteban Echeverría). This project took place during the summers of 2011, 2012, and 2013, and for nine months in 2014. The results were 950 pages of notes, 133 interviews with current and former activists from nine different piquetero organizations, and more than 4,000 photographs and videos. While I include a detailed discussion of my methodology in Appendix A, this section provides basic information on my data collection and analysis before moving ahead.

With the exception of ten meetings with national leaders in the movement, the bulk of my recorded conversations consisted of life-story interviews with rank-and-file members (Atkinson 1998). My purpose was to
obtain a detailed description of the personal history of each subject in his
or her own terms and to explore how their involvement in a piquetero
organization related to other events in their lives. In other words,
I followed the advice of Jack Katz (2001, 2002) of asking "How?" instead
of "Why?" questions. I used interviews to reconstruct chronologically the
experiences of respondents instead of asking interpretative questions. In
part, the reason for this is that people's statements about motivations are
usually poorly associated with their actual behavior (Jerolmack and Khan
2014). In addition, the fact that I am Argentinean meant that activists
were less likely to perceive me as a neutral observer, given the contentious
nature of the movement in public opinion. Since respondents know that
most observers have strong viewpoints about them, they may have felt
compelled to provide a "proper response" that obscures their experiences,
perceptions, and ideas. Only at the end of each interview did I ask
a general question on their reasons for staying or leaving.

I recruited my respondents by asking during participant observation if
they wanted to be interviewed, usually setting up a separate time to meet.
In addition, I used snowball sampling to contact dropouts and other
activists who were not regularly present at the sites where I did research,
with the purpose of increasing the diversity of experiences represented in
my sample. I made sure to ask for referrals after every interview and from
different people in each organization, to reduce the potential bias caused
by respondents referring me to people with similar views as them.

The purpose of including dropouts among the respondents was to
understand how the experiences, perceptions, and stories of those who
stayed and those who left differ (for a similar approach, see Klandermans
1997; Passy and Giugni 2000; White 2010; Corrigall-Brown 2011).
Consequently, I had recorded conversations with fifteen former participants. While contacting, meeting, and talking with former members was
a substantial challenge, I was able to take advantage of many relations
developed over the length of the fieldwork to interview activists before
and after their withdrawal.

In addition to providing opportunities for recruiting respondents, participant observation served as a source of evidence in its own right. While
interviews were a window into the personal history and perceptions of
each activist, participant observation gave me an opportunity to witness
their routines in the movement. The everyday life of organizations is the

context in which activists spend most of their time while mobilized and where personal experiences consequential for their subsequent trajectories are more common. As Belinda Robnett (1997) and Wendy Wolford (2010) argue in their studies of the civil rights movement in the United States and the Landless Peasant Movement in Brazil, it is at the grassroots level that the general agenda and meanings of a social movement get translated into particular appeals that resonate with the life histories of participants. Thus, daily events within groups of activists may be more meaningful to people than the overall characteristics of the movements to which they belong (McAdam 1988; Blee 2012; Shapira 2013). Therefore, as the fieldwork progressed and my interest in the experiences of rank-and-file activists deepened, I increasingly centered on what some respondents call "those days when nothing happens." I continued attending demonstrations and special events but also took part in the unremarkable tasks that occupy most of their time: fulfilling the requirements of workfare programs, having endless meetings, and doing paperwork.

I analyzed fieldnotes and transcripts using open and focused coding (Emerson, Fretz, and Shaw 1995). I first read over each of them in detail, writing down on small note cards the trends and issues that emerged. I used these note cards to create a more specific tree of nodes, which then served as a guideline to repeat the systematic line-by-line analysis of the data. I used NVivo software to code all this evidence. By this means, I was able to identify both commonalities and variations in the experiences of respondents.

Once I concluded the analysis of the evidence, I selected the stories and examples that most clearly illustrated and illuminated the different mechanisms I identify. In other words, the following chapters use interviews, fieldnotes, and photographs to provide a "thick description" (Geertz 1973) of how individuals engage in the process of becoming a piquetero activist. My goal is to help readers, no matter their familiarity with my case of study, place themselves in the shoes of the residents of Buenos Aires' most marginalized communities and visualize how behaviors that may make little sense to an outsider are completely logical for my respondents. Why do people commit to a political organization despite ideological disagreements? How do grassroots networks thrive even when their members face substantial obstacles to participation? What can we learn about mobilization when we stop idealizing protesters and see collective action as what it really is: an activity done by people who have a complex history and sometimes contradictory motivations yet are determined to live according to what they see as wholesome and right for them?

1.6 LOOKING AHEAD

In order to achieve its goals, the book is structured in the following way. Chapter 2 analyzes the transformations in Argentinean society since the 1970s, describing how the symbolic and material repercussions of deindustrialization were concentrated on vulnerable segments of the population. Neoliberal reforms not only undermined the means of sustenance for poor families but also dislocated much of the taken-for-granted attitudes and habits that organized life in working-class neighborhoods. Widespread joblessness affected the set of agreed-upon expectations and meanings at the core of working-class culture, which allowed people to organize their daily lives and interact with each other with a degree of confidence. The result was great anxiety and pervasive distrust.

Chapter 3 presents the trajectory of piquetero organizations as part of a broader wave of contention in Latin America. I show how they developed as networks of neighborhood groups coordinated by a central leadership, with extensive connections to preexisting instances of community life such as political parties, local associations, unions, and land occupations. Organizers were able to draw on established cultural and political traditions at the local level to develop an effective repertoire of contention, which in turn helped their groups become efficient problem-solvers. The chapter then explores how, over the past two decades, these groups succeeded in accumulating resources and developing cores of committed members, leading to an enduring presence in Argentina's popular politics.

Chapter 4 focuses on how older activists use their practices in the movement to reconstruct routines that once constituted an essential component of their personal identity, but that social changes have rendered impossible. In addition, I elaborate on how the reconstruction of routines varies for men and women: While the former engage in activities associated with blue-collar occupations, the latter reenact the type of household duties seen as the counterpart of factory work.

Chapter 5 describes the way in which younger members of the movement develop daily practices associated with an otherwise infeasible honorable lifestyle. In an environment with limited opportunities for personal growth, the movement offers a working-class ethos, plus the resources and training to exercise it. The chapter concludes by showing how the expectations inculcated to young members also reflect the ideal of a proletarian family with a gendered division of labor.

Chapter 6 analyzes how activists of all ages protect communal habits threatened by the expansion of unemployment. In a context of material deprivation, expansion of interpersonal violence, and decay of public spaces, organizations become oases of socialization where interpersonal trust and altruism are still possible. Just like reconstruction and development, protection of routines is a gendered process. I outline this effect by describing the role of two typical shared tasks within piquetero groups: the male-dominated "security teams" in charge of self-defense and crowd management during protests and the "milk cups," soup kitchens for minors that are almost entirely run by women.

Chapter 7 explores the trajectories of those activists who fail to develop attachment to their organizations, arguing that the key difference is between those individuals whose reasons for leaving are external (i.e., they face unsurmountable obstacles to continued involvement) and people whose motives are internal (i.e., they do not find participation appealing enough). Consequently, I introduce the distinction between potential dropouts (those who continue participating because they lack a better alternative), voluntary dropouts (those who choose to leave the movement for a more effective source of income), and reluctant dropouts (those who leave forced by special circumstances). I conclude with a return to the overall argument of the previous three chapters. The one thing potential and voluntary dropouts have in common is that participation does not become an end in itself for them but instead is just "a helping hand" to get through tough times. In contrast, reluctant dropouts share with long-term participants what I refer to as "resistance to quitting": a strong tendency to overcome obstacles to participation. However, this attitude has its limits, as even enthusiastic activists are not immune from life events that impede participation.

I outline my conclusions in Chapter 8, where I summarize the book's findings and analyze its main implications. I follow this conclusion with an appendix describing in detail the book's methodology, including a discussion of the practicalities and dilemmas of planning, funding, and implementing my fieldwork. A second appendix lists all recorded interviewees, along with basic demographic information.

For over two decades, piquetero organizations have been one of the most effective ways for marginalized Argentineans to support their families and assert their rights. In the process, they have played a crucial role in the still fledging Argentinean democracy. Exploring the complex processes through which individuals develop attachment to these groups is thus essential because it allows us to understand how people react to socioeconomic challenges in ways that contribute to an inclusive and stable political regime. Strong community organizations worldwide create channels for the expression of collective demands, support public life, and encourage civic engagement, especially among the most vulnerable segments of society. Consequently, the following pages aim not only to engage in key scholarly debates but also to serve as a humble tool for furthering the goals of grassroots activists around the globe.

2

"I Became a Bum"

Economic Reforms and Everyday Life in Argentina

The demonstration seems to be a success. Alejandro's organization, along with other allied groups, has completely blocked Buenos Aires' main intersection for about three hours. The whole event has been quite demanding: We gathered early in the morning, took two trains and a subway, remained standing for a long time, and marched for several blocks, all under the intense summer sun. The group's leaders decide to give the following day off to those who participated. I ask Alejandro if he wants to reschedule an interview we had arranged, but he tells me he is going to be at the organization's building anyways.

The next morning, as I arrive at the place, I find a small group of activists angrily talking among themselves. Apparently, some people who did not go to the march assumed the day off also applied to them. To make things worse, Carlos, the district coordinator, is refusing to call the no-shows to tell them to come. As soon as I arrive, Alejandro asks my opinion saying, "perhaps you see this thing differently." He goes on:

There are women here who have five children, earn 800 pesos. When they come and ask for something, you have to say yes. There are others who have a cooperativa, earn 2000 pesos. It is not much, but it is a salary. And they wear sneakers that cost at least 1000 pesos. Then you go to their home, and they never cook, always order delivery. And those are the people who complain to you! (Fieldnotes, February 26, 2014)

Alejandro's strong opinions about the value of austerity and responsibility are a reflection of his personal history. Born almost sixty years ago in a small village in the province of Tucumán, he has worked all his life in manual labor. His parents separated in his early childhood, and he lived for a few years with another family in the community, where he helped on a farm. He was still a minor when he hopped on a cargo train and made it to Buenos Aires with the idea of finding his father. However, he was unsuccessful for a while and ended up joining a group of street children who survived through begging and petty theft. He eventually got a job in a produce market, reconnected with relatives, and began a more stable life. He worked off the books in different occupations until he reached the legal age in which he could apply for formal jobs. Once he began working in a factory, he realized that it was his favorite kind of activity:

My thing was the factory. I do not care what it makes, stuffed toys, whatever, but I liked, you know, entering in the mornings and being there until six in the afternoon or ten at night. It was like, you know how you get used to being locked inside? That was my thing. (February 26, 2014)

For decades, he built a reputation as a trustworthy employee. He proudly tells stories of employers giving stellar references for him and of neighbors knowing that he was a hardworking man. He worked in meatpacking, textiles, and metals until factories began to close. Around the late 1990s, the last company he worked for went bankrupt, and for the first time, he could not find another job. He tried self-employment, from selling footwear and pastries door-to-door to mowing lawns, until even those jobs became unsustainable.

It was about this time that Alejandro was invited to join a piquetero organization. He had political experience, but the way he learned about the movement was completely different. An old lady in the neighborhood, who knew him from childhood and would yell at his friends when they tried to play soccer in the streets, let him know about an organization where he could find help. According to Alejandro, the reason she told him was precisely his reputation in the community:

She knew I was out of work. You know, people from the neighborhood know you, because today you cannot distinguish people, but in the past you could tell who worked and who did not. If you saw a person who never worked in his life, you are not going to tell him, "hey, come over here," because he never cared about it. So she knew I had worked all my life and I was mowing lawns, then told me "come with us." I do not know, she bothered me so much that I came here. I was doing quite badly because I could not find a job anymore. (February 26, 2014)

In the more than fifteen years since then, he has never left the group. Throughout my field research, he was a constant presence, working in a community improvement cooperative, attending meetings, and coordinating the security group. Not even medical troubles, brought about by a life of hard labor, were enough to hinder his involvement. When working with tools became too difficult, his fellows switched him to more administrative tasks, yet he still showed up every day wearing work clothes, barely missed an event, and took on the responsibility of managing different projects.

Alejandro's trajectory within the movement is not shared by all: Many people who joined around the same time as him are no longer participating, and some of his closest associates have dropped out. Yet the circumstances that led him into an unemployed workers' organization are very common. Almost every activist I talked to, regardless of their experiences prior to recruitment, joined the movement "due to necessity," seeking to obtain resources needed for survival. Alejandro's story, in other words, exemplifies the consequences at the individual and community level of long-term socioeconomic decline.

Despite political and economic instability, Argentina remained the most developed Latin American nation until very recently. A combination of extensive state intervention, a large light industry sector oriented toward the internal market, and powerful unions caused relatively high salaries, generous welfare policies, and low informality. However, as did many other areas of the world, the country experienced a paradigm shift in policy-making toward pro-market reforms since the 1970s. First implemented by the 1976–1983 military dictatorship, these structural transformations were either ineffectively resisted or actively promoted by subsequent democratic administrations. In particular, the 1990s presidencies of Carlos Menem saw an intensification of neoliberal policies and a dramatic acceleration of an already ongoing deindustrialization process. The result was a substantial growth in long-term unemployment, inequality, and marginalization, which peaked in the early 2000s but whose effects are still felt today.

This chapter explores these consequences. However, it will focus not just on the material effects of mass unemployment in Argentina (which have been thoroughly researched), but also on its symbolic and psychological ones. Neoliberal reforms not only undermined the means of sustenance for poor families but also dislocated much of the taken-for-granted attitudes and habits that organized life in working-class neighborhoods. Widespread joblessness precluded the type of life these communities associated with respectability, centered on the recognition of work experience, the prevalence of the breadwinner/homemaker domestic model, the accumulation of wealth in the form of a self-built home, and the reliance on local institutions for support.

In other words, regardless of their specific experiences, people like Alejandro highlight that when jobs were plentiful, life was difficult yet predictable and honorable. Residents of poor areas had a sense of what they needed to do in order to make a living, keep their relatives safe, and obtain resources. Mass unemployment disrupted the expectations and meanings at the core of working-class culture. As Alejandro insists, things like being used to spending long days in a factory and having a clear understanding of which neighbors were reliable workers allowed people to organize their daily lives and interact with each other with a degree of confidence. The collapse of these assumptions resulted in increasing uncertainty and distrust, which was as damaging to people's experiences as the material hardships imposed by increasing marginalization.

2.1 FOUR DECADES OF INEQUALITY AND DEINDUSTRIALIZATION

It is commonplace for Argentineans to describe their country as defined by drastic fluctuations in economic policy. Public discourse (of various ideologies) fixates on the inconsistencies of government plans, despairs about the incapacity of elites to reach long-term deals, and idealizes other nations that supposedly have been able to sustain stable policies (Grimson 2018). As with any myth, there is some truth to these claims. It is undeniable that Argentina's economic standing has declined since the early twentieth century (Gerchunoff and Llach 2003; The Economist 2014). In addition, distributive conflicts between an export-oriented agricultural sector on the one hand and an import-substituting labor-intensive industrial sector on the other have historically undermined the overall stability of the country (Gerchunoff and Llach 2004; Gerchunoff and Fajgelbaum 2006; Alvaredo, Cruces, and Gasparini 2018). However, narratives linking these disappointing economic results to a tendency toward irresponsible, inconsistent decision-making are overly simplistic. In fact, despite its volatility, in broad terms, Argentina has followed the policy paradigms prevalent in the region and the world at different times. After a period of high inequality and limited government, starting in the 1930s and 1940s, decades of industrialization by import substitution, coupled with strong state intervention, distributed wealth and improved the living conditions for working- and middle-class people. However, since the 1970s, pro-market reforms have led to growing disparities and worsening labor market opportunities. Even though at times (especially since the turn of the century) governments have tried to ameliorate the consequences of neoliberal policies, the structural constraints imposed by an increasingly interconnected global economy have limited the success of these initiatives. The myth of Argentina as a uniquely unstable nation is belied by the fact that other societies in Latin America and beyond faced comparable challenges at around the same time and followed relatively similar courses of action.

In the thirty years between the mid-1940s and mid-1970s, Argentina reached the lowest levels of inequality in its history, developed one of the most extensive welfare states in Latin America, and exhibited very low rates of unemployment. The social policies implemented by the 1946–1955 government of Juan Domingo Perón caused a massive redistribution of income, which not even its most ardent adversaries were able to reverse completely. The recognition of labor rights, the creation of various public assistance programs, and the establishment of the women's vote cemented the legacy of Peronism as a broad source of identity appealing to large (and very diverse) segments of the population, particularly among the working class. Despite intense political conflicts and recurrent military interventions, the combination of strong unions, a growing industry oriented to the internal market, and widespread government intervention kept poverty at bay for several decades. By 1974, when household surveys began to collect data, joblessness was 2.4 percent, less than 5 percent of the population lived under the official poverty line, and measures of inequality were among the lowest in the region (Groisman 2013; Alvaredo, Cruces, and Gasparini 2018).

Since then, however, the country's productive structure entered a period of profound transformations associated with sweeping neoliberal reforms. The 1975–2003 period includes years of rapid economic expansion along with increasingly severe crises, which reached their peak between 1998 and 2002, when Argentina's GDP shrank by 18 percent. As a result, in the roughly three decades after the mid-1970s, the country's GDP per capita remained stagnant, and disparities in wealth and income became entrenched (Lozano 2002; Gerchunoff and Llach 2003). Unemployment rose from the low single digits in the 1970s to 7.4 percent in 1990 to more than 20 percent in 2002. Underemployment grew from about 5 percent in 1974 to 20 percent in 2002 when three-fourths of part-time workers were involuntary (Neffa, Oliveri, and Persia 2010). Inequality also rose, with the Gini index and income ratios reaching levels comparable to the highest in the region (Groisman 2013; Alvaredo, Cruces, and Gasparini 2018).

These transformations had drastic effects on Argentina's working classes, as individuals with lower levels of formal education were among the
hardest hit by a shifting economy (Groisman 2013). Not only did stable
occupations become harder to attain, but the quality of jobs available also
declined. The percentage of employees in the manufacturing industry
more than halved, from 39 percent in 1974 to 17 percent in 2006. In
contrast, employment in areas requiring more credentials, such as government, professional, and business services, increased from 21 percent in
1974 to 41 percent in 2006 (Alvaredo, Cruces, and Gasparini 2018).
Informal labor and self-employment, which frequently have no benefits
and offer less stability, rose substantially. In 1980, one-fifth of employees
were off the books. In 2003, the percentage peaked at almost 50 percent
(MTEYSS 2010; also see CAC 2013; Bertranou and Casanova 2014).

After 2003, economic recovery and changes in public policy improved
these numbers slightly. However, the effectiveness of recent redistributive
interventions is limited by structural transformations in Argentina's labor
market, which has become more segmented and service-oriented.
Consequently, while inequality, unemployment, and informality have
fallen since their peak in the early 2000s, they remain far above their
1970s levels (Neffa, Oliveri, and Persia 2010; Groissman 2013; Salvia,

FIGURE 2.1 Recyclables collection center. La Matanza, August 2014.
*"When factories began to close, many fellows were kicked out. If you have to feed
kids and you do not want to go steal, you have to do something, gather cardboard,
anything"* (Lázaro).

Vera, and Poy 2015). Accessing stable employment and a living wage has become a greater challenge, particularly for poor Argentineans. In 2018, less than half of the economically active population had access to a job with full benefits, and workers in low socioeconomic status households were 13.5 times more likely to be employed in the informal sector than their upper-middle-class counterparts (Donza 2019).

In sum, Argentinean society seems to have entered a new normal in which a large portion of the population faces remarkable obstacles to access the educational and occupational opportunities that offer prospects for upward mobility. The progressive deterioration of the labor market over the past forty years concentrated in the poorest segments of society, with long-term consequences for the lives of individuals and the well-being of their communities.

2.2 UNEMPLOYMENT AND ITS IMPLICATIONS

The most direct consequence of unemployment is the undermining of the means of sustenance for an individual and his or her household. Faced with the loss of a source of income, families have a difficult time making ends meet, which becomes increasingly harder the longer it takes for the laid-off member to obtain a new job. This situation is compounded by the fact that in many societies, access to essential services such as healthcare, retirement plans, and social insurance is contingent on formal employment. In addition, the existence of biographical constraints such as dependents, coupled with the difficulty in translating skills specific to one occupation into another, creates barriers to finding a new job with similar pay and benefits as the one lost. In other words, being out of work means a shortfall of earnings both directly (through a period without pay) and indirectly (because of reductions in future income even after finding a new job). These effects tend to be more pronounced for lower socioeconomic status households, whose members are more likely to experience episodes of joblessness and have fewer financial and community resources to cope with them.

However, the implications of unemployment go beyond material deprivation. Work is central to people's lives in many intangible ways. First, it affects their identity: Who they are is determined to a great extent by what they do for a living. Studies of working-class culture have emphasized that manual labor is as much a source of identity as it is a source of income. It provides a comprehensive set of ideas about how the world operates and helps individuals interpret their place in it (Thompson 1971; Willis 1977; Charlesworth 2000; Lamont 2000). In addition, given the intimate link between a person's sense of self and his or her public image (Cooley 1902; Mead 1934; Goffman 1959), it is not surprising that occupation also influences how other individuals perceive someone. Consequently, exclusion from the job market undermines a person's claim to desirable social roles related to specific economic activities, gradually imposing membership in the disempowering and stigmatized category of the idle and jobless (Bourgois 1996; Sherman 2009).

Second, work fosters the creation of interpersonal connections. Leaving home, traveling somewhere, engaging in coordinated tasks, and even having conflicts generate all sorts of interactions with strangers, colleagues, customers, and supervisors. The experience of unemployment can thus be very isolating, as it drastically narrows the set of relationships an individual enters into every day. In addition, the loss of income caused by joblessness affects the capacity to spend on recreation and socialization, further reducing opportunities for sustaining meaningful associations (Kessler 1997).

Finally, and most crucially, having a job endows daily experiences with purpose (Bird 1966; Bourdieu 1997). It means being needed somewhere, having a schedule to follow, and tasks to complete. Involuntary idleness causes changes in a person's very notion of time, as discovered by Marie Jahoda, Paul Lazarsfeld, and Hans Zeisel in their classic 1930s study of the Austrian town of Marienthal:

Anyone who knows how tenaciously the working class has fought for more leisure ever since it began to fight for its rights might think that even amid the misery of unemployment, men would still benefit from having unlimited free time. On examination this leisure proves to be a tragic gift. Cut off from their work and deprived of contact with the outside world, the workers of Marienthal have lost the material and moral incentives to make use of their time. Now that they are no longer under any pressure, they undertake nothing new and drift gradually out of an ordered existence into one that is undisciplined and empty. Looking back over any period of this free time, they are unable to recall anything worth mentioning. (1977: 66)

The negative effects of unemployment largely depend on its temporal extent. In other words, the more difficult it is for people to obtain a new job, the more profound the consequences for their well-being. As failed searches accumulate and the perspective of being employed in the near future fades, workers confront the devastating realization that their exclusion from the labor market emerges not out of temporary circumstances but out of their structural unemployability. Simply stated, they do not have a role to play in the economy and are left to survive at the margins.

Denis Merklen uses the metaphor of the "urban hunter" to describe this situation. Unlike "farmers," who can rely on a predictable relation between efforts and income, "hunters" are at the mercy of forces beyond their control:

Hunters do not plan their lives according to an annual harvest, programmed in harmony with natural cycles. Neither do they have special means of saving which would allow them to adapt to periods of scarce prey or bad harvest. They do not have the possibility to participate in the reproduction of an economic cycle. Using the modern equivalents of fishing, gathering or hunting they live off what their habitat can offer, extracting it from that nature which they belong to: the city. What characterizes their way of acting is their relation of immediacy with their environment. The hunters know their territory perfectly and have developed effective strategies to catch a prey, based on what "nature" offers them. However, given that he or she exploits only "wild" resources (undomesticated) the hunter does not control reproduction. This is the key point. He or she knows the proper means to catch a prey, but he or she still needs to find one. (2005: 174, my translation)

The consequences of this exclusion are also felt at the community level. Mass unemployment weakens the social networks and institutions that provide cohesion to neighborhoods (Wilson 1996; Kessler 1997). As more and more residents are laid off, local businesses have fewer customers; religious and civic organizations lose resources; and public life in general declines. Informal means of social control lose efficacy; violence increases; and interpersonal trust weakens. This has the effect of further isolating individuals who have been expelled from the labor market, generating a vicious cycle of self-reinforcing marginalization. As William Julius Wilson explains in his study of joblessness in the United States:

Social isolation deprives inner-city residents not only of conventional role models, whose strong presence once buffered the effects of neighborhood joblessness, but also of the social resources (including social contacts) provided by mainstream social networks that facilitate social and economic advancement in a modern industrial society. (1996: 66)

In sum, the negative effects of unemployment go far beyond the individual loss of income. The removal of work-related sources of identity, relations, and purpose becomes more pronounced the longer a person is excluded from the labor market. When joblessness becomes persistent and wide-spread, the investment of individuals in the well-being of their community enters into a downward spiral:

Employment is the support, if not the source, of most interests, expectations, demands, hopes and investments in the present, and also in the future and the past that it implies, in short one of the major foundations of *illusio* in the sense of involvement in the game of life, in the present, the primordial investment which – as traditional wisdom has always taught, in identifying detachment from time with detachment from the world – creates time and indeed *is* time itself.

Excluded from the game, dispossessed of the vital illusion of having a function or a mission, or having to be or do something, these people may, in order to escape from the non-time of a life in which nothing happens and where there is nothing to expect, and in order to feel they exist, resort to activities which, like the French *tierce*, or *totocalcio*, *jogo de bicho* or all the other lotteries or gambling systems of all the bidonvilles and favelas of the world, offer an escape from the negated time of a life without justification or possible investment .... And, to try to escape from the sense, so well expressed by the Algerian subproletarians, of being the plaything of external constraints ("I'm like a scrap of peel on water") and to break out from a fatalistic submission to the forces of the world, the younger of them especially may also use acts of violence which in themselves count for more than, or as much as, the profits they procure, or death-defying games with cars or motor-bikes, as a desperate way of existing in the eyes of others, for others, of achieving a recognized form of social existence, or quite simply, of making something happen rather than nothing. (Bourdieu 1997: 222–223, emphasis in the original)

Nevertheless, the disruptive effects of job loss are rarely enough to undermine cultural dispositions emphasizing hard work, discipline, and stability. In other words, despite the well-documented link at the neighborhood level between widespread unemployment and prevalence of antisocial behaviors (Wilson 1996; Ihlanfeldt 2007; Fougère, Pouget, and Kramarz 2009), studies have consistently found that most residents in communities affected by exclusion from the labor market continue to play by the rules and seek legitimate occupations (Wilson 1996; Newman 1999; Sherman 2009). The appeal of a life centered on stable manual employment remains in place even when social transformations make such existence impossible (Bourgois 1996; Wacquant 2004). This is precisely the situation in Argentina, where events since the final decades of the twentieth century deprived countless people of the opportunity to live the lives they see as most fitting to them.

2.3 SOCIOECONOMIC DECLINE IN GREATER BUENOS AIRES

The deterioration of the labor market since the 1970s did not happen equally across Argentina. Indicators in the twenty-four districts surrounding the federal capital, which concentrate over eleven million residents (a quarter of the nation's total), have consistently been worse than average.

FIGURE 2.2 Dilapidated health post. La Matanza, May 2014.
"I do not get anything from the state, what do I get? Hunger, I get hunger. There is no health, there is no education, there is nothing, I receive nothing from the state" (Olivia).

Working-class neighborhoods in these districts, where the largest piquetero organizations developed and where almost all of my respondents live, were hit particularly hard by transformations in the economy (Delamata 2004; Grimson, Ferraudi Curto, and Segura 2009; Auyero and Berti 2015).

These dynamics had enormous effects on the lives of people in the piquetero movement. Deindustrialization caused drastic increases in unemployment and informality. As countless factories closed, carrying with them all sorts of small local businesses, obtaining stable employment with a decent salary and good benefits became increasingly difficult. Middle-aged respondents ended up being too young to retire but too old to be retrained for the kind of jobs available in a postindustrial society:

For the law, your working age is until sixty-five, then you retire, when you reach sixty-five. But if you had the bad luck, like most of us who are here in a movement, that when you were fifty you lost your job, or when you were in your forties, you have no way to enter again. Because you have a child, or they want you to work in a particular way, or they have thirty people waiting in line. (Tito, May 25, 2012)

[When] they started to bring all sorts of imported goods, the person who had a factory closed it because he could not sustain it. I had experience working in lots of factories, because when I came to live here, in 1980, you opened a newspaper then and got a job, you had the luxury of choosing jobs instead of losing jobs. Then all that generated that when you saw yourself unemployed, and the families, obviously that was terrible in the neighborhood. Those of us who felt we still could do things, we were desperate. (Federica, June 6, 2012)

For younger interviewees, the problem is different: Necessary credentials and experience are frequently out of reach for them. Poorly funded elementary and secondary schools, limited availability of jobs, residential segregation, and discrimination conspire to prevent a successful transition into higher education and well-paying occupations:

I tell you as a young person, the primordial need that shows up in all conversations is employment. Because kids leave high school, and cannot get a job because everywhere they ask for experience. You finish high school, have no experience at all, how can you start your first job? I think that the biggest problem of young people is the lack of jobs. Take for instance, they go to high school, you need two or three pesos every day for the bus, you have to go to physical education in the morning or after school, you have to buy books and photocopies, and a lot of kids have a mother that has a lot of children, she cannot facilitate that. So what do kids do? "Well, I'll go and work." And drop out of school. They get some odd job, but they already lost the school and those odd jobs will end in nothing. (Leila, July 30, 2011)

There is this vision that the country has improved ... but you do not see that in Greater Buenos Aires, in the outskirts. What you see is the growing decay of youth, with the issue of crime, drugs, and lots of issues that we need to exterminate in the future. For instance, in a neighborhood we made a survey and saw that of seventy or eighty kids, only eight go to college. Only twenty finished high school. Almost thirty have not finished elementary school. That is the social conglomerate that tomorrow will have to lead this country. The state is absent there. (Carlos, July 20, 2011)

The result is that even after a period of relative growth since the early 2000s, a large portion of the population remains excluded from the formal labor market, forced to rely on unstable survival strategies that combine odd jobs, public assistance, charities, and in a few cases, lawbreaking (Auyero 2001; Quirós 2006, 2011):

2001 were terribly convulsed times. And that extended for a few years. Then a relative economic stability, sort of, due to the high prices of export commodities, caused things to calm down a bit. Not because the real necessities were solved, but because there was an opportunity, as we say here, of making it a bit. He who had no job could get an odd job, or a precarious job, in a country that has 40% off-the-books employment. Some were even luckier and got a regular job, [but] these are few. (Patricio, July 21, 2011)

We have the everyday problems, salary, income, work. There is a very large portion, some statistics say that forty, fifty percent of industrial workers are off-the-books. That is concentrated in the poorest neighborhoods, because the percentage of fellows in those neighborhoods who work in informal jobs, odd-jobs reaches seventy percent. They are discriminated because of where they live, they live in a slum and then cannot give their true address because they do not get hired. Businesses today will check where you worked, where you live, and you can only get a job selling hot dogs. The informality of work, the precarization of work, is one of the greatest problems we see in the neighborhood. (Humberto, July 21, 2011)

The effect of these transformations for the material and psychological well-being of residents in these communities was profound. Individuals and families experienced a sharp decline in living conditions, which generated conflicts within their homes and in many cases led to severe mental health problems. These dynamics can be illustrated with the cases of Diego and Lourdes, who belong to two different organizations yet live in the same district.

For more than a decade, Diego worked in a pharmaceutical company. As a registered, unionized worker, he had access to regular pay increases and social benefits. Yet all that progress came to an abrupt end when he was fired in the 1990s:

I used to work in a very important pharmaceutical company. And then I became a croto [bum]. A hungry person. A guy who could not find a job, who had failed to obtain a good standard of living, because I had a precarious house. I moved from being a worker who had a good salary. What do I mean? I did not even work digging ditches, which is not a dishonor. I worked in a company, in a pharmaceutical factory, I had a job in which I am not saying I was an intellectual nor a member of the middle class, but I had, a way of life, a status. Afterward I was in little more than rags, without a way out, when I lost my job. (June 9, 2012)

Being laid off completely shattered the daily routines Diego was used to. From "being a guy who lived focused on filling my work hours," he was now stuck at home with no role to fulfill. Becoming a *croto* was more than just the physical manifestation of material deprivation; it also was a visible sign of unemployability. As weeks turned into months and rejected applications multiplied, people like Diego suffered many forms of humiliation, which made scarcity even harder to bear. Experiences like being told repeatedly by prospective employers to wait for a phone call that never came were painful demonstrations that their work experience, once their most valuable asset, was irrelevant to the few jobs available.

For Diego and countless others, extended unemployment also meant a threat to an ideal of masculinity centered on providing for the needs of their families. Raised to be good fathers and husbands, being involuntarily idle in the middle of their active years had devastating consequences:

We saw men, some older than others, who after a lifetime of working, many took their own lives, because they felt they were at the bottom of the sea. We moved from being the generators of the family budget and the structure of our families, to being the lumpens who were always at home lying down. Because the issue of depression showed up, moral decay, "I am useless." That's how they made us feel, a guy older than thirty had no place in a factory. (June 9, 2012)

The combination of material impoverishment and psychological distress was of course not limited to men. Lourdes, a woman in her fifties, experienced similar challenges when she went bankrupt. After working for five years in a factory, she and her husband built a small grocery store in front of their house so she could stay home and take care of their child. For seventeen years, this business was her pride, offering a source of independent income and a constant connection to neighbors and customers. However, as the economic situation in her community deteriorated, her clientele diminished rapidly. The store, which used to be a crucial source of money for the household, now became a drain as beggars replaced shoppers:

I was like angry with the world, because I said, how is it possible after so much sacrifice so I could have my store? I first began with a small kiosquito [shop], and then I added one thing and another until I had a larger store. I paid all taxes, everything was legal. And I could not pay business taxes because I could not make ends meet. Because I always thought I had a strong character. But I cannot say no to children. That is what happened, children came and asked for milk and bread. You need to realize that they were not asking for soda, but milk and bread. How can you say to a little child "I cannot give you anything," or "send your dad to come and buy"? So I gave to them, and I could not do that, because I was practically giving away stuff. Kids had no way of paying, they said the mom sent them, and moms sent them because it was the only way I would give them something, out of pity. And I could not live out of pity, I had to buy the bread and milk I gave away. It got to the point when I had to close to store. (August 1, 2011)

With her business closed, Lourdes sought employment elsewhere. Nevertheless, finding a new job in a tough economy, after years of working in a store, was very difficult:

With a lot of pain I closed my store, and I began to look for jobs, even for a few hours, I did not care because I was not afraid to work. But due to my age, I did not get anything, where was I going to find a job? Besides, I needed some recommendation from someone to begin working, in whatever place, a store, as a housecleaner, whatever, I was not afraid. And no, I could not find anything. (April 24, 2014)

Fortunately, Lourdes's husband did not lose his job, so while the family had to cut expenses substantially, they never experienced the extreme deprivations many of their neighbors suffered. However, the collapse of a business for which she had worked so hard took a very heavy toll on Lourdes's health. Desperate to fill the time previously occupied working and isolated from the social life the store sustained, she began obsessively doing household chores:

What happened? I began in my house to clean, to clean. I lived obsessed, I did not realize it was a depression, because I felt like a failure, having to close the store, which had taken me so much effort. Because it had taken a lot of work to build it little by little, it was not from a moment to another that we set up the store, it was a lot of work … that is how depression works, it was being locked at home, until one day my sister came and said, "what are you doing here stuck all day cleaning and cleaning?" Because I was obsessed cleaning every spot, I could not sleep, I was used to work from six in the morning when I got up, because I got up to clean, prepare everything, and then work at the store. I opened from seven in the morning to ten at night. I did not close, and I talked with one person, another, my neighbors, I knew everyone. (April 24, 2014)

The struggles of people like Diego and Lourdes were not limited to the individual level. As unemployment became the norm, the challenges faced by working-class families were compounded by a substantial decline in their communities. Changes in social policies and the deterioration of the labor market disrupted many of the institutions that used to structure daily life in working-class neighborhoods across the nation (Merklen 2005; Grimson 2009). Not only did factories and businesses close, but communal spaces such as schools, clubs, and parks also suffered. These transformations contributed to an increase in interpersonal violence and the undermining of public life (ODSA 2011; Auyero and Berti 2015). When asked about changes in their neighborhoods, most respondents highlight what they see as an explosion in criminality and substance abuse. What used to be taboo, hidden activities have taken over shared spaces. Interviews are full of references to *la esquina,* "the street corner," as the archetype of a place previously occupied by wholesome activities (children playing and adults socializing) yet now controlled by young men who are both victims of addiction and victimizers of peaceful residents:

There's too much drugs, every corner you see people doing drugs, there is too much crime, too many thefts … they drink in the street, they do drugs in the street, they piss on the street. They curse at you, "hey, dude, leave some money for the booze," all those things people did not do in the past, or at least I did not see it. (Lázaro, June 27, 2014)

People used to consume marijuana and cocaine. That stuff always existed, only that in the past it used to be at parties and between four walls. Now they do that in the streets. (Bianca, July 8, 2014)

I live in a precarious neighborhood, a neighborhood where all the little houses are the same. There are a lot of drugs there. Until last year there was a [dealer's] place in front of my home, two or three houses down the street another, and in the other block another. And I walk past every day, and every day in the same corner you see the same kids. Destroyed. (Jonathan, June 1, 2012)

Question: How has your neighborhood changed since you have lived there?
Melina: Lots of drugs. It used to be a humble neighborhood, people looked for jobs, they really did, and now it is like the more easy life, drugs, prostitution, and other things.

Q: And what are the other things?
M: Being on the corner, harassing the neighbors. You used to see that there were two or three or four people who bothered, but they did not bother the neighbors, if you were with someone they did not know, they would not bother him, now it has changed. Things are more visible, more violent. I think it is because people have no jobs. (Melina, June 20, 2013)

The consequences of rising crime and drugs are exacerbated by decades of underinvestment in public infrastructure and services (education, health, safety, recreation, and transportation), which deprives residents of basic needs and hinders the development of socialization spheres:

Life in poor neighborhoods is tough, it is tough because buses do not reach there, because hospitals are far away, because there are few schools which do not have enough open seats, because there is no sanitation, because there is no sewage, there are open air ditches where the waste water flows in the open. (Osvaldo, August 9, 2011)

What happens in our zone is that we do not have places where teenagers can have recreation. . . . Now we have a place that the municipality built, it used to be a huge empty lot. They made a shed. And it is only open a few hours. They do activities, but it is mostly closed. That place needs to be open, so they can go play soccer, do exercise. But it is almost always closed. (Bautista, August 5, 2011)

My neighborhood is a neighborhood that, like all neighborhoods here, you lack public lights, there are many outages. There is no water, sidewalks, paving, sewage. I think that the health post in the neighborhood is not enough for the quantity of people who live there. Housing is really needed, the houses are very humble. I think we need a playground, there is no playground for the kids, so they can play. There is not a cultural or recreational center for the kids in the neighborhood. (Iván, June 9, 2012)

To make matters more difficult, local actors that traditionally served as spaces for collectively addressing these problems many times lack resources and influence. Mariana complained about the incapacity of the neighborhood association in her community to live up to its historical function as representative of the residents' interests. Even though the institution is supposed to be run collectively and offer free services, in practice, it is controlled by local politicians who charge fees for everything:

In our neighborhood we have a neighborhood association and a club, a cultural center, and a health post. The three are taken by the ruling party in this district. Like, look at this: a kid has to pay a monthly subscription of fifteen pesos to play soccer. But if you have no money, no job, how can you include that kid so he can play? (July 30, 2011)

Analía described a similar problem. Due to the inadequacy of garbage collection, a large empty lot in front of her house risked becoming an illegal landfill. In addition, squatters had tried to occupy the space, and drug users frequented the location. Together with a group of neighbors, she made inquiries with the municipality and discovered that the lot was designated for public use. However, residents were ultimately unable to organize and pressure the authorities to turn the space into something that addressed the area's many needs:

First we had spoken about doing a small playground. Well, after a long talk with the neighbors in one meeting, people said it was not convenient to make a playground, because there are so many drugs around there, and we will not take the kids in the middle of the day to a playground so they can see all those things. You have to imagine, in front of my house there is a big wood where they do drugs, they inject themselves, and if you take the kids there they see the needles, everything. So in the end the neighbors wanted not a playground, but a neighborhood center, or a kindergarten. Because in a center you can have nurses who take your blood pressure, perhaps a physician, even if only once or twice a week. Or a pediatrician, because the health post is many blocks away from where we live. But neighbors began to get tired, everything we did was in vain, nothing worked. So all that began to weaken, we did not complete it, what we had organized was dismantled. (August 5, 2011)

2.4 THE PAST AND PRESENT OF EVERYDAY LIFE

In sum, economic changes associated with neoliberal reforms drastically undermined the living conditions in the most vulnerable communities in the nation, as the challenges faced by individuals, families, and neighborhoods reinforced each other (Auyero and Berti 2015). Joblessness, crime, and violence became commonplace aspects of everyday life, locking people into a spiral of decreasing opportunities. Olivia, a mother of nine and survivor of domestic violence, used the metaphor of a locked room to describe the combination of accumulating problems and declining solutions:

They used to be older boys [doing drugs], now ten-, twelve-, thirteen-, fourteen-, fifteen-year-olds. They are sadly lost in the drugs and it hurts, because the kid is sick, it is a twelve-year-old kid, the family gets sick, because what can they do? It is like you are in a room with four walls and you hit one wall, hit another, you find no solution. There are no free places around here for kids to rehabilitate. You have to pay for it and it costs lots of money. Then the kid gets out, at any job they will ask for an education. And most kids who get out, what kind of education can they have? They do not get anything, and fall back [into drugs]. I see it, they go back into crime . . . I think that the state should create jobs, because many kids get out of prison, but now they have a record. Many kids maybe really want to change, go search for a job and they are told no, because they have a record. And perhaps that kid, at age sixteen already has a family, they already have kids, and the kid perhaps, as we say here, wants to rescue himself, change his life. Unfortunately we, as a society, condemn them. (January 15, 2014)

Residents make sense of these transformations by contrasting a dangerous and uncertain present with a past in which life was hard but orderly. In other words, deindustrialization not only undermined the financial stability, psychological well-being, and overall safety of individuals, households, and communities but also affected the material conditions at the root of Argentina's working-class culture, the set of agreed-upon assumptions that organized daily life in the country's poorest neighborhoods. These communities always struggled with material scarcity and unsatisfied needs. However, the availability of formal manual labor, coupled with the network of institutions supported by such activity, allowed residents to structure their days around a set of specific routines (people leaving early in the morning for work and returning late in the afternoon, the entry and exit times at schools, the schedules of community and union-related events). In addition, as Alejandro recalled at the beginning of this chapter, extensive job opportunities helped distinguish "who worked and who did not," who was a responsible person that could be trusted and who was not.

The widespread exclusion from the labor market caused the collapse of the domestic, professional, and communal routines that conveyed a sense of consistency and respectability to the everyday life of working-class Argentineans. Even those who had played by the rules, working long

FIGURE 2.3 Entrance to shantytown. Autonomous City of Buenos Aires, February 2014.
"Crime gets worse every day. These days you leave your home and find all sorts of things in the streets. You cannot speak on the phone because someone will steal it from you, you cannot have a purse because people know that if you have a purse it means you have some money" (Lía).

hours, accumulating experience, and contributing to their families, found themselves idle. Adults lost their lifetime occupations; youngsters could not find their first job; and public life broke down under the combined weight of resource deprivation, rising interpersonal violence, and state neglect.

As the following chapters will explain, the comparison between an idealized past and a problematic present is central to understanding not only people's perception of their neighborhood's evolution but also the reasons why participation in a grassroots organization becomes so enjoyable for some. In other words, the appeal of involvement in the unemployed workers' movement cannot be understood without paying attention to the symbolic and psychological consequences of mass unemployment. Piquetero groups became essential for the financial survival of countless families, but contrary to what many detractors of the movement argue, that is far from the only reason people participate in them. In fact, long-term involvement seems to develop out of processes that are only partially related to the distribution of material resources. Practices in the movement allow people to earn their livelihood in morally sanctioned ways, obtaining refuge from the context of marked socioeconomic decline that has affected working-class communities in Argentina in the past four decades. Through the reconstruction, development, and protection of routines perceived as wholesome, some activists solve crucial deficits in their lives, such as the feeling of being unable to affect one's condition, the lack of public appreciation, and the isolation from meaningful relationships.

3

"The Struggle Is on the Streets"

Democracy, Neoliberalism, and Piquetero Mobilization

For many reasons, December is a contentious month in Buenos Aires. The beginning of summer brings uncomfortable, humid heat, and the city's lack of public pools and clean bodies of water denies residents a place to escape the weather. The growing use of air conditioning puts strains on the electric grid, and blackouts are frequent. The proximity of Christmas, which most Argentineans observe, causes extra tension as many people face difficulties affording gifts and celebrations. Anxiety becomes palpable and only subsides in January when those who can leave for vacation.

The final weeks of the year have always been complicated times, and Argentineans like to joke about the stress that comes with the holiday season. However, this tendency has become more acute since 2001, when a combination of food riots and nationwide protests caused the fall of the national government. Besieged by widespread disapproval and the biggest economic crisis in the country's history, the administration of Fernando de La Rúa resorted to increasingly desperate measures and declared a state of emergency on December 19. When this decision failed to stem the surge in collective action, the next day security forces launched a brutal repression. After hours of violence, the president resigned.

Ever since then, social movements, unions, and political parties commemorate the victims with annual demonstrations. That is the reason why more than a decade later, on the morning of December 19, 2013, piquetero activists in the district of La Matanza are getting ready to march. Things are particularly tense this year. Reports about possible lootings always surface around this time, but in recent weeks, they have been particularly strong. Power cuts also seem to be happening more frequently. This morning, as I took two buses and walked a mile to get to

49

an organization's building, I saw in several separate places the remains of tires burnt the night before by people demanding the restitution of electric service. A few young participants tell me that the original plan was to protest tomorrow, but there are rumors that supermarkets will be attacked then (one of the largest associations of shop owners called for its members to close their stores just in case). Hence, the demonstration was set for today to avoid any association with potential plunderers.

Preparations end around 11 AM, and we depart in three rented buses. The final destination is a rally from the National Congress to the Palace of Government in downtown Buenos Aires, but first, we will participate in a small local protest. The buses park; we get out and wait for people from other neighborhoods. A woman with limited mobility begins greeting everyone. Someone invites her to get back on the bus: The march has not begun; why not wait seated? She responds loudly, "[T]he struggle is on the streets, not on the buses," and keeps saying hello to those around her.

Eventually, everyone arrives, and we begin marching five blocks to a metallurgical company that is in the process of firing several employees. The streets are largely empty under the midday sun, and the appearance of several hundred people marching together triggers nervous reactions. The few open businesses hastily close their doors; residents standing outside hurry to their homes; and a loud security alarm goes off. By the time we get to the factory, an improvised stage with big speakers has been prepared on the back of a truck. The leaders of the march discuss the details of the event with the company's private security, which is accommodating: This kind of protest is commonplace in Argentina. As long as the demonstrators stay in the street and let people enter and leave the place, there will be no conflict. A few people (including one of the affected workers) give speeches, relating the struggle in this specific company with the overall history of the movement and the larger march we will join later.

After half an hour, we walk back the way we came. The tension has not subsided: Stores remain closed, neighbors are still behind doors, and the alarm goes off again. We get on the buses and start the trip downtown. I talk with Milagros and Renata, two middle-aged friends who have been in the movement for more than a decade. They tell me that originally they were skeptical about the organization. However, over time, they began to see things differently. Today, it is clear that they feel pride in the many sacrifices they made over the years. They share stories of exhausting demonstrations, compare themselves to younger participants who "want everything right now," and insist, "people say we are lazy, but we work a lot."

FIGURE 3.1 March in support of striking teachers. La Plata, March 2014.
"In here, no one is going to gift you anything. Here you earn things, with your effort, you earn things" (Milagros).

Finally, we make it to the central event of the day. Thousands of demonstrators occupy five to six blocks of *Avenida de Mayo* (May Avenue), a traditional location for protests in the city. Most piquetero organizations opposed to the national government are attending, along with some far-left political parties and unions. It is early in the afternoon on one the hottest days in the year, yet the atmosphere is cheerful. Demonstrations in Argentina borrow heavily from one of the country's passions: soccer. Drums, fireworks, flags, and trumpets make the protest noisy and fun. Songs originally used to cheer for different teams have their lyrics changed into political statements.

The march advances slowly until it reaches *Plaza de Mayo* (May Square), the most politically charged place in the city. Crucial events in Argentina's history, such as the declaration of the first autonomous government in 1810, the massive demonstration of October 1945 that saved Juan Domingo Perón from incarceration, and the gatherings of mothers of the disappeared during the 1976–1983 dictatorship, all took place here, in front of the presidential palace and other official buildings. Here too was the epicenter of the revolts that we are commemorating. Some of the palm trees in the square remain charred after being set on fire that day. Leaders of many groups (including the one I am marching with) give speeches that combine homage to those killed in 2001 with more recent demands: minimum wage increases to combat the rising cost of living, the end of a controversial plan to surveil protests, and improvements in the working conditions of public employees.

A whole day's worth of activities wraps up. It has taken more than expected, and everyone is tired. However, people seem to be in a good mood as they return to the buses in an orderly manner. Despite rumors, nothing out of the ordinary happened. The fear of widespread riots will not materialize, and tomorrow newspapers will cover the rally extensively, highlighting the different types of groups which took place in it.

Protests like the one just described, combining diverse elements and agendas, were typical during my research. Over the three and a half years my fieldwork spanned, few of the demonstrations I attended included only organizations of unemployed workers. Much more frequently, these groups marched along with student associations, political parties, human rights advocates, and unions, either as part of a formal coalition, or as a temporary alliance around a particular topic. For all of their innovative and unique aspects, piquetero organizations have been embedded from the beginning in dense institutional networks and complex political cultures, at both the local and national level. This immersion influenced their trajectory, allowing them to remain influential for over twenty years.

This chapter outlines the history of this movement, highlighting both its participation in a wave of mobilization that affected South America over the past few decades, and its close relation to a rich tradition of popular politics in Argentina. Piquetero organizations developed as networks of neighborhood-based activists coordinated by a central leadership, with extensive connections to preexisting instances of community life. Organizers were able to draw on established cultural and political conventions to develop an effective repertoire of contention and a flexible internal structure, which helped them adapt to changes in their context, capitalizing on opportunities and overcoming challenges.

Moreover, the enduring presence of the piquetero movement in working-class communities across the nation is also associated with processes at the individual level. A crucial aspect of the movement's persistence is the way in which it functions as a refuge for practices associated with an appealing but increasingly uncommon proletarian lifestyle. The opportunity to engage in habits threatened by deindustrialization is a key reason why some recruits eventually develop a strong attachment to their organizations, helping these groups maintain one of their central assets: a core of seasoned, loyal members.

3.1 REGIONAL MOBILIZATION AND THE PIQUETERO MOVEMENT

Starting in the 1980s, Latin America experienced a combination of substantial political liberalization on the one hand and growing inequality due to neoliberal reforms on the other. As mentioned in Chapter 1, this scenario has proven fertile ground for the development of various experiences of grassroots organization throughout the region, which have proven their strengths in many ways. First, they have contributed to the "deepening" of democracy in different countries, playing a central role in efforts to expand the social rights recognized and enforced by the state (Almeida 2007; Roberts 2008; Delamata 2009a; Silva and Rossi 2018). Second, they obtained increasing influence in institutional spheres of power, especially during the first decade and a half of the twenty-first century. Governments in the "pink tide" in Latin American politics sought to incorporate parts of social movements into their coalitions. The result was an expansion of the role that social movements played not just in the streets but also in the political system at large (Baiocchi 2005; Baker and Greene 2011; Levitsky and Roberts 2011; Prevost, Oliva Campos, and Varden 2012; Burbach, Fox, and Fuentes 2013). Finally, they have developed connections beyond national borders. Assisted by events such as the World Social Forum and the struggle against the Free Trade Area of the Americas, activists in the region have had a growing influence over events at a global scale (Johnson and Almeida 2006; Stahler-Sholk, Varden, and Kuchner 2008; Silva 2013).

However, this road has not been free of obstacles. First, the immersion of activists in a political process marked by neoliberal principles of governance creates powerful dilemmas (Alvarez 1999, 2009; Roberts and Portes 2006; Svampa 2008). In particular, grassroots groups that developed in opposition to pro-market policies face the quandary of offering services to underprivileged communities in ways that sustain the very social order they want to transform. By providing essential public goods such as food, health, and education, civil society organizations allow the state to delegate some of its basic social responsibilities (Gómez and

Massetti 2009; Hale 2011). Second, the increased access to institutional spheres of power has caused its own problems. Lawmakers, officials, and activists frequently operate under different logics, priorities, and strategies. This situation has generated occasional conflicts and pressures to accommodate agendas and tactics, even from allied or sympathetic administrations (Park and Richards 2007; Lapegna 2013, 2016). Finally, right-wing political coalitions in the region have made consistent progress, especially since the mid-2010s. Much of their electoral appeal seems to be the result of backlash against progressive policies, highlighting the existence of limits to the influence of grassroots organizations (Ellner 2020; Ferrero, Natalucci, and Tatagiba 2019).

As one of the most visible instances of collective action in Latin America's recent history, the piqueteros exemplify the opportunities and challenges faced by grassroots organizations in the region. Most organizations in the movement are relatively loose networks of neighborhood-based groups coordinated by a central leadership that stage disruptive events such as blockades of roads and pickets in front of factories, supermarkets, and government offices. In the ensuing negotiation with the authorities, they pressure for the distribution of social assistance, usually in the form of foodstuffs, positions in workfare programs, and funding for small cooperative projects. If successful, they distribute what they obtain among participants, following criteria based on need and merit: Whoever has more dependents and contributes more time and effort to the organization is prioritized. Moreover, activists use part of these resources to develop a vast array of social services in areas where the welfare arm of the state has retreated. The prospect of accessing material support draws many people into these organizations, which in turn helps them continue demonstrating for more "jobs, foodstuffs, and plans."

The ideological spectrum of the movement covers almost every current in Argentina's left-wing politics.[1] In general terms, most organizations in Buenos Aires (where my fieldwork took place) belong to three loose (and frequently overlapping) ideological families. First, some groups align with various Marxist traditions and parties, such as the Maoist *Corriente Clasista y Combativa* (Classist and Combative Current); the Trotskyist *Movimiento Sin Trabajo "Teresa Vive"* (Jobless Movement "Teresa

---

[1] For overviews of the different organizations in the movement, see Svampa and Pereyra (2003, chapter 2); Pereyra, Pérez, and Schuster (2008, introduction); Rossi (2017, chapters 1 and 2).

Lives") and *Polo Obrero* (Worker's Pole); the Leninist *Movimiento de Liberación Territorial* (Territorial Liberation Movement), and the Guevarist *Movimiento de Trabajadores Desocupados "Teresa Rodríguez"* (Movement of Unemployed Workers "Teresa Rodríguez") and *Movimiento de Trabajadores Desocupados "Aníbal Verón"* (Movement of Unemployed Workers "Aníbal Verón"). Second, there are organizations that combine elements of left-wing nationalism, liberation theology, and Peronism. Examples are the *Federación Nacional de Trabajadores por la Tierra, la Vivienda y el Hábitat* (National Federation of Workers for Land, Housing and Habitat), *Barrios de Pie* (Neighborhoods Standing Up), the *Coordinadora de Trabajadores Desocupados "Aníbal Verón"* (Coordinator of Unemployed Workers "Aníbal Verón"), the *Movimiento Evita* (Evita Movement), and the *Movimiento Independiente de Jubilados y Desocupados* (Independent Movement of the Retired and Unemployed). Finally, a number of groups define themselves as autonomists, seeking to create self-reliant forms of employment and production. Among them are the *Frente Popular "Dario Santillán"* (Popular Front "Dario Santillán") and several *Movimientos de Trabajadores Desocupados* (Unemployed Workers' Movements) with presence in the southern part of Greater Buenos Aires.

Ideological disagreements have thwarted past attempts to develop a unified coalition covering all these organizations. However, in practice, activists, allies, and adversaries recognize them as belonging to the same movement (Svampa and Pereyra 2003; Rossi 2017). To a great extent, this recognition is related to the prevalence of functional and structural similarities. Despite divisions and particularities, three factors cause most piquetero organizations to operate internally and externally in relatively homogeneous ways.

First, the immersion of piquetero organizations in a shared political culture undermines the weight of their ideological differences. The historical predominance of Peronism among working-class communities in Argentina (Auyero 2001; Rossi 2017), coupled with long-standing political practices such as the neighborhood-based organization of collective action and the existence of relations of trust and reciprocity between organizers and constituencies, generates commonalities in the daily work of grassroots organizations. Whatever their specific agendas, groups of unemployed workers cannot function successfully without following established traditions and expectations at the local level.

Second, the internal structure of most piquetero organizations promotes a remarkable tolerance to diversity of opinions among ranks.

Since their emergence, a majority of them have functioned as networks of local groups (Merklen 2005; Grimson, Ferraudi Curto, and Segura 2009; Quirós 2011; Manzano 2013). The immediacy of the goals bringing these groups together (securing the livelihood of vulnerable families, obtaining the resources necessary to address indigence, and providing basic social services) contributes to a situation in which the enforcement of ideological conformity takes a backseat to the solving of urgent problems affecting the survival of communities.

Finally, while disagreements between leaders caused many splits and prevented piquetero organizations from establishing an all-encompassing umbrella confederation, smaller alliances based on particular objectives have also been frequent (Fornillo, García, and Vázquez 2008; Pereyra 2008; Forni 2020). The recurrence of contingent partnerships between different groups limits the influence of their individual platforms, as it forces them to share resources, meet with each other, and coordinate strategies. In addition, organizations in the movement recurrently engage in joint activities with other actors such as unions, political parties, and human rights groups. By emphasizing common grievances and tactics, these coalitions further reduce the influence of organizational specificities in the daily lives of activists.

These factors have not only generated parallels in the everyday work of different piquetero organizations but also contributed to their capacity to overcome substantial challenges. Since its emergence more than two decades ago, the movement has been affected by changes in political alignments, economic conditions, and public opinion (Delamata 2004; Svampa 2005, 2008; Epstein 2006; Massetti 2006; Garay 2007; Wolff 2007; Pereyra, Pérez, and Schuster 2008; Gómez 2009; Manzano 2013; Pozzi and Nigra 2015; Rossi 2015, 2017; Kaese and Wolff 2016). However, organizations of unemployed workers have remained a constant presence in countless poor neighborhoods of Argentina, contributing to the sustenance of families in need, providing social services, and generating opportunities for citizen and community empowerment. Their resilience reflects the capacity of activists to adjust to the ebbs and flows of contention cycles, pragmatically making decisions in response to variations in their context.

3.2 1996–2003: EMERGENCE AND EXPANSION

The direct precursors of the unemployed workers' movement were localized uprisings in different provinces of Argentina (Barbetta and

Lapegna 2001; Auyero 2002, 2003; Svampa and Pereyra 2003; Pereyra 2008; Ramos 2009; Benclowicz 2013). In them, protesters occupied public spaces and buildings, as well as blocked roads, to demand attention to the consequences of layoffs, budget cuts, and lack of payment of salaries. The term *piquetero* itself (Spanish for road blocker or picketer) became commonplace between 1996 and 1997 during protests in the provinces of Neuquén and Salta, where the privatization of the national oil company by President Carlos Menem (1989–1999) caused a sudden leap in unemployment. Shortly after, a number of groups in the periphery of the country's largest cities, especially Buenos Aires, began to emulate these protests, developing an efficient repertoire of contention and a flexible internal structure, which remain the norm to this day.

Although narratives at the time described the movement's emergence as a spontaneous reaction to deprivation, it is clear that political processes played a central role. As Javier Auyero (2002, 2003) and José Daniel Benclowicz (2011, 2013) have shown for the cases of Neuquén and Salta, respectively, the uprisings that gave piqueteros their name were only possible thanks to the work of preexisting political actors, which catalyzed widespread discontent into organized collective action. In the case of Greater Buenos Aires, previous experiences of popular organization were essential to the emergence of piquetero groups, providing expertise, connections, and leadership (Svampa and Pereyra 2003; Delamata 2004; Merklen 2005; Pereyra 2008). For instance, the National Federation of Workers for Land, Housing and Habitat developed out of the experience of community organization in El Tambo, a former land occupation in La Matanza, and benefited from its association with the *Central de Trabajadores Argentinos* (Central of Argentinean Workers), a confederation of hard-line unions. The Classist and Combative Current was created in a similar way by activists from different political traditions (mostly Maoism, but also Peronism) in another area of the same district. Organizations such as the Worker's Pole and the Jobless Movement "Teresa Lives" were founded by initiative of the *Partido Obrero* (Worker's Party) and the *Movimiento Socialista de los Trabajadores* (Socialist Movement of Workers), respectively, two small but well-organized Trotskyist parties that helped them develop extended territorial networks. In other words, piquetero groups, like many other instances of collective action, emerged out of the remnants of past cycles of mobilization. During times of reduced activism, networks of militants do not disintegrate completely. Although their influence is reduced, the persistence of these groups helps generate resources that allow future protests to take place (Rupp and Taylor 1987; Melucci 1989; Staggenborg 1998).

In addition to the contributions of previous experiences of collective action, it is impossible to explain the development of the piquetero movement without paying attention to the marked deterioration of economic conditions in the country. Starting in 1998, Argentina entered a four-year-long recession that caused unemployment to rise to record levels. This situation led countless individuals and their families to join the movement (Svampa and Pereyra 2003; Epstein 2006). Piquetero groups functioned as channels through which they could obtain essential goods and services (Quirós 2006, 2011; Ferraudi Curto 2009; Frederic 2009). As long-term unemployment became widespread in numerous neighborhoods, the networks on which poor families had traditionally relied for assistance were rapidly exhausted of resources. As a result, piquetero participation emerged as a central component of the strategy of survival (Lomnitz 1975; González de la Rocha 1986, 2006; Hintze 1989) of many Argentineans.

Economic troubles also created opportunities for the movement. Piquetero organizations were capable of obtaining resources from the state, benefiting from the weakness of the federal government and the different local administrations, which offered concessions to keep protest under control (Epstein 2006; Massetti 2006). Activists combined habitual demands of the urban poor (housing, basic services, and pensions) with a new agenda centered on jobs and the provision of social assistance to the unemployed (Svampa and Pereyra 2003; Delamata 2004; Schuster et al. 2006), gaining not only recognition in their communities but also relatively positive media coverage (Gómez 2009).

In sum, in its first years, the unemployed workers' movement went through a period of rapid expansion. In October 2000, a six-day-long blockade of *Ruta 3* (National Route 3), one of the main arteries of Greater Buenos Aires, demonstrated the strength that the movement had achieved. A few months later, another protest in the same location lasted for eighteen days (Svampa and Pereyra 2003; Merklen 2005). In less than five years, piquetero organizations had consolidated their position as a crucial component of Argentina's political scene.

This centrality would only grow during 2001 and 2002 when the nation suffered one of the greatest economic collapses in its history. Living standards fell rapidly as the country faced a combination of deficits, mounting debt, and a fixed exchange rate policy that caused a severely overvalued currency. In addition, the administration of Fernando de la Rúa, inaugurated in late 1999, showed a clear lack of capacity for dealing with the situation, as increasingly drastic adjustment plans followed each other without success. By the end of 2001, debilitated by massive capital flight, a crushing defeat in legislative elections, and a growing lack of support, the government made a final desperate attempt to save the financial system by setting limits to the amount of money that individuals could extract from their bank accounts. The result was a wave of social unrest. In mid-December, food riots occurred in the periphery of major cities. The government responded on December 19 by declaring a state of siege, which protesters ignored. On the 20th, after days of turmoil and repression that took the lives of approximately thirty people, President De la Rúa resigned. Following a period of ten days in which three different people served as president, a pact between party elites led to the appointment by Congress of a new interim government led by Eduardo Duhalde to finish De la Rúa's term.

Duhalde was able to sustain governability and implement changes in the economic policy. After years of recession, by the end of 2002, the economy began to show the first signs of recovery. However, his legitimacy was never strong due to the irregular circumstances of his designation and his association with the Menem administration (as vice president between 1989 and 1991 and governor of the province of Buenos Aires between 1991 and 1999). In addition, some of his measures had been enormously unpopular (for instance, the conversion to pesos of all accounts and debts in dollars, which implied a massive regressive distribution of income). In June 2002, police forces assassinated two unarmed piquetero activists during a protest in the district of Avellaneda, Greater Buenos Aires.[2] As a result, Duhalde was forced to move forward the elections for a new president, which were held in April 2003, six months before scheduled, and which gave a narrow victory to Néstor Kirchner, a Peronist governor from the southern province of Santa Cruz.

The consequences of years of recession were extreme.[3] Between 1998 and 2002, Argentina's GDP fell by almost one fifth. In May 2002, 21.5%

---

[2] What came to be known as the "Avellaneda Massacre" was probably the most famous case of police repression of the piquetero movement, but sadly, it was far from the only one. Between 1997 and 2002, more than ten people were killed during piquetero demonstrations (CELS 2003; FPDS 2003).

[3] The source for these data is the National Institute of Statistics and Census, the official statistics center of Argentina. Historical series were last accessed on July 31, 2019. Data on

of the labor force was unemployed. In October of that year, 57% of Argentineans lived below the poverty line, and 27.5% were indigent, meaning their income was below the amount necessary to buy enough food for sustenance. These numbers were even worse in Greater Buenos Aires: 24.2% of workers were unemployed, and poverty affected 64.4% of the population, while indigence reached 30.5%.

These years coincide with the highest point in the movement's overall influence, not only with regard to their presence in the streets (Schuster et al. 2006; Nueva Mayoría 2008) but also in terms of cohesion, policy leverage, and public support. First, never was the objective of creating a unified coalition of all piquetero groups closer to being achieved than it was in 2001–2002. Although in the end they were unsuccessful, the "National Piquetero Assemblies" of July and September 2001, in which most organizations participated, constitute the moment in time when the overcoming of differences seemed most possible (Svampa and Pereyra 2003). Second, the movement's impact on public policies reached its peak in this period. After De la Rúa's resignation, the leaders of the largest organizations became recognized interlocutors of the Duhalde administration. Protests forced the government to offer concessions, in particular, a new workfare program with about two million beneficiaries. As an example of the influence of the movement, the leaders of the two largest organizations were incorporated Into the national advisory body that was created to supervise the implementation of this program. Finally, the legitimacy of the movement was very high. In spite of their use of a repertoire that disrupted urban life, by early 2002, opinion polls showed that more than 50 percent of the population supported the piqueteros (Savoia, Calvo, and Amato 2004).

In sum, in 2001–2002, the unemployed workers' movement reached its peak of influence. The combination of organizational legacies, effective repertoires, flexible structure, and worsening economic conditions helped the movement become one of the most visible instances of resistance to neoliberalism. However, changes in political and socioeconomic conditions since 2003 substantially modified this scenario, forcing organizations to adapt.

the GDP are available under www.indec.gob.ar/indec/web/Institucional-Indec-InformacionDeArchivo-5. Data on poverty can be found at www.indec.gob.ar/indec/web/Institucional-Indec-InformacionDeArchivo-2 and information on unemployment at www.indec.gob.ar/indec/web/Institucional-Indec-InformacionDeArchivo-6.

3.3 2003–2015: DEMOBILIZATION AND ORGANIZATIONAL STRENGTHENING

Starting in 2003, piquetero organizations faced a number of important challenges (Pereyra 2008; Svampa 2008). First, economic recovery caused a reduction in unemployment, which despite the persistence of high levels of informality and precariousness (Groissman 2013; Donza 2019) led to an expansion of labor opportunities for working-class Argentineans and reduced the centrality of piquetero groups for the survival of many families.

The end of the recession also facilitated a vigorous reconstitution of the political system that had been affected by the crisis (Pereyra, Pérez, and Schuster 2008). That is, the capacity of representative institutions to provide governance at all levels improved significantly. The rebound in the economy caused a budget surplus and an increase in the reserves of the treasury, which allowed more generous government-run assistance networks. As a result, these years witnessed a growth in the legitimacy of the system, as well as in the public confidence in the capacity of the government to solve the problems of the country (UTDT 2011). In addition, overall support for urban protests declined, due in part to an increasingly hostile media that framed roadblocks as an excessive tactic which violated the public right to transit (Svampa 2008; Massetti 2009).

The central actor in this new context was what came to be known as Kirchnerism. After winning the presidential elections in April 2003 with less than a quarter of the votes, Néstor Kirchner soon proved to be an intelligent leader who was able to create a coalition of forces behind a political project that distanced itself from previous administrations. In particular, the new government adopted a nationalistic and anti-neoliberal discourse, which was reflected in many public policies and which had the effect of depriving the piquetero movement of the clear association between government and antagonist that had prevailed during previous years. Some organizations perceived Kirchnerism as "more of the same," that is, a realignment of the same actors that had led the country to economic collapse. In contrast, other groups saw the government of Kirchner as the opposite of neoliberal policies and as the Argentinean expression of a new wave of left-wing governments in Latin America. As a result of this division, some organizations sought to sustain contention, while others became part of the political coalitions of Néstor Kirchner (2003–2007) and his wife and successor, Cristina Fernández de Kirchner (2007–2015).

In sum, the post-2003 context was characterized by economic recovery, improving state capabilities, a reconstitution of political elites, and changes in public opinion. As the labor market and political system recovered from the worst years of the economic crisis, the piquetero movement as a whole lost much of the influence it enjoyed early in the decade (Pérez, Pereyra, and Schuster 2008; Svampa 2008; Delamata 2009b; Pozzi and Nigra 2015).

However, an exploration of dynamics at a lower level of analysis offers a more complex story. Although they failed to maintain their momentum, piquetero organizations did not vanish (Kaese and Wolff 2016). Over the years, some of them accumulated substantial resources and expertise. Even though opportunities for large-scale protests became more limited after the 2001–2002 crisis (Pereyra, Pérez, and Schuster 2008; Svampa 2008), the post-2003 context was not entirely negative for grassroots organizations within the movement. Two factors explain this dynamic. In the short term, the political scenario created various opportunities for activists, as a new national administration sought to incorporate them into its coalition of support. In the long term, social policy reforms enacted since the 1990s expanded the possibilities for civil society groups to administer state resources.

The short-term political context benefited organizations that allied themselves with the government. Similarly to what happened in other countries of the region (Alvarez 2009; Rossi 2015), the Kirchner administrations, which came to power with only 22.2 percent of the vote, sought to incorporate grassroots organizations into their coalition of support (Boyanovsky Bazán 2010; Perelmiter 2012). The need for the government to obtain the allegiance of these groups generated openings for piquetero activists who had been mobilized for years in their communities. Pro-government organizations received substantial funds for the management of workfare plans, aid for infrastructure and productive projects, positions within state agencies, and even opportunities to win legislative seats. Moreover, this support came from a government that (at least rhetorically) shared many of their ideas and in a regional context where several Latin American countries elected left-leaning presidents. The tactic followed by the Kirchner administrations was backing the development of already sympathetic grassroots groups, directing resources toward them to ensure their cooperation (Rossi 2015; Kaese and Wolff 2016).

However, although the Kirchner administrations privileged the relationship with allied groups, organizations that did not support the government still benefited from state resources. To a great extent, this was due to the continued negotiation power of disruptive collective action and the potential political cost of repression, which led authorities at different levels to use workfare plans and foodstuffs as bargaining tokens to defuse conflicts. However, this outcome also stems from long-term transformations in the management of social policy. Starting in the 1990s, welfare policies in Argentina and other parts of Latin America moved from a universalistic logic to a more targeted one, in which the state relinquished control over certain areas of social assistance (Lo Vuolo et al. 2004; Barrientos and Santibañez 2009). This transformation helped state agencies delegate a significant portion of the management of social policies to all sorts of grassroots organizations (Alvarez 1999, 2009; Park and Richards 2007). This "focalized" nature of public intervention allowed piquetero groups, regardless of their ideology, to become distributors of assistance, which provided a source of organizational resources and a way to recruit members (Garay 2007; Manzano 2013).

In other words, piquetero organizations and state officials gradually entered a symbiotic relationship that remained in place after the crisis. While the latter were able to delegate the responsibility for the implementation of social policies to other actors, the former acquired resources necessary for their functioning. Given the context of poverty in which they are immersed, piquetero groups cannot obtain the funds and assets they need to function from their members. Quite the opposite, activists usually need material support from the movement in order to maintain their fulltime involvement. Thus, the goods and money needed to sustain long-term collective action in these marginalized neighborhoods are provided by different state programs through a constant process of negotiation with the authorities.

Thus, while organizations allied with the government received more resources, opposition groups also managed to obtain some degree of state support. Combined with their alliances with other actors (such as hardline unions, opposition parties, and NGOs), piquetero organizations that were less favored in the distribution of resources still received a great deal of public funds, which allowed many of them to remain active. Authorities and activists developed a complex yet relatively stable partnership, especially at the local level, where the interests of both actors frequently align.

Therefore, after 2003, political opportunities for the piqueteros gradually shifted. From a context that encouraged disruptive collective action to extract concessions from a debilitated government, a new environment emerged in which short-term calculations by political elites and longerterm transformations in social policy generated avenues for the growth of grassroots organizations. As a result, even though their overall mobilization capacity and number of followers declined, in other aspects, many piquetero groups strengthened.

3.4 2015–2019: NEOLIBERAL RESURGENCE, POLITICAL REALIGNMENTS, AND SUSTAINED RELEVANCE

In late 2015, twelve years of center-left government ended with the election as president of Mauricio Macri, whose campaign centered on a rejection of the Kirchner's economic policies. His platform of pro-market measures and denunciation of "populist" legacies was similar to other right-wing alliances that made substantial progress in the region in the last decade, bringing the "pink tide" of progressive governments to a halt (Ellner 2020; Ferrero, Natalucci, and Tatagiba 2019). Macri's strong performance at the polls surprised many and generated a substantial change in the country's political environment. Seeking to revitalize the economy and combat inflation, the new administration implemented a program of fiscal austerity, deregulation, and trade liberalization with the goal of attracting foreign investment. In addition, it adopted a more confrontational stance with regard to grassroots mobilization. The results were challenging for piquetero organizations in three distinct ways.

First, the new government eliminated many of the institutional links between piquetero organizations and state agencies. Not only were officials associated with the movement fired, but social programs and funding lines that supported the work of many organizations were also cut. The elimination of these resources and connections was a strong hit for some of the most ardent opponents to the new administration.

Second, there was an increase in repression of activists throughout the country, raising the alarms of national and international observers (HRW 2016; Amnesty International 2017; CELS 2017; OAS 2017). In Buenos Aires, Luis D'Elía, one of the most visible figures in the piquetero movement, was arrested in late 2017. In the province of Jujuy, the local government succeeded in dismantling one of the country's largest grassroots groups, the Tupac Amaru Neighborhood Organization. Many of the group's leaders were prosecuted and incarcerated. In 2017, the National Guard suppressed small roadblocks by indigenous groups in the provinces of Chubut and Río Negro, leading to the deaths of two protesters. While episodes of violence during demonstrations also took place during the 2003–2015 period (in some instances with deadly consequences), human rights organizations expressed increasing concern over the hard-line approach of the Macri administration toward social protest (CELS 2017; Amnesty International 2018).

Third, the austerity programs implemented since 2015 produced mediocre results. By 2019, inflation had increased; the economy remained stagnant; and unemployment had risen. A strong devaluation of the currency (between April 2018 and December 2019, the Argentinean peso lost more than half its value) compounded an already delicate situation. As with other times in the country's history, vulnerable communities were hit particularly hard by these developments. Piquetero organizations were thus confronted with a rising social emergency in which larger numbers of people required assistance.

However, the new situation also generated opportunities for the strengthening of piquetero groups. The expansion of unemployment increased the number of people who approached these organizations in search of resources, boosting their mobilization capacity and thus their leverage with the government. In addition, while short-term opportunities for accessing state resources through alliances with the authorities mostly closed, the long-term dynamic in which government agencies delegate responsibilities into grassroots networks remained largely unaffected. In other words, officials in the Macri administration could not dispose of piquetero groups, as they function as one of the most effective ways in which social assistance is distributed in vulnerable communities. Due in part to the pressure exerted by these groups, the government was forced to pass a Social Emergency Law, which despite its uneven implementation led to an increase in the number of workfare programs available.

Consequently, it is not surprising that the unemployed workers' movement remained a very visible actor in opposition to the resurgence of neoliberal policies in Argentina. By negotiating with the authorities at different levels and navigating political shifts in a pragmatic way, piquetero organizations managed to continue providing support to countless families and influencing public policies. In particular, an alliance of three large networks, the *Confederación de Trabajadores de la Economía Popular* (Confederation of Workers of the Popular Economy), Neighborhoods Standing Up, and the Classist and Combative Current, increased its public presence substantially. These groups played an important role in the campaign for the 2019 presidential elections, which led to the defeat of Macri's reelection bid and the establishment of a new administration led by Alberto Fernández (chief of the cabinet of ministries between 2003 and 2008). With the inauguration of the new president in December 2019, figures associated with the movement obtained important positions in legislative bodies and state offices.

3.5 THE STRATEGIC IMMERSION IN ESTABLISHED POLITICAL TRADITIONS

The fact that piquetero groups were able to respond to diverse challenges, obtaining official recognition, accumulating resources, and strengthening their core structures along the way, indicates the importance of acknowledging the agency of activists. Social movement organizations and their members are almost never passive objects of structural forces (Goodwin and Jasper 1999), instead actively seeking to adapt (with varying degrees of success) to the ups and downs of contention cycles. As Pablo Lapegna demonstrates in his study of mobilization surrounding genetically modified crops in Argentina (2016), activists play a central role in their own accommodation to varying contexts.

In the case of the piqueteros, organizations modified their strategies in response to changes in their environment. In their first years, they expanded aggressively, adopting repertoires of protest that had been proven effective in other parts of the country, capitalizing on government weaknesses, and attempting to create movement-wide coalitions (Auyero 2003; Svampa and Pereyra 2003). Since 2003, they began to rely less on large-scale disruptive collective action and more on electoral participation, community projects, and institutional development (Pereyra, Pérez, and Schuster 2008; Boyanovsky Bazán 2010; Kaese and Wolff 2016). Since 2015, political realignments and the restoration of neoliberal policies faced these groups with a difficult context marked by decreased links with the state, rising repression levels, and growing needs in their communities. Yet this new environment also brought opportunities, which activists sought to exploit.

In other words, contextual factors have both constrained the courses of action available to piquetero activists and offered avenues for them to sustain their presence. As Federico Rossi (2017) argues, these groups adjusted to their changing environment by choosing from a set of available strategies in their interactions with different actors in public, semipublic, and private arenas. The options available to organizers at particular points (what Rossi calls "repertoire of strategies") were determined by the history of collective action in Argentinean society (what he terms "the stock of legacies"):

The concatenation of past struggles, which, through the sedimentation of what is lived and perceived to be lived as well as what is intentionally learned, produces an accumulation of experience that adds or eliminates specific strategies from the repertoire of strategies as both a self-conscious and oblivious process. (2017: 42)

Consequently, it is impossible to understand the persistence of the unemployed workers' movement without paying attention to its active engagement with political conventions that predate its emergence. Piquetero groups were responsible for substantial innovations in popular politics in Argentina (Svampa and Pereyra 2003; Pereyra, Pérez, and Schuster 2008). In addition, the movement has contributed to expanding the public debate by incorporating new issues, encouraging other actors to adopt more radical agendas, and constructing coalitions that challenged established political alignments (Pereyra 2008; Delamata 2009b). However, piquetero activists have also drawn heavily on previous traditions in Argentina's popular politics. Much of the capacity of some groups in the movement to overcome challenges has been due to the resonance between their actions and a preexisting organizational, cultural, and spatial environment.

Regarding organizational links, piquetero groups had from the beginning extensive connections to long-standing community actors such as unions, religious institutions, land occupations, and political parties (Svampa and Pereyra 2003; Merklen 2005; Benclowicz 2011, 2013; Battezzati 2012). Such connections were essential to the growth of the movement, for several reasons. First, they funneled resources into organizations, helping them sustain their work. Second, they granted crucial know-how to activists, especially with regard to the management of state-funded social assistance. Third, they congregated organizers that otherwise may not have encountered each other and generated valuable contacts with politicians, officials, and civic leaders that would serve as allies.

Piquetero groups also benefited from their adherence to established notions of local political behavior. As Robnett (1997) and Wolford (2010) have emphasized for the cases of the United States and Brazil, the success of activists at mobilizing support depends on their ability to connect the work of their organizations to context-specific cultural scripts concerning right and wrong, what Wolford calls "localized moral economies" (2010: 19). That is, in order to appeal to participants, the overall agenda of a movement must undergo a process of translation into symbolic frames that are meaningful at the micro level. In the case of the piquetero movement, organizations have been embedded from the beginning in the political culture prevalent in working-class neighborhoods, which has been heavily influenced by the legacy of Peronism and a rich history of various forms of grassroots mobilization. These traditions emphasize relations of reciprocity and trust between patrons and their constituencies, which in turn sustain collective mobilization and the implementation of state policies at the community level (Auyero 2001; Levitsky 2003; Grimson, Ferraudi Curto, and Segura 2009). Despite their competition for resources with other networks of social assistance, the piquetero movement shared the set of norms, dispositions, and expectations that have characterized popular politics in Argentina for the last few decades.

Finally, much of the strength of piquetero organizations has relied on their strategic utilization of space in ways already familiar to their constituencies. The reliance on neighborhood networks as basic units of organization, the occupation of public places to gain visibility, and the use of blockades to force authorities to negotiate have been present in many instances of working-class collective action in Argentinean history (Merklen 2005; Pereyra 2008; Grimson, Ferraudi Curto, and Segura 2009). As with other experiences of mobilization in Latin America (Wolford 2010; Oslender 2016), piquetero organizations took advantage of established spatial dynamics in poor neighborhoods to recruit members, advance their goals, and obtain resources (Svampa and Pereyra 2003; Quirós 2011; Battezzati 2012; Manzano 2013).

In other words, to a great extent, it has been their resonance with local political traditions, more than their break from them, that allowed piqueteros organizations to expand and remain active. Since their emergence, these groups have functioned in a similar way as other cases of political life in their neighborhoods (Quirós 2011; Lapegna 2013). In particular, an influx of leaders knowledgeable in community activism, a flexible internal structure, and an effective repertoire of contention have allowed them to operate as efficient problem-solving networks (González de la Rocha 1986; Auyero 2001) on which residents can rely when unemployed. Despite their innovative aspects, the movement for the most part has attempted to reconstruct past forms of social organization, rather than create new ones. As Rossi (2017) explains, the piqueteros, like other cases of collective action in the region, are better interpreted as efforts to reconstitute links with the state that have been severed by neoliberal exclusion:

Neoliberal reforms have produced a change in the focus of protest in Latin America: since the 1980s it mainly occurs in the quest for recognition by the state …. This quest for recognition is part of what I call the *struggle for (re) incorporation*. I use this term because although most actors in this quest present discourses of radical societal transformation, those discourses have actually unfolded as types of collective action that can be deemed "bridging with the state" (apart from the unintended transformations produced by the incorporation of the actors). By "bridging with the state," I mean types of collective action that aim to (re)connect excluded segments of society with state institutions to recover – or, for the first time, gain – access to rights and benefits that the state has ceased to secure or provide. (2017: 17–18, emphasis in the original)

The struggle for reincorporation mentioned by Rossi also explains the appeal of participation in the movement. One of the main motivations for the men and women who develop commitment to their organizations is precisely related to the desire to return to an idealized past centered on the experience of manual labor. In fact, the effectiveness of organizations in providing this experience is one of the reasons for their resilience.

3.6 ACTIVISM AND THE REMARKABLE PERSISTENCE OF THE PIQUETERO MOVEMENT

The trajectory of the unemployed workers' movement combines innovative elements with adherence to traditional notions of labor, family, and community that permeate political culture in Argentina's working-class neighborhoods. The capacity of piquetero organizations to adapt to a changing environment, pragmatically choosing from different strategies of action available, allowed them to become an established presence in countless vulnerable communities. Despite changes in their political context and in the economic conditions of the country, over time, activists developed a relatively steady relationship with state authorities, maintained their status as recognized managers of social assistance, and accumulated important organizational resources.

However, the enduring influence of piquetero networks is not only the result of macro-level (movement-wide) and meso-level (organization-wide) factors. Processes at the individual level have also been crucial in the persistence of this movement. Since their emergence, many piquetero organizations have been able to turn a portion of the people who join "due to necessity" into committed cadres. Despite the fact that few recruits enter the movement due to ideological sympathy, most lack extensive political experience, and almost all face significant barriers to participation, some of them gradually develop a strong attachment to their groups. Thus, while the overall membership of most piquetero organizations has varied throughout the years, many of them have solidified an inner core of reliable and experienced participants (Quirós 2011; Manzano 2013; Pérez 2018).

Therefore, any analysis of this movement's history will be incomplete unless it explores the processes affecting the experiences of participants. How do people join a piquetero group? Why do they follow different paths once recruited? How do their personal characteristics interact with their experiences while mobilized? All these questions are relevant to explain the trajectories of both the movement as a whole and the organizations within it. In this, my case of study is hardly exceptional. As Jocelyn Viterna argues in her book on the FMLN guerrillas in El Salvador:

At present, most social-movement theory focuses on how macro-level phenomena (typically, political opportunities, political threats, and amorphous "resources") and meso-level structures (typically, networks of organizations) create the conditions that initially generate an episode of social mobilization. Yet, at a fundamental level, a social movement's power lies in the numbers and types of participants it can amass. Understanding how *individuals* initially come to participate in a movement, why the early risers choose to stay or defect, how new recruits are generated along the way, and what happens to people after the movement ends is a critical component for understanding a movement's power to transform society. ... Attention to micro-level processes can extend existing macro- and meso-level approaches to improve our understanding of how social movements begin, when they endure, and whether they have lasting consequences for individuals and societies. (2013: 6, emphasis in the original)

In the case of piquetero organizations, their capacity to retain a portion of their new members is related to the ways in which they function as a refuge for practices associated with an appealing but increasingly uncommon proletarian lifestyle. Through their involvement, some participants reconstruct, develop, and protect habits seen as wholesome yet threatened by deindustrialization. The opportunity to engage in a romanticized set of working-class routines is a key reason why some recruits eventually develop a strong attachment to their organizations, thus helping these groups maintain cohesion and develop a core of committed members despite personal obstacles and ideological dissension. The following chapters demonstrate how this process takes place for people of different ages and genders.

4

"I Know What It Means to Follow a Schedule"

Reconstruction of Past Routines

It is one of the busiest kinds of days for piquetero activists. A few days ago, the Ministry of Social Development sent a truckload of foodstuffs, and today, it is time to distribute these among the different neighborhoods where the group is active. There are many things to do: check amounts, fill out paperwork, and move heavy stuff from a deposit into cars, trucks, and wagons. The work is demanding, but people are in a good mood. Mauro, a short man in his late fifties, seems to be the center of attention, telling all sorts of spicy jokes to his friends Lázaro and Edgar as they transport boxes from one place to another.

Around lunchtime, Mauro asks me to join him for a quick trip to get some auto parts. We walk a few blocks to the neighborhood's main avenue. He stops at one store to buy oil and in another to get an engine filter. Throughout our walk, he explains technical details about how to keep an old car in good shape, saving money by doing repairs yourself. He also tells me about yesterday's march, which ended super late because he had to give a ride to a guest of the organization. On the way back, we find a man gathering discarded wooden crates from the street. Mauro tells me to be careful around this person, who has a reputation of being a violent addict. A few days ago, he stopped by the organization with an open box of wine, looking for trouble. Mauro took care of the situation by giving him a cigarette and telling him to go bother someone else.

Mauro is a friendly fellow with a down-to-earth approach to life's problems and a skill for making others laugh. Like most of the people I interviewed, he organizes his personal history around the different jobs he has held. He dropped out of high school to work as an

71

apprentice in a small workshop located in front of his parents' house. He remembers with pride the confidence his employers placed in him:

I did not like to study much, I liked to work more, have my own things, be independent. I was fifteen years old and they gave me the keys, I was in charge of the workshop, I was the one who opened, closed. I already had responsibilities back then despite my age. (April 21, 2014)

His experiences in the workshop reinforced what would become a strong interest: car mechanics. Ever since he purchased a moped as a teenager, he has always had a car or motorcycle: "[T]o me, having a car is not a luxury, but a necessity." This passion, coupled with a remarkable work capacity, helped him climb positions until he reached his dream job: the assembly line at one of the country's largest automobile factories. He describes his time in this company as a golden age. Being an autoworker validated his identity as a self-made man who compensated for a lack of formal education with experience, good references, and hard work. Moreover, his employment came with significant social status. His pay was enough to give his family a comfortable standard of living and gradually build a small house:

When I got together with my wife we came to live in this district, . . . and I bought the plot where I live now. First we had a shack, until I could build a house. We built it over time, as best as we could. Luckily I always found a way and worked, money I made, money I invested in the house. It's a modest house but I live a block from [a major thoroughfare], thanks to God I do not owe anything to anyone. (April 21, 2014)

Nevertheless, this lifestyle came to an end in the mid-1990s, as the company's restructuring led to Mauro being laid off. Like many workers who faced a similar situation around the same time in Argentina, he tried self-employment. However, his new profession as a taxi driver was risky and scarcely profitable. After his car was stolen and the insurance company refused to pay for it, Mauro found himself jobless and, more importantly, feeling useless. The work experience and skills accumulated since he was a teenager, which once qualified him for the best-paying blue-collar positions, were suddenly not enough to get him even the simplest job. For a man used to sustaining his family, the effect was devastating:

It was hard, because I went to look for jobs and they asked for young people with formal education. I had only my elementary school, back in my time with that you got hired, if someone recommended you. Now they demand high school, that you study mechanics, it used to be that with good experience and references you got a job, now they want specialized machines, they use computers, you need a high school diploma. (April 21, 2014)

Even before he was laid off, Mauro's wife, Guadalupe, participated in a soup kitchen run by a piquetero organization. What started as charity toward others gradually turned into part of a survival strategy. The couple realized that since many friends were losing their jobs, economic troubles were likely. In her own terms:

We suffered no deprivations because my husband worked at the company and made good money, it used to be that a worker at that company was a big deal. Now not anymore, but then it was a big deal, we suffered no deprivations because we had our vacations, our car. When I entered this organization we had two cars and a truck, so you have an idea that we were not in need. I did not lack money for food nor for my children, not even for education because my youngest children went to private schools. But I always saw that the situation would worsen. I was in contact with other people who were losing their jobs, the unemployment crisis had begun. I said then, "well, my husband has a job today, but if he is fired from the factory what is he going to do? At his age he is not going to be able to enter in another factory." (June 13, 2013)

Despite the increasingly desperate financial situation, Mauro was reluctant to join an organization whose members were stigmatized as lazy and violent. His self-image as an honorable worker was inconsistent with a movement he saw as causing trouble to others:

When I was in a factory, I did not see these things. I saw the piqueteros demonstrating and cursed at them. Because there was a time when I was a driver that my wife used to tell me "careful because we are going to block here," and I was driving and had to avoid them. (May 5, 2014)

However, eventually Guadalupe's insistence and the prospect of obtaining resources led Mauro to sign up. For a long time, he participated in exchange for foodstuffs until he was enrolled in a workfare program. Despite his initial reluctance, as he got involved, something resonated with him. He uses the term *rebuscármela*, roughly translatable to "finding a way," to express how the movement allowed him to react to exclusion from the labor market:

It was not a change from one day to the next ... perhaps I entered due to curiosity and then stayed due to necessity. Because circumstances take you. Governments promised things, and as I said, after your forties you are out of the labor system and you have to find a way. And well, one way of finding a way was precisely this, entering the organization, having a plan, being able to enter into a cooperative. It helped me to move ahead, you know? (May 5, 2014)

In the fifteen years since he joined, Mauro has fulfilled all sorts of roles in the group. For a long time, he worked in different cooperative projects, first cleaning streets and then in housing and sanitation, until a spinal disk herniation caused him to be assigned to do administrative work. Ever since then, his daily activities take one of two forms. During demonstrations, he is in charge of security. He spends hours keeping a close watch on the actions of the police, as well as ensuring that activists do not wander off, drink alcohol, or misbehave. Most days, however, Mauro arrives around 8 AM at the organization's main building, a set of improvised offices and storage rooms in one of Buenos Aires' poorest neighborhoods. His job is to help with paperwork, and he should not make substantial physical effort. Nevertheless, almost every time I visited, he was engaged in different forms of manual labor: distributing foodstuffs, fixing cars and machinery, preparing flags, or helping with the building's maintenance. He usually goes home between 5 and 6 PM, after most people have left. Mauro seems to love being busy. As he frequently repeats with pride, "I know what it means to follow a schedule":

I wake up at half past six, so I can be here before eight so I can see what is new, what do we have to do, what can I help with, what do we have to organize. There are days when there are very few things to do and days when you do not have enough time, days in which you have to be here until late, like when they bring foodstuffs, you take, move, everything. Those of us who work here, sometimes we have neither holidays nor free time, because if you have to come here on a Saturday or Sunday, when there are national meetings, those of us who have responsibilities know we have to be here. (April 21, 2014)

Mauro is one of the many middle-aged activists for whom participation in the piquetero movement becomes a way to reconstruct routines associated with a golden past. His attachment does not seem to depend on ideological agreement with his organization. He credits the movement with teaching him about politics and opening his eyes about the structural causes of his community's economic relegation. He also highlights that activism made him a more avid reader and undermined his initial hesitancy to engage in debates with his fellows. However, he remains an independent thinker who openly expresses opinions diametrically opposed to the group's main stances. For example, he supports the reinstitution of mandatory military service and believes in a punitive approach to drug addiction. Instead, his commitment relies on the capacity to partake in valuable practices. Soon after joining, he learned that he could use the organization to reenact the type of life he was used to. The movement became a surrogate assembly line, where he could feel useful and needed:

I stayed in the organization because it is a place where, after all, I felt comfortable. That is also why I took on the commitment to go forward, to participate, to talk with the folks, make them understand. That makes you feel that you are necessary too in the organization, because it is a small contribution, you see, but if we all contributed a bit, things would be different. (May 5, 2014)

The reconstruction of routines provides Mauro with two things that were lost as factories began to close. First, being a piquetero offers predictability. Activism becomes an excuse for him to get up early and show up at the organization at a certain hour because there is always something that needs to be done. In his many years in the movement, he learned of countless ways in which he could fill unwanted free time with purpose, fixing things, moving stuff, and learning new skills such as installing water pipes or arranging people in a demonstration.

Moreover, getting his body sweaty and his hands dirty conveys respectability to Mauro's experiences. He is not a taker or freeloader. Instead, he earns the benefits he receives. Cash transfers and foodstuffs are not charity; they are a salary he deserves in return for his efforts. He often compares himself to people who are paid more and yet work fewer hours or who want to obtain resources without first making an effort:

I got hooked in the movement, organizing the cooperatives, helping my people. You can see that I am here from eight in the morning to five, six in the afternoon, every day, even Saturday and Sunday. And there are fellows who perhaps are in a cooperative and earn much more than me, but see me here in the administration and say "hey, dude, buy us a drink." They should buy me one, because they have a better salary, but it is ok. You are here so many hours, earn less than them, they do not believe it but that is how it is. (April 21, 2014)

The remainder of this chapter will describe how this process takes place for people like Mauro. In the piquetero movement, some middle-aged participants are able to use their everyday practices to reconstruct their experiences from a time in which factory jobs were more easily accessible. However, this process reflects a division of labor by gender. While men engage in routines associated with blue-collar occupations, women reenact the type of household duties seen as the counterpart of factory work. The idealized working-class life activists seek to reenact is itself gendered, and consequently, the experiences of men and women vary substantially.

4.1 DEINDUSTRIALIZATION AND THE FRAGILITY OF WORKING-CLASS MASCULINITY

Interviews with men in their forties or above show a remarkable consistency in terms of labor history. Most respondents had their first job in their early teens and never finished high school. Through relatives or acquaintances, they began working informally in different manual occupations (workshops and construction sites, with a few cases of retail or street vending). By the time they were old enough to apply for formal jobs, they had amassed significant practical knowledge and embraced habits such as waking up early, following regular schedules, and devoting part of their income to supporting their families. Official employment granted them stability, a higher salary than when they were minors, and the possibility to learn a trade. For years, their main professional assets were good references from employers and a set of marketable skills gained through work experience.

However, the economic transformations described in Chapter 2 severely affected these trajectories. Deindustrialization left countless people in limbo: too young to retire but too old to reinsert themselves in the labor market. For men, three particular aspects of this situation made their predicament especially powerful.

First, the male-dominated institutions that were supposed to provide support to jobless workers failed to operate properly. Faced with a weakening of their political influence (Levitsky 2003), many of Argentina's largest mainstream unions reacted to neoliberalism in an accommodating way, choosing to negotiate with governments and employers instead of fighting layoffs (Svampa and Pereyra 2003; Rossi 2017). Unemployed men accustomed to union-based protections suffered not only a lack of material support but also a crushing blow to their identity as workers. Many refer to being "abandoned" by the very groups whose purpose was to assist them. Mario's union boycotted the attempts to prevent the firing of 500 employees in his company:

The defeat in the 90s was total. I worked in a cable company, and was a delegate. Then the guys fired five hundred people. They fired us in '92, '93. I went and arranged an assembly, to try to occupy the place. I was 27 years old. To take the place, the assembly was more or less about that. Who fired us? The unionists, the older ones, they betrayed us. They disclosed what we were going to do. (July 28, 2011)

For Mario, this betrayal contrasted markedly with the role that unions had played in his upbringing. His father was affiliated to the *Unión Obrera Metalúrgica* (Metallurgical Workers Union), the country's powerful federation of steelworkers. In addition to providing a good salary and benefits, the union served as a source of identity and socialization for his family: He recalls weekends spent in the large sports complex built for card-carrying members and their relatives.

Sadly, Mario's negative experience is far from uncommon. In the case of Nahuel, not only did union officials do nothing to protect him and his fellows from being fired, but they were also the ones communicating the management's decision:

Our union representative ... said, "well boys, the company says you need to clear the place," so I told him, "well, you are a union representative, you are not a representative of the company; [the company] has to tell us this, and we have to attack it, but not you, you have to defend us." We had to stop the boys when he said that, when he opened his mouth that way, because many went over to him, we had to stop them ourselves so they did not hit him. (July 6, 2014)

The accommodating strategy of many unions with regard to pro-market reforms meant that countless men found themselves isolated from supportive institutional networks at precisely the time when they needed them the most:

The debacle of the late 90s came with the army of the unemployed ... We believed that the ideal was that the unemployed of each union was supported by his union. But obviously, it did not happen that way. (Diego, June 9, 2012)

Second, for many male respondents deindustrialization meant the devaluation of their most prized asset. A reputation as a responsible and capable worker, backed by employer's references, was not only a way to obtain jobs but also a source of validation. For many interviewees, the most difficult aspect of joblessness is the feeling that although they followed all rules good men were supposed to follow, learning a craft, working hard, and accumulating practical knowledge, they eventually ended in a society that has no need for them. Bautista describes the frustration he felt when, after losing his job in a plastics factory, he had to undergo formal job interviews instead of proving his skills with a machine. Accustomed to a world in which actions spoke louder than words, he failed to understand why "professional" behavior and speech mattered at all:

I did not expect an interview, because in the place I was before they asked "you know how to work?" checked how you worked, and that was it. And when I lost my job, I found out what an interview was. I had no idea. It used to be that they saw how you worked, you wanted to work, and you stayed. Not anymore. They check how you sit down, how you speak. They do not even see how you work. (August 5, 2011)

Tito describes a similar degree of exasperation. Practical experience is no longer the way to acquire valuable skills, and even jobs that are much simpler than the one he worked on for decades (automaking) require what seem to be unreasonable credentials:

Back in the time when I began working, my experience was that I started cleaning pieces in a workshop, and went from there. Today, just to work refilling shelves in a supermarket you need to have a high school diploma. And they also demand that you know something about computers. Things like that, to work at a supermarket, to put a can on a shelf. (May 25, 2012)

Third, health issues frequently compounded the effects of long-term unemployment for older men. Occupational hazards, the effects of aging, and the lack of preventative healthcare caused many people in my study to experience different degrees of disability, which further reduced their employment prospects and severely affected their self-esteem. Men whose sense of masculinity is strongly linked to their capacity to endure hard work without complaining are confronted, as they age, not only with joblessness but also with accidents and illnesses:

Extract from fieldnotes, February 19, 2014
[Alejandro] began speaking with the other woman and told her that he is in bad health. The doctor told him "the only thing you are capable of doing is to direct the traffic," and he responded "too bad I am not like you, doing nothing all day," "yes, I totally cursed at [the physician]." Two of his vertebrae are out of place, he also has other "bones that are fucked," and now they told him that he has renal colics.

Extract from fieldnotes, March 5, 2014
[An activist] told me, "Yes, I did all sorts of jobs. I built sidewalks, those bus stops, all kinds of things until I had the accident." The accident he had is he fell from a six-meters-tall scaffold and broke his hand pretty badly. He showed me his hand, which required surgery, and it had a large cut, it is clear he had an important surgery based on the scar. Thus he now has a workfare plan because the doctor told him he cannot do any strenuous activity.

Older men in the piquetero movement tend to react to physical ailments with public displays of sexuality or aggressiveness. For instance, when some activists jokingly teased Alejandro about his use of a chiropractic belt, to everyone's amusement, he waved his hands as if holding a woman while making love to her and said that until his forties, he "used to grab a 150-kilo woman and took her like this, a block back and forth." The same respondent who showed me his injured hand also bragged about his role in the organization's security team, hinted that he got "eighteen scars" more due to fights, and highlighted his participation in the 1982 Malvinas war. As research has suggested, perceptions of disability vary by gender (Gerschick 2000; Meekosha 2006). Health problems are widespread among older participants in the piquetero movement, who like most poor Argentineans are disproportionately exposed to pollution, accidents, and violence and who lack access to proper medical care. However, while female activists speak of disability largely as an obstacle to employment, for their male counterparts, it seems to be much a stronger threat to their masculine identity. Throughout my fieldwork, I witnessed older men lightheartedly describing past sexual achievements and engaging in visible demonstrations of bodily strength, such as moving goods and participating in security teams, despite the evident risk of further injury. In contrast, such displays are almost completely absent from interactions with female activists coping with disability.

In short, the elimination of factory jobs affected working-class men in particular ways. The choices and behaviors that used to lead to reliable occupations and social respectability (an early entrance in the job market, the accumulation of experience and good references, and the investment of savings in a self-built home) no longer were effective. Left in a limbo between retraining and retirement, abandoned by their unions, deprived of marketable skills, and increasingly affected by health issues, these people became almost unemployable, which had a devastating effect on their sense of self. This is the situation that older male recruits in the piquetero movement face, as the cases of Horacio and Lázaro illustrate.

4.2 RECONSTRUCTING LIFE IN THE ASSEMBLY LINE

I interviewed Horacio about a year after he had joined a piquetero organization. He is a man in his late fifties with decades of work experience. He was born to a single mother in Paraguay and moved with her to Argentina when he was still a child. As soon as he finished elementary school, he began working in the shoemaking industry, first with odd jobs, later in factories, and finally as a subcontractor. Companies would make orders, which he would then produce in a workshop he built in his own home. For decades, this occupation allowed him not only to sustain his family but also to train younger people in the fine art of turning raw leather into high-quality footwear. The work was not very profitable given how demanding it was, but it paid the bills and was a source of pride. As he insists, there are few people remaining with his skills:

I am a professional shoemaker, anyone says "make this shoe" and I will draw, make, and create the shoe. I am a professional, but nowadays I do not think there are many like me. For instance, I made fine high-heel shoes, I sewed them on the machine, but I think it was ten years ago that I taught the last shoemaker. (June 6, 2014)

Horacio explains that the reason why few people remain in his profession is the same as why he no longer has a job: Over the past few decades, trade liberalization led to an influx of cheap, imported shoes. The demand for the premium merchandise he can make plummeted:

In the past there were jobs everywhere, we shoemakers did not rest. Because back then there were exports, they exported from here to the outside. Now it is the other way around, now they bring from other countries, everything is upside down. Now if you go buy a shoe there are no [leather] shoes, it is all made of cloth, they bring them from I do not know where, China, I do not know. (June 6, 2014)

To make things worse, Horacio suffered a medical crisis triggered by the death of his beloved mother. Hypertension and other heart problems frequently prevent him from doing the occasional construction gigs that he relied on during lean times:

It depends on the physician, whether he says "yes, you can do this" or "no, you cannot," because certainly I am sick, first of my heart, but thanks to God the heart seems to be recovered, but hypertension not. I cannot be under the sun for long, because the sun, I do not know what it does, but it raises your blood pressure. Then I cannot be under the sun, so I have to find a job like this, coming and being with [the organization]. (June 6, 2014)

The overall result was not so much material deprivation, because his wife and two daughters are employed and supported him during his periods of inactivity. However, his skills in leatherwork, which took him years to acquire, are not as valuable as in the past. For Horacio, using the remaining machines in his home would not only be unprofitable but also be humiliating:

I am 58 years old now, I do not have a job, nobody gives me a job, even though I am a professional. Why? First because I am old already, and second, they do not want a guy who knows, because I will charge them what I am worth, otherwise I am not going to work. Then no one hires you, because I am a professional, I am not going to work for you for a hundred pesos a day. (June 6, 2014)

In other words, shoemaking took a lot of time and was never very well remunerated, yet at least companies paid more for people with talent and expertise. However, over the past decades, economic transformations and health issues have conspired to exclude aging workers like Horacio from the labor market. What used to be assets (decades of experience and the ability to make high-quality products) end up being drawbacks at a time when most shoes are imported. The consequence is a demoralizing feeling of being superfluous. He cried as he described the adult men applying for workfare programs:

I saw all those people, all of them my age, there were only two or three young men, that made me sad, because we are, in one word, rejected. Old people have experience, but we are losing that experience ... A country is built by people working, all the people working, using all the people, no matter how old. In this country, if you are old, you are rejected, you are useless, but the knowledge we have, who are we gonna give it to? Who are we gonna teach it to? We will take it to the grave. (June 6, 2014)

The way Horacio joined his organization is very similar to others I talked with. He had petitioned at a government office for assistance, without success, until a relative who participated in a piquetero group offered to help with the application. Shortly afterward, he received a small subsidy equal to approximately 30 US dollars and as a result began to attend events. The amount gradually increased: By the time we talked, he received about 100 US dollars monthly and was hoping to enroll in an even more generous workfare program:

Horacio: One day my sister in law says, "do you want to sign up?" "Yes."

Question: How long ago was this?
H: About a year. Of course, I signed up to see what happened, I did not know. I signed up here and later she said "you are in," I did not know what "being in" was. She said, "you have to go to the bank to get paid," "but why would I go to the bank to get paid if I never had money in the bank, and I barely have any money – I said to my in-law – you are kidding me." "No – she said, and gave me a piece of paper – go to the bank there in [this district]." "Ok." The truth is I went, showed my ID, showed the piece of paper, and they gave me 150 pesos. "Well – I told her – I made 150 pesos." ... The second month I was paid 225 pesos, and the third month I do not remember if it was 200 or I was already paid 750. To this day I am earning 750, now I am part of a cooperative, I joined after a month, and I am still here, we go out, every day I have to come here, at eight in the morning I have to be here, or if we have a rally we have to go. (June 6, 2014)

Despite the organization's financial support and the likelihood of receiving more funds that would reduce his dependency on his wife and daughters, Horacio is still very skeptical about the movement he joined. In particular, he compares it unfavorably with the other significant experience of political participation he has had in his life when, fifteen years ago, he mobilized with his neighbors to demand the formal recognition of their home titles:

Horacio: We never blocked roads, never did that. I never liked that, because people now for any reason block roads. No, no, we went directly [to the government] never blocked the road. "We are neighbors," I said. "Let's not block the road, let's got there, what is the use of blocking the road here, if the problem is there?" ...

Question: *And when you go out and block roads here with the organization, what do you feel?*
H: I feel the same. To be honest, what can I say? I just entered here and still do not understand this place, what they do, because they do not explain things to you. You know what I am saying? The other day we did a roadblock and I do not know why, because they do not talk to you, they need to communicate, if they do not talk I am not going to know, I go to comply, or to say, "I went." Nothing else, because I do not know anything. (June 6, 2014)

Nevertheless, Horacio does not just criticize the organization. He also describes the kind of things that would make him appreciate it more. For him, the problem with the group is that the relation between efforts and benefits is broken. That is, his small plan requires him to show up every day, but other than meetings, demonstrations, and a few hours of community improvement work, there is not much for him to do. He vented his frustration with "the politicians" who run the organization by describing the different machines in the building, which the group obtained years ago to develop a textile cooperative, but that today are idle. In his view, he could easily use these tools to teach his trade to younger people, both giving them an education and revalorizing his occupation:

If [the organization's leaders] have all these machines here, I do not know why they have them, why do you want these machines if you do not use them? Anyone here can learn the trade, but how can they learn if the machines are idle? That is why I tell you, these people are politicians, they think of other things, they think about signing people up, they do not think about working. (June 6, 2014)

In other words, Horacio's main grievance against the movement is about unrealized productive potential. He has the skills, and the organization has the machines: It would be simple, in his view, for him to return to an activity that offered purpose and pride. He wants to make money but through what he sees as constructive activities. Yet coordinators do not seem to care, and consequently, his knowledge and experience remain as unrecognized as they were before he joined:

I would like a chance to teach people. I do not have a degree, but I make my degree, you know what I am saying? It is not like I say "I have a degree," no, I sit down and do the job, that is my degree, I do not have a paper that says "he is this." Because there are all types of things, but I can make them all. So I ask God that tomorrow, if I have the opportunity to teach people, like in this place, that I teach. (June 6, 2014)

Lázaro has been in the movement for longer than Horacio, but his original attitude was very similar. At fifty-two, he is a big man with an intimidating presence and a personal history to support that impression. He dropped out of elementary school (he attributes it to rebelliousness and the constant fights between his parents) and took a job in construction. Over the years, he specialized in plumbing and worked in metallurgy, footwear, and meatpacking assembly lines, until he lost his last stable job in the 1990s.

FIGURE 4.1 Activists fixing a bus. Highway on the way to Buenos Aires, May 2014.
"My life was always about mechanics. Since I was eleven I worked in mechanics" (Tito).

There is also a more negative side to his past, which he regrets. For a long time, he was associated with some of the most violent soccer gangs in the country. As is frequent in Argentina (Veiga 1998; Grabia 2015), his hooliganism overlapped with an active involvement in grassroots politics. Before rallies, local candidates would give him money to organize cookouts and distribute wine to entice people to attend. Lázaro says it was not a good environment: There were too many drugs and too much alcohol, and many of his friends ended up behind bars. However, he did not truly leave it until after he joined a piquetero organization. He had very negative views of the movement but was told that through his participation, he could obtain a small pension for his elderly mother:

I always had the idea that the people here were some fucking piqueteros, that blocked the road, why didn't they go search for jobs instead, they bothered people. But when things got tight for me, when I could not find a job, nothing, then I came here, and a great fellow I have, she told me, "why don't you begin participating, at least for your mom?" because my mom had no retirement, no pension, nothing. (June 27, 2014)

By participating on his mother's behalf, he eventually obtained a spot for her in a social program. At that time, he was invited to remain engaged so he himself could receive assistance. He was reluctant but did not have much of a choice: The year was 2001, and the country's economy was collapsing. Gradually, his distrust toward the movement eroded:

My mom got a Bonaerense,[1] *I slowly began getting in, getting in. They told me, "why don't you participate for yourself?" "No, these piqueteros block roads, why don't they search for jobs." I was in a tight spot and everything, and yet I kept that ignorance of not knowing what the organization was about. Until well, I am telling you, I met the organization through a friend and began living things inside here that are impressive, like how fellows discussed politics, how they discussed their children's needs, that was a hard time because there was a lot of hunger, a lot of misery.* (June 27, 2014)

Ever since then, Lázaro has not left the movement. He is a constant presence in his organization: In the morning, he collaborates on sanitation projects, and in the afternoon, he stays longer than required, giving a hand to others and participating in meetings. A recent diagnosis of diabetes limits the work he can do, but he still helps with the everyday operation of the many cooperatives the organization runs. Over the years, I saw

---

[1] The *Barrios Bonaerenses* was one of the largest social programs administered by the government of the province of Buenos Aires. It started in the late 1990s.

countless instances of him volunteering extra time. For him, spending each day in the organization has become a habit:

Lázaro: They took me out of ditch maintenance due to diabetes, because it is a job in which you risk hurting yourself a lot, because when cleaning a ditch you find trash, run into stuff that scratches you a lot, you are always injured, if not on your hand on your leg. And with my illness an infection can cost you a leg, so they decided I would be an assistant.

Question: How is a routine day for you?
L: I go to work in the morning, I arrive at eight. I see what the guys need, talk to them, make comments, we talk, and then around one or two I come here to the [organization's building]. It is like a thing that if I am not here I feel something is missing, it has been many years, every day coming here.

Q: And what do you get by coming here?
L: Not being at home sitting watching TV. I am here, you share things with your fellows, discussions, opinions, a lot of things, it is nice, I like it. (June 27, 2014)

Lázaro's tattoos are a sign of his violent past, as is his ability to organize security at demonstrations. However, his everyday interactions with other activists indicate a completely different present. He frequently jokes and has an easygoing attitude. He credits the organization with helping him escape violence and addiction by keeping him busy:

When I entered the organization I lived drunk, I even got to the point of using drugs. And inside the organization they gave me tasks and responsibilities and with all that I started to forget all the barbarities I did, then here the fellows supported me, and they made me see that what I was doing was wrong. I do not claim to read the Bible and all that, but I did change a lot my way of life, because of the support I have. (June 27, 2014)

Lázaro also highlights the care he receives from others in the movement. In particular, he credits his partner (who he met through the group) with preventing him from relapsing into bad habits and companies: "Sometimes I get a bit crazy and say 'I am going with the guys, to have some beers,' and she stops me, 'do not be an idiot, why would you do that?'"

In other words, for Lázaro, activism constitutes a safe haven that isolates him from an enticing but self-destructive lifestyle. From the moment he joined, he was surrounded by people who did not share his old ways, and his time was filled with routines that kept him busy. This estranged him from circles that sustained his addictions and allowed him to lead a less violent life. He was able to put his knowledge of plumbing and construction to use, contributing to dozens of infrastructure projects that benefit his community. As he got more and more involved, his increasingly busy everyday activities became far more predictable and honorable. His attachment to piquetero activism emerged out of its contrast with a past life where many of his friends ended up incarcerated and leaders "preferred to give me a bottle of wine rather than a plan or something."

I think that by being busy, the organization kept me busy, gave me a job, took me out. By letting me express myself at meetings, letting me speak, I changed a lot, for the better, because otherwise I may have ended up thrown dead on a ditch. I lived drunk and causing trouble, I liked to party, liked to drink, and all that began changing as I got involved more in the organization. They taught me, and what is more, I learned to listen, which is something I did not use to do, you would talk to me and I "blah, blah, blah," I did not listen, I did not care no matter what you did. I was a big guy and pretty stupid too. Now well, that changes you, life is like that, the essence of the organization is that it made me realize many things. By keeping me busy in something I did not think about "I have to go to the store to have a beer" or "I have to go with someone to fuck around," so much of your time is occupied, so much time, that you are worn out when you get home, you get tired, want to rest, lay down, watch TV a bit and sleep. And the next day again, come over here and "hey, you got to do this, this, and this." (June 27, 2014)

It is impossible to predict Horacio's trajectory in the movement. Yet it is possible to identify the processes that led Lázaro from a similar skepticism to the point where he is now. For Lázaro (and potentially for Horacio), participation in the movement offers a way to reconnect with his past as a worker. The routines of getting up early, showing up for work, and participating in a productive project provide him with respectability and consistency, shielding him from even his most self-destructive behaviors. He wakes up thinking about what needs to be done in his cooperative, spends his waking hours busy at work, and by the end of the day is tired and wants to go to bed. He is also constantly interacting with people in ways that validate his attachment to the movement's routines. Consequently, despite occasional disagreements with others in his organization, he is deeply committed to it.

4.3 COMMUNITY DECAY AND FEMINIZED DOMESTICITY

In addition to the idealization of certain types of work, interviews with middle-aged activists of all genders also show adherence to a family model centered on a male breadwinner and a female homemaker. In fact, as Chapter 1 showed, respondents see the expansion of unemployment and the decline in their communities as mediated by the disruption of family structures. As fathers were laid off, the narrative goes, mothers had to work long hours outside the home, neglecting the supervision of children who then were more likely to engage in anti-social behavior.

While some aspects of this narrative are true, others are not. Deindustrialization severely affected families by undermining their material well-being, reducing their capacity to plan for the future, and cutting their links to community institutions. In addition, interviews suggest that joblessness was associated with an increase in intra-family conflict and addiction, especially among men. Nevertheless, the life histories of female participants also indicate that most engaged in paid occupations for extended periods even before unemployment became widespread. Industries were largely segregated by gender (for instance, metallurgy, meatpacking, and construction were overwhelmingly male, whereas housecleaning, textiles, and retail hired mostly women). Yet overall, the women I talked to were not excluded from the labor market.

The fact that discourses about the past of families in working-class neighborhoods of Argentina are partially inaccurate does not deny their influence. As Stephanie Coontz (1992) argues in her study about household structures in the United States, myths about how things used to be in the past inform ideas about how they should be today. Within piquetero organizations, a romanticized image of domestic life linked to plentiful manufacturing jobs affects the expectations of activists. Women's paid employment is not seen as an ideal long-term family condition but instead as a short-term alternative during times of crisis or as a part-time way to finance nonessentials. In other words, the proletarian lifestyle that activists seek to reconstruct is itself gendered, and hence, men and women reconstruct different sets of habits based on what they see as proper to them. In the case of middle-aged activists, this becomes evident in three forms.

First, women are far more likely to enroll in projects involving traditionally domestic tasks (cooking, cleaning, and doing paperwork) and to highlight these activities as the most gratifying and impactful aspect of their work. Both men and women describe feeling useful and being busy as key rewards of participation. Yet the specific meanings of such rewards are connected to ideals surrounding gender. For instance, Tatiana is part of the administration team in her organization's main office, but she highlights cleaning and cooking as the tasks that make her feel most fulfilled:

Feeling useful is, for example, seeing that you do something and another person enjoys it. For example, when you see that here they tell me, "Tatiana, on this date there is a national meeting." And I know that on that day I have to be here from very early in the morning, until very late at night, because I have to cook, make breakfast, meals, lunch. And when you do those things and see that others eat them, enjoy them, at least for me I like doing that. O when they say, "Tatiana, can you do this thing?" I like having things to do. They make me feel like I am useful to them. (February 27, 2014)

Second, even though organizations sometimes appoint women to tasks usually seen as masculine, this situation is mostly described as an anomaly imposed by the circumstances. Luisa, an activist in her seventies who runs a piquetero cooperative in the district of Esteban Echeverría, blames government neglect and corruption for the fact that women are assigned to work in the streets:

Luisa: If they want us to produce, then they should give us work the way it is supposed to be. And neither the municipality, nor the president, should forget that a majority of us here are wo-men [emphasizing each syllable: mu-je-res]. In the cooperatives, women.

Question: How is that?

L: Most are women. They should not be given work using a spade. They should not be given work building sidewalks. They should send more developed work, where people can produce. Here I have people who are bakers, pastry makers, cooks, women can work doing that. Making products, not being sent with a spade to build stuff. The best projects are taken by politicians: working at an office, working at a hospital, cleaning a hospital. Why don't they send those projects to social movements too? (June 12, 2012)

Several men in the movement also share this perception. Mauro describes the involvement of women as a major hindrance to the first infrastructure projects his organization undertook:

In 2004, when [President Néstor] Kirchner came here, we could obtain the first sanitation cooperatives, in this neighborhood. They made three projects, I was in one, it was the first project. And it was very difficult because we had women fellows, our movement was mainly women, you were forced to include women, due to the need. So the thing was mixed, but women did not perform as well as men, we made little money, it was very annoying. (April 21, 2014)

The point here is not whether women's involvement undermines the efficiency of certain workfare projects. In the case of Luisa, I witnessed men and women shoveling dirt together more than once and could not tell any difference in their productivity. For the case of Mauro, other activists attributed the problems in the organization's first endeavors either to issues unrelated to gender (such as delays in government funding) or to problems they say are more common among men (such as addiction). However, regardless of their factual accuracy, these perceptions affect the experiences of people in the movement and generate specific ideas as to which activities are more fitting to different participants.

Third, even some of the most active middle-aged female participants in the movement express ambivalence and guilt about what they see as neglect of their domestic duties, a viewpoint that is far less common among male respondents. Activists of all genders describe female participation in the paid labor force as a temporary solution rather than a desirable situation and refer to housework as the primary responsibility of women. Thus, it is not uncommon to find cases like Sabrina:

My family never forbade me from anything. But I find the time. For instance, I get up at five in the morning, clean everything, if I have to do laundry I do, if I have to iron clothes I do. And at night, of course except perhaps when it gets too late here for me to cook, but at night I cook, I leave food, feed them, I do everything. They never lack clothes nor anything. Nor the cleaning, nor anything. So I comply, you know, with both sides. (June 2, 2014)

Sabrina's work capacity is remarkable: In addition to coordinating a neighborhood and overseeing several cooperative projects for her organization, she also does all the cleaning and cooking for her family. Just as significant is the fact that after years of intensive activism, she feels compelled to clarify that she fulfills her duties to "both sides." Almost none of the men I talked to had a similar attitude.

In short, women's efforts at reconstructing proletarian routines vary from men's. While for the latter, this process involves engagement in practices associated with industrial jobs, for the former, it is more about domestic labor. Life histories reveal that activists of all genders worked outside the home throughout their lives. Yet female respondents tend to see paid occupations as secondary to household responsibilities. Consequently, their perception of the piquetero movement is different from their male counterparts, as Brenda and Constanza show.

4.4 PRESERVING AN IDEALIZED PROLETARIAN DOMESTIC LIFE

Brenda joined a piquetero organization approximately two years before our interview. She migrated in the 1990s from her native Peru, drawn, like many others, by tales of economic success and the policy of fixed dollar-to-peso parity ("one to one"), which raised the exchange value of salaries earned in Argentina. She was in her twenties and had finished high school, worked in both retail and factories, and even taken some vocational courses. However, the only jobs she was ever able to secure in Buenos Aires were housecleaning and street vending. She married another immigrant, a construction worker, and together with him purchased a lot and built a home.

Twenty years later, in her late forties, Brenda does not seem to regret migrating. She has a positive attitude and is constantly seeking job opportunities. She buys cheap items ("a little of everything, tupperware, a few toys, in the winter hats, gloves, socks") in the downtown district of Once, where wholesalers operate, and sells them by the unit in the streets and open-air markets. She also makes children's garments for sale and repairs clothes for her neighbors. Her husband is frequently hired to do construction or maintenance projects and, when these gigs are not available, helps with the street vending. Together with renting one room in their house to a relative, the family makes just enough to get by.

Brenda's immediate survival does not seem to be at risk. However, decades of depending on odd jobs, constantly adjusting with her husband to make ends meet, have left in her a deep desire for a reliable occupation. Moreover, her options are narrowing because asthma now prevents her from doing heavy housecleaning work. She has enrolled over the years in many government-run vocational courses, such as dressmaking, manicure, waxing, makeup, nurse assistant, and basic computer skills, but has not found a better job.

People in the neighborhood always talked about political networks that helped people get assistance, but being a foreigner, Brenda was not entirely familiar with them. The way she joined the piquetero movement, hence, was by a combination of chance and curiosity: One day while selling in the streets of another neighbor-hood, she saw a demonstration and decided to speak with its leader. It turned out they were from an organization a few blocks from her house:

One day I was in San Justo² selling, in the street, about two years ago, and I saw a lot of people with banners that went in front of the municipality building. And then I said, "what would these women want?, I will get close." I was thinking in my head, "I know girls who are in these movements and they get jobs, I would like a job, I want to sign up. Are these people them?" I asked someone to keep an eye on my things, got close to a woman, and asked, "madam, what are you asking for?" "We are [organization] from [location]," from my neighborhood they said, and since I live there I said, "so, you guys have a boss, something?" "yes," they said, "we have a coordinator and here they give you a job, social plans." "Uh, this is what I am looking for, who is the coordinator?" "Doña Josefa." That is when I met Josefa, and told her, "Doña Josefa, good morning, I am looking for a job because I am selling on the streets, I do not have a job, I have nothing, what can I do?" She gave me the address of this place, and said, "come over on this date." (May 22, 2014)

Josefa took copies of Brenda's documents, put together an application, and told her to wait. For a while, nothing happened, until she obtained a small plan of about 50 US dollars. For more than a year, Brenda participated in demonstrations and special events, until she was enrolled in a more generous program that paid double that amount and required her to show up a few days a week to participate in a productive project. She chose sewing and joined a group of five to ten women who fix clothes and make stuffed toys. However, a paperwork issue caused her to lose this plan and return to the previous one after only three months. Neither she nor Josefa know the reason: It is frequent for officials to communicate bureaucratic decisions without explaining much. Perhaps some document was missing; perhaps there was an eligibility problem; or perhaps the papers got mixed up. Yet despite not being required to attend regularly anymore, Brenda remained involved as if nothing had happened, con-stantly reminding Josefa of her situation. She is also adamant about not wanting a need-based subsidy (what she calls "plan") but a merit-based workfare program (what she refers to as a "job"):

I told her, "Doña Josefa, I want to sign up for stuff but I want to work, because I can still work. I do not want a social plan, I want a job." (May 22, 2014)

² San Justo is an important commercial center and the administrative seat of La Matanza, the largest district in Greater Buenos Aires.

Like many other participants, Brenda's first experiences in the movement were marked by uncertainty and confusion. In particular, she was ashamed of being involved in demonstrations because of widespread prejudices about welfare beneficiaries and piquetero activists. However, with time, she became more comfortable, to the point that she does not mind canvassing in her neighborhood:

Brenda: At the beginning I had a bit of shame, I said "what am I doing here?" and then I began to get used to it, because it was like relaxation, something I never did, everything is like a laugh, fellowship, walking through the streets, carrying the flag, all those things.

Question: How is it that at the beginning you were ashamed?
B: Because sometimes one thinks, "ay, someone can find me, someone can see me, someone who knows me" and now let me tell you that when we went to gather signatures, the entire neighborhood saw me, and I do not care at all, let everyone look.

Q: And why that change?
B: I do not know why, because I say, I am not doing anything, I am not stealing, I am not prostituting myself, I am just gathering signatures, talking to people, why should I care? (May 22, 2014)

Nevertheless, our conversation made clear that even though she has a more positive attitude toward the organization and enjoys the company of other people in the sewing project, the main reason Brenda keeps going is the expectation of getting a spot in a better program. In particular, she hopes to enroll in a cooperative under the *Argentina Trabaja* ("Argentina Works") program:[3]

I am still with the 225 pesos plan, see how slow things are, but Doña Josefa told me that perhaps I will enter the cooperative too, so that makes me more happy, that is also why I keep coming. So I am here in the movement, doing what I can. (May 22, 2014)

The *Argentina Trabaja* plan (frequently referred to as "the cooperative") is not only better paid (although beneficiaries remain under the poverty line) but also implies a more regular schedule. Unlike her current situation, in which she works a limited amount of hours a week, the *Argentina Trabaja* program would mean showing up early each day at the organization's offices, going to the room where the sewing machines are, and

---

[3] At the time of the interview, this program paid 2,000 Argentinean pesos, or the equivalent to about 250 US dollars.

working with other women for several hours. It would free her from the need to go to different locations each day, juggling various short-term gigs each week, and leave time for her responsibilities at home. Moreover, even though it is a workfare program, beneficiaries are still officially registered, which for someone who has worked off the books since coming to Argentina twenty years ago is an important symbolic reward:

Being here is convenient for me because for me, this is, I take it like a job, I like being here, because first I do not have a job, it is convenient because I know that if I enter into the cooperative I will have an on-the-books job. I never had an on-the-books job here, I always worked in people's homes, but no one registered me, I had no health insurance, nothing. (May 22, 2014)

In short, enrollment in this particular plan would imply additional income, but its main appeal, which keeps Brenda engaged, is regular hours and recognition. She does not seem interested in the group's politics (a topic largely absent from our conversations). As she insists, the possibility of working every day in the same project "lifts my spirits and makes me want to come here more, I signed up to work, I want to work, I always worked." Brenda has found an activity that resonates with her self-image as a hard worker and good woman. Being awarded a spot in the *Argentina Trabaja* would help her sustain her involvement in such an activity, validating her identification with a positive category (people who "still can work" and "want to work") in contrast to those who are either unable or unwilling to earn their living. When I asked her at the end of our interview whether she wanted to add anything, she insisted:

Brenda: I think we have talked about everything, a bit about everything. But as I told you, I would like to be here, but to work, to be in the cooperative.

Question: What do you mean?
B: I mean working, being in the cooperative. There are people here who work and are in the cooperative, but I still do not know. I may, or may not. But I would like to be in the cooperative working, being stable, come and say "I am going to work" and then leave at a certain time and go home. (May 22, 2014)

Like Brenda, Constanza's early years in the movement were defined by ambiguity. Yet over time, she developed a fierce loyalty to her organization. A longtime resident of one of the least advantaged areas of the Lomas de Zamora district, she is in her fifties and joined her organization around the turn of the century, as everyone around her began losing their jobs.

Constanza's situation was particularly dire because of a heart condition that prevented her from doing physically intensive chores. She did not know much about politics and had previously had a bad experience with another piquetero group. However, her current organization had built a reputation in the neighborhood as an effective place to find help:

I came here because I had stopped working, because I have a health problem, I stopped working. I always worked, so when I stopped working there was this place, and people knew there were social plans. It has been eleven years since I am here. People knew there were social plans and all that, and well, I came, signed up, I got a plan, and since then I stayed with them forever. Always, I joined the struggle here, and I liked it, I liked it, and I stayed here. (July 28, 2011)

Constanza's organization is an example of the ways piquetero activists have adapted to a changing environment. During 2001–2002, it was one of the most disruptive groups in the district. As Mario, one of its leaders, told me once: "[W]e were the baddest guys around here." However, over the years, they developed a more congenial relationship with the government and concentrated on providing education services to the community. Today, the organization administers not only workfare plans but also vocational courses and remedial high-school classes for more than a thousand students a year. The accumulation of resources has allowed the group to continue serving the area, even though the number of people they mobilize for demonstrations has declined:

Compared to the end of 2001, this feels like Europe. Let me tell you, I am talking to you now and I am figuring out how I can buy more computers [for a classroom]. Back then I used to go house by house asking for rice, in solidarity, because if we gathered ten kilos of rice and made a big stew for all, the big pot fed more than if everyone ate rice separately, at their homes. (Mario, July 28, 2011)

The organization's building is a series of rooms constructed over the years around a central yard. Most serve as classrooms for courses on sewing, electricity, welding, and computer literacy. The nicest of all, the only one with tiles on the walls, is the kitchen, where for many years, Constanza has taught a cooking class that offers an official diploma. With it, her mostly female students (over the years, I only saw a handful of men attending) can apply to be janitors and cooks at public schools.

In three and a half years of fieldwork, Constanza was present almost every single time I visited the organization. In addition to teaching her course, she usually arrives early in the morning to open the place, takes care of maintenance and cleaning, helps with errands and paperwork, and organizes special

FIGURE 4.2 Constanza's cooking class. Lomas de Zamora, March 2014.
"I'm trying to teach the girls here to cook, so they find a husband" (Virginia).

events such as demonstrations. Her presence is essential to the group's capacity to offer educational services to the community, which is a source of pride for her. Even though she only finished high school as an adult, her course is the one that fills fastest, and she keeps a long handwritten waitlist among her papers. As she said once, while interrupting an interview with younger activists:

I am not interested in diplomas, things like that do not interest me, otherwise when I finished my high school I would have kept going. I am not interested because when I got here I got into the social side, and I like the social side. What we say we do . . . I like that, because in reality at this age I am not interested in diplomas. They [other activists in the interview] are in the educational part, they are younger, it is great what they are doing. She [pointing to a particular activist] keeps studying, and all that. But I am in the social side, and I like it. (May 17, 2012)

Moreover, Constanza insists that her success in the classroom has not come at the expense of her contribution to the organization's broader mission, nor of her responsibilities at home:

Things also depend on you, I can be a teacher, come teach, and then do not do any other activities, that is not useful. It is like going to a school, go to any of the schools around here. Teachers there go, teach, and do not give a shit about other people. They do not give a fuck about students ... That is why we need to raise consciousness, if I am a teacher or anything, I am aware of the other activities. Slowly, those who like it will continue. And those who do not like it, "I do not like it and that is it, I want to go teach and then go home." That is in the conscience of each person. And I have a family, I am not on my own. And well, my husband got used to it, because I, when I get home, I do stuff around the house, I cook too, maybe I can leave something ready for the next day, or I leave it ready for them to do it, I move around. Today I have a meeting, I am going home around seven, and I will take care of cooking also at night. It is not that I abandon, leave everything, that if you go to my house you will find chaos. No, very orderly it will be. Because I am very active. (May 17, 2012)

The majority of people who participate with Constanza are indeed younger, and many are studying to become teachers. Yet they are deferential to her, mostly because of her long experience. She emphasizes to anyone who wants to listen that she has been in the place for many years and that she never left despite divisions with other groups and generous offers to go somewhere else. She describes in detail the many protests she went to during the contentious times of the great crisis of 2001–2002, including some that involved walking for hours under the sun or camping for days in the winter:

Now all we do are events, they are not marches. In reality everyone who is here, no one knows the marches we used to make. We once made a march, which I will not forget as long as I live, from here on a rainy day, they did not suspend it, we went from here, walking, we concentrated in Puente La Noria *(La Noria Bridge), everyone else was there, it was a lot of people back then. With the leaders we went from La Noria, all the flags, everything, to Saavedra walking non stop. And the next day, besides that, we walked from Saavedra to the Ministry.*[4] *Two complete days. Some fellows abandoned because their legs could not take it anymore, they were a bit out of shape. But I walked both days.* (May 17, 2012)

By insisting she is not interested in credentials and recalling difficult protests, Constanza is drawing a line between herself and younger activists with higher levels of formal education. She is reframing her limitations as strengths and emphasizing the contributions she has made to the place. However, even though she likes to pull rank, her hostility is not directed to

[4] From *Puente La Noria* to Saavedra, the distance is about 20 kilometers. Usually, "the Ministry" refers to either the *Ministerio de Trabajo, Empleo y Seguridad Social* (federal Ministry of Labor, Employment and Social Security) or the *Ministerio de Desarrollo Social* (federal Ministry of Social Development), both of which deal with workfare programs. The two locations are in downtown Buenos Aires, so the walk on the second day was between 15 and 20 kilometers.

those who teach classes at the place. Instead, she criticizes those who, in her view, only participate for money:

Extract from fieldnotes, May 13, 2013
Constanza told me that Elena is her friend, but she is not a real activist, because during elections she and her daughters go around asking who needs help and they work for whoever pays more. Constanza says she lets Elena come use the sewing machines when she needs them, but that "we are the real activists, who do not earn one peso."

Extract from fieldnotes, May 21, 2013
[A man came asking a question about workfare plans] Constanza in particular criticized this man a lot, saying that he had been with the movement, but left when they stopped distributing foodstuffs. Like other times, she said "that is the way it is, there are people who come only if you give them something."

Extract from fieldnotes, April 30, 2014
As always, Constanza compares herself favorably with those who left, or with those she criticizes. At one point I asked her if she knew about people who had been in the organization but left. In other words, I asked her about dropouts. She said no, that she is not in contact with people who left, and immediately moved on to an eulogy of her commitment: "I was here in good and bad times. I never left. I have not even worked during elections." A topic that comes up every time I talk to her is her disdain for people who do politics for money, that "during the elections they work with those who pay them."

In other words, Constanza builds a righteous sense of self by comparing her political experience to that of others with seemingly illegitimate motives. From her perspective, the key difference is not that she and her fellows do not make money through their activism. It is that they are willing to participate for free if necessary. This moral criterion is particularly important to her because she is among the few in her organization who were around during the lean times of the early 2000s, when resources were far scarcer and all the movement could spare her was a meal in a soup kitchen.

In short, through a piquetero organization, Constanza has obtained what Brenda seems to be looking for: the resources and rationale for engaging in particular routines, which in turn provide two key rewards. First, she obtains respectability (both in- and out-group): Other activists recognize her effort and contributions; students value and seek her knowledge; and community members know of her positive work ("in the neighborhood, even the dogs know who I am"). Moreover, her substantial contributions to the organization do not impede her from being a good mother and wife. Second, she gains stability: Each day, there is something that needs to be done for the organization to continue operating. Each semester brings a new iteration of her popular cooking course, and each season has its own specific events like congresses, commemorative demonstrations, or graduation ceremonies. For a person who not that long ago was excluded from the labor market, this is a remarkable achievement. Thus, her loyalty to the group is completely understandable:

Extract from fieldnotes, May 10, 2013
Once again it was clear that Constanza feels at home in the building's kitchen, as if it was her kitchen. I never saw her in a bad mood, even when she criticizes others. She spends the day doing things, cooking (she made a rice and lentils stew for noon, and then made an apple pie for her younger daughter). Cooking well is a source of pride for her: she told me that two of her daughter's friends "invited themselves to eat" because their own mothers do not cook as well. She also sews things and teaches the cooking course. Besides, she is the one that informally runs the place day to day. She is always there. Around 3pm, when I was sitting in the kitchen, she told me referring to the things she was doing, "See, Marcos? This way the day flies for us."

4.5 THE SEARCH FOR GENUINE JOBS

The previous sections compared the experiences of recent recruits to the movement with people who have been involved for at least a decade. Like Horacio and Brenda, new participants tend to be skeptical of their organizations but also eager to obtain employment. Many of them eventually drop out as they find a better opportunity somewhere else (usually a pension or job that pays better than the small amount of a workfare plan). In contrast, others follow a trajectory like Lázaro and Constanza, who through their practices in the movement and interactions with other activists learn ways to reconstruct the routines of an idealized past centered on manufacturing and domestic labor.

However, regardless of their (potentially) different outcomes, all the respondents mentioned in this chapter share a similar set of dispositions. They come from different backgrounds; their specific professional careers vary; and their personal viewpoints reflect the diversity of opinions in Argentinean society. Yet all have been directly affected by large-scale socioeconomic transformations that made everyday life in their communities more uncertain. Consequently, they all seek the consistency and respectability that comes from partaking in the kind of life they have been socialized to see as most fitting to them.

Central to this romanticized lifestyle is an ideal type of employment. Respondents frequently talk about their desire for "genuine jobs." In broad terms, this label means decently paid, stable blue-collar work. More specifically, people in the piquetero movement emphasize certain characteristics of "proper" occupations. First, they have to do with manufacturing, producing a concrete good rather than an intangible service. Second, they are supposed to pay enough for the earner to support a family and offer an array of basic social services (health, recreation, and retirement). Third, they are expected to be demanding, meaning that the normative association between effort and rewards must go both ways. Hard work should always be compensated, yet only those who put in the effort are entitled to its benefits. Finally, and perhaps most importantly, interviewees insist that good jobs reward a series of dispositions. Employers are supposed to seek out and pay more for workers who accumulate practical experience, show up on time, and avoid unprofessional behaviors like drinking, quarreling, or lawbreaking.

In sum, activists perceive deindustrialization as undermining the kind of work that makes a healthy, moral life possible. Interviews are full of contrasts between the odd jobs frequently available to participants (sometimes through government-funded programs) and their ideal type of employment. Both Tito (who is assigned to a street cleaning crew in Florencio Varela) and Priscila (who is part of a small textile cooperative in La Matanza) agree that projects involving the production of goods are better:

Do you think I like being called lazy? I am working in a cooperative and people still yell at me "lazy." I mean, I am not against the cooperative, but give me a cooperative that produces. I do not say that cleaning a curb, cleaning a park is a dishonor. But I am not reactivating anything. Let me produce. If I produce, I know I will get something. Because if instead of $1200 [paid by the government], with my production I get $800, I got it with my production. . . . So that is what I am looking for. Let me produce bricks, produce mops, whatever you want. But I reactivate things, I am doing something to reactivate things. (Tito, May 14, 2012)

I fulfill my hours. If we have to be here at eight, we are here at eight. And if we have to do something we do it. To do useful things, not to fool around. Because at least for me, sweeping streets is not an occupation. It may be nice for the neighborhood, but I do not think it is very useful. Like in here we make pants, all sorts of things. That is useful, because from that we buy more cloth, we buy flour for the soup kitchen. Whatever we need for the soup kitchen, we sell and use that money to buy. So it is useful. Sweeping streets is not that useful. (Priscila, May 19, 2014)

In other words, manufacturing labor (and, by extension, those involved in it) is seen as generating value. The idealization of this kind of work does not only inform the experiences of older participants. Blue-collar jobs, with their set of obligations and benefits, are also seen as the solution to the troubles of marginalized boys and girls. In the words of Lázaro:

In reality what we want is not a social plan, because that is not useful, we want a dignified job. Look how the youth are getting lost, under drugs, under alcohol, and all those things that are emerging. Why instead of letting kids kill themselves don't you find them a job, you open factories or something, so they can get out of where they are? Because you will see, if you live in a neighborhood like the one I live in, all the kids are on a corner, smoking a joint or drinking. It is a bad life, sadly. (June 27, 2014)

In other words, the wholesomeness of occupations related to manufacturing labor is instilled on younger generations, but Argentineans who came of age in or after the 1990s have been exposed to a labor market in which those kinds of jobs are much scarcer. The imbalance between the employment aspirations learned from their parents, on the one hand, and their limited capacity to enact them, on the other, is crucial to understanding the appeal of piquetero mobilization for some of them, as the following chapter will show.

5

"If It Rains or Hails, You Still Have to Show Up for Work"

Development of New Habits

Their official name is the "health commission," but everyone calls them the "health girls." They are a group of women in one of the organizations in my study who engage in different activities related to the well-being of children. They distribute resources to soup kitchens, share information with parents, and keep track of low-weight infants. This work can be challenging, yet their only income is a workfare plan obtained through the movement. Moreover, two factors beyond their control complicate their task. First, state neglect in the form of bureaucratic delays and lack of supplies frequently prevents them from doing their job. Second, they are also usually required to help with paperwork and demonstrations. Consequently, the days of these activists alternate between almost idle and extremely busy.

Not surprisingly, this situation generates conflict. The women in the group complain about being asked to do a lot, even with regard to things unrelated to health. In addition, the fact that sometimes they have nothing to do generates accusations of laziness. The members of the commission insist that others do not see the most demanding parts of their work, such as walking from place to place collecting data or having training sessions in other parts of the city.

Such is the situation on this hot January morning. Paloma, a member of the commission in her early twenties, is getting ready to resign from her position of *planillera*: the person who verifies other people's attendance and entry times. The group's coordinator unilaterally assigned this additional task to her, and she recently got in a strong argument with a number of older women that arrived late for a separate project: "[Y]ou must be drunk if you think I will get up at seven in the morning because you fucking kid think we should be here at eight." As we wait for the coordinator to arrive, Giugliana joins us. She is the head of one of the organization's newest locations and does not work in health. Yet she is a good friend of Paloma, who tells her about the situation. Giugliana is supportive: "Those women, if they had to go work at a factory would die! What would they do if they had to wake up at four in the morning?"

Giugliana is a thin woman in her thirties who jokes with everyone and is well liked by her fellows. However, her cheerful attitude evaporated once I sat down with her for an interview: She shared a story of struggle, suffering, and resilience. She dropped out of high school and began working different gigs at age thirteen: She made boxes, cleaned houses, and learned to produce shoes. She remembers the ease with which she learned new trades and the confidence her father had in her, as a responsible teenager who worked hard, did not do drugs or alcohol, and was careful with boys. Her good sense, she says, made her an independent child.

When she was nineteen, however, Giugliana made a decision that would affect her life. She met a police officer and moved in with him. At the beginning, the couple worked well together, yet after a while, he began abusing her, using beatings and withholding money in response to what he saw as transgressions. Giugliana endured in silence and terror for two years. Eventually, after an occasion in which her partner placed a gun to her head, she decided that unless she left him, she would be murdered sooner or later. She called the police and moved with her two children to her best friend's house.

Nevertheless, the problems persisted: Not only did her husband ignore restraining orders and continue threatening her, but he also declined to support their children. To survive, Giugliana relied on the solidarity of friends and relatives. Yet the risk remained that financial vulnerability would force her to return to an abusive relationship. What made the difference were two things. First, her sister offered her a place to live for free in the back of their parents' lot. Second, a few years before her separation, she had become involved in a piquetero group. Her husband refused to let her work, but she realized the need to have an independent income and signed up without his knowledge. For a long time, she participated sporadically, helping with a soup kitchen and attending demonstrations. When she left her abusive partner, Giugliana asked whether she could have a better-paying plan. The organization, recognizing her desperate situation, prioritized her case. When they obtained additional positions after many protests, Giugliana began earning more money and working every day:

That's when I began working. When they signed me up I remember going and asking my coordinator, "Are you sure that I will work?" I said, "Are you sure that I will be selected?" I drove him crazy. And well, thanks to God, we could get the plans. It was a big struggle that we had, to begin earning 1200 pesos per month. We even had to go out to the streets, camp in places to have a raise. It took us a lot of sacrifice. (February 26, 2014)

The organization played a crucial role in Giugliana's recovery. The resources she obtained were more than a material help. They were essential to regaining a sense of personal autonomy and definitely breaking with a toxic marriage:

My ex-husband once told me as he was leaving: "You will come to me crying for money." And to this day he is still waiting. I did the legal paperwork, yes. But to denigrate my children by crying, telling him "come back, your kids miss you," no. I do not do that. (February 26, 2014)

More importantly, Giugliana made friends in the organization, and these relations became essential when a new crisis hit. After more than a year without seeing anyone, she began dating another man. However, when she became pregnant, he decided to disappear. The baby was born premature and died within days. Confronted with a terrible tragedy, her fellows had the opposite attitude her boyfriend had shown:

Here the fellows, the organization, helped me a lot. They paid for the funeral. I was alone and you know how hard it is to do that paperwork, they took care of everything. Of everything they took care. I cannot complain, they were very good fellows with me. They took care of going to see me at the hospital, of bringing my family. They were in every moment, my family and the organization. And they took care of the funeral. They did not leave me alone even for a minute. I am very grateful. Very grateful, because it did not happen like "oh, she is a fellow who had a problem, that is it," quite the contrary, they were all the time with me. Helping me get ahead so that I did not enter in a depressive state. (February 26, 2014)

As a result of these experiences, Giugliana became an enthusiastic member of the group. She worked for a few years assisting other women and helping with administration until her coordinator asked if she would be interested in opening a new office for the organization. Activists in her neighborhood had to walk twenty blocks in order to seek help or fulfill the requirements of workfare plans. Having a separate location would help serve the community better. It would be a lot of work and involve using her personal residence, but she agreed:

[The coordinator] put us in this area, so I take care of the people this side of the avenue who come to work. He had the idea, "why don't you do it in your house, so people see us?" So I started slowly. Little by little neighbors began to get interested, what did we do, which projects we had, and well, I recruited people. People who need a plan, who go to marches for foodstuffs, I have a group of fellows who are in the Argentina Trabaja *cooperatives, like I am, only that they have to go to work improving clubs and schools. They have fewer responsibilities than me. Because I take care of checking that they go to work, I have to go to meetings, I take care of the common fund to pay rents. I am the one who gathers the money, keeps it, and takes it so others pay.* (February 26, 2014)

As the previous quote describes, Giugliana's days are very busy. In addition to recruiting people, she has to do paperwork, control attendance, participate in meetings, and take care of the locale's finances. Nonetheless, she claims to love it (an assertion that my interactions with her over the years confirmed). Being in the organization provided a supportive group who helped her in the worst moments. Moreover, becoming a coordinator also gave her recognition for her efforts, by leaders (who asked her to open a new location), her fellows (who trust her with their money), and the community (whose members show up at her home to ask for assistance). Moving from helped to helper has been a deeply empowering experience. A few years ago, she needed others to escape domestic violence. Today, she is the one lending a hand, using the organization's connections, expertise, and reputation:

Giugliana: I like all this thing of working with people, helping people. Let me tell you, sometimes I am sick and get up anyways, I go, come, I grumble but still like this.

Question: What do you like about this?

G: I like helping people get a plan. Or give them foodstuffs. Or tell them "well, you've got a problem, let me go with you to do the paperwork" or "you have got to do it this way." Because there are people who are in a worse situation than me. For instance, thanks to God my house does not flood, but there are people who do: "well, let's go to the municipality to talk." Since they already know our organization, then they meet with you faster, you know? (February 26, 2014)

Empowerment has also meant the capacity to help women going through a similar experience as her. Giugliana is not the only victim of domestic violence in the area, but her painful experience can be used to rescue others:

I had a fellow who was suffering domestic violence. From my own experience, I always told her, "look, you should not let anyone hit you. He does not have the right, you have the right to report him, if the relationship does not work anymore, it does not work anymore. Do not stay with him for your children's sake, because the worst thing you can do is stay. Your children will cry, will miss him because it is the father, but by you staying with that person, seeing that that person keeps hurting you, the ones that suffer the most are the children, because they see that." (February 26, 2014)

Giugliana's organization has pushed for some of the most progressive legislation in the country, from universal basic income for children to gender identity laws. The group is also part of human rights advocacy networks and has been at the forefront of initiatives to control police abuse. Giugliana has repeatedly demonstrated, canvassed, and camped to support these activities. However, her personal views are more ambiguous. For instance, even though her abusive ex was a cop and her attempts at obtaining support from the police were not always effective, she still complains that due process limits the capacity of security forces to do their job:

I think that the police sometimes are overwhelmed, they do not have the means. You perhaps get a thief and then the Mothers of Plaza de Mayo [Argentina's most iconic human rights movement] argue about human rights. What, only thieves have human rights? What about the people? I do not agree with that. I do not agree with the Mothers of Plaza de Mayo. (February 26, 2014)

In addition, despite the difficulties trying to access resources to support her children, Giugliana shares the opinion that offering needs-based welfare for single mothers (in contrast to programs based on merit) encourages young women to get pregnant before they are ready:

They give you a universal income [asignación universal], how many young girls are pregnant because they know they will earn a plan? They should not give that. They should give it, but in another way, so they study, become someone tomorrow. They should open factories, so people have jobs. I do not want to depend on a social plan. I want to work and have a dignified salary. (February 26, 2014)

An unsympathetic observer would argue that Giugliana's views are the result of ignorance or prejudice. Yet such an interpretation fails to explain other aspects of her life. The fact that she does not have a lot of formal education does not mean she is uninformed. Quite the opposite, she is an avid follower of news media and participates regularly in meetings to critically discuss current events. She emphasizes how participation in the movement helped her become a more inquisitive person, who is not afraid to demand what she sees as her rights and argue with others:

I used to know nothing about politics. It is not like I know a lot now, there are things I do not understand, or that I need to learn more about. How can we change people's mentality in our society, so they realize, they are not fooled with a small subsidy or a pension? So [the government] does not give you something to cover your eyes and ears? Things like that open up your mind. (February 26, 2014)

More importantly, Giugliana actively contributes to an organization that helps the most destitute in her community, including recovering addicts and youngsters with criminal records. A possibility is that she is forced to do this work, yet in our private conversations, she expressed genuine passion for the movement, and I repeatedly saw her volunteer extra time for it. How are we then to reconcile her activism with her private opinions?

As argued in Chapter 1, the fact that someone's actions do not necessarily correspond to his or her viewpoints should not surprise us. In fact, inconsistencies between political participation and private opinions are a frequent aspect of collective action for two reasons. First, as Javier Auyero and Debora Swistun (2009) argue in their study of environmental suffering in Buenos Aires, individuals may share certain convictions publicly while endorsing other views in private. This situation is not the result of willful lies or self-deception. Rather, it is part of a front-stage strategy in response to what people perceive others want from them (Goffman 1959; also see Cooley 1902). Second, as case studies of grassroots mobilization have shown (Wolford 2010; Quirós 2011; Viterna 2013), an individual's support for a movement does not require unconditional adherence to its overall agenda. The program and goals of organizations and coalitions undergo a process of translation at the micro level, through which generalized appeals turn into context-specific meanings and tactics, which in turn resonate with the experiences of particular activists.

When combining both factors outlined previously, it becomes possible to understand the apparent contradiction between Giugliana's personal beliefs and the agenda of the organization she enthusiastically supports. While demonstrations and roadblocks are the most visible aspects of her participation to outsiders (the media, the public, bystanders, and officials), for her, they are secondary. What really matters is the day-to-day work that occupies the vast majority of her time in the movement. In this context, the overall political goals of her organization recede from view, and in their place comes a litany of routines that allow her to feel useful, necessary, and above all, moral.

For Giugliana, days are filled with almost endless tasks: getting up early, showing up to meetings, making sure participants do their job, and completing paperwork. She also devotes substantial time to solving the countless problems neighbors bring to her, sometimes during weekends or late at night. Through this work, she faces frequent decisions regarding who to prioritize in the distribution of help. From her perspective, there are two kinds of individuals: those who earn their benefits through hard work and those who seek to be paid without doing any effort. While she praises the former as people who "want to progress," she derides the latter using the word *chanta*, an Argentinean term meaning a mix of liar and good-for-nothing:

[Some people] you realize are chantas. *Do not want to progress. I am not going to do the work for you. I am going to give you a hand, the rest do it yourself. You understand? There are people who are waiting to be given things without doing anything. And that is not the way things work. You understand? Because if I can go out to work, so can you.* (February 26, 2014)

The establishment of a boundary between those who earn their benefits and those who just live off the generosity of others is crucial to understanding Giugliana's commitment. For her, participation is not so much about adherence to a set of policies but about the opportunity to engage in the practices she associates with honorability. Activism allows her to be more than a taker, to obtain resources not thanks to charity but through hard work. In her view, the attractiveness of the organization lies in the balance of costs and benefits but in a way opposite to what one would expect: The resources she obtains in the movement are valuable precisely because they entail sacrifices. From the beginning, she could tell that the organization was not a place for slackers:

At first they just made us go every day to the organization, because there were people who never worked, or did not like to work, so that they get used to having a job and going every day. You know, because in this place, if it rains or hails, you still have to show up for work. That is something some fellows do not get. Because if you go to any job and say "oh, it is raining, I am not going to work," they will kick you out! (February 26, 2014)

Giugliana's attitude is consistent with psychological research on people's tendency to attach more value to things when they demand a higher effort (Festinger 1957; Kruger et al. 2004; Inzlicht, Shenhav, and Olivola 2018). Through her activism, she is able to associate benefits with hard work. As a result, she both assigns worth to her labor (it is valuable because it leads to remuneration) and also claims membership in the category of those who "want to progress" and are not "*chantas.*" Her demanding routines in the movement turn her social plan from a mere handout into something akin to a "dignified salary." Moreover, the recognition by other activists allows her to cement this identity even further:

I am today a coordinator and lead a neighborhood because others chose me. You understand? I did not ask for anything. They had me do a job, I did it. And they know I am responsible. For me to not go to work, something really bad has to happen. I have to be very sick or something with my children, otherwise I am there every day, I go to every place, I am very responsible in that sense. (February 26, 2014)

The importance of activism for Giugliana also emerges from the scarcity of alternative ways of accessing resources. She is among the millions of young working-class Argentineans who experience substantial barriers to stable, formal employment. The reduction in blue-collar occupations in recent decades affected them in a different way than their parents: While older people remember the certainties and meanings of a life centered on factory labor, individuals like Giugliana, below forty, are too young to have ever experienced that. Most have been socialized into the dispositions of factory jobs and learned crafts from older relatives. Yet their expectations of organizing their lives around the experience of manual work clash with the reality of changes in Argentina's economy, which is now more service-oriented and in which the educational credentials necessary to access good jobs are often out of reach for the poor.

Therefore, for many young activists, participation in a piquetero organization provides the chance to develop an otherwise infeasible honorable lifestyle. In a context with limited opportunities for personal growth, the movement offers a working-class ethos, plus the resources and training to exercise it. However, while for their parents this is a work of reconstruction of past habits, for them it is a labor of development of new routines.

Moreover, just as with their elders, the experiences of young piquetero activists also reflect the ideal of a proletarian family with a gendered division of labor. Men tend to enroll in infrastructure and community improvement projects, while women are far more likely to be assigned to programs associated with household chores. In addition, even though all young members are compelled to have discipline at work and self-restraint at home, the actual meaning of these ideals is gender-specific. For men, being a responsible worker is associated with manual labor and public life, while for women, expectations are framed in terms of administrative work, motherhood, and domesticity.

FIGURE 5.1 Roadblock on *Puente Pueyrredón* (Pueyrredón Bridge). Avellaneda, June 2012.
"I complain sometimes about being tired. But if you get involved in this, it is because you like it. What I like of all this is that every day, even if it does not look like it, you contribute to growth. One's growth and also growth for others" (Gisela).

5.1 YOUTH UNEMPLOYMENT AND LABOR MARKET EXCLUSION

Almost every respondent I talked to describes youth unemployment as a major problem. Transformations in Argentina's economy mean that younger generations of workers came of age in a very different environment than their parents. The decline of manufacturing and the increasing prevalence of the service sector cause great difficulty for working class youth to insert themselves in the labor market. Lacking extensive formal education and unable to accumulate practical experience, they face low levels of employability that worsen with each passing year. Even jobs that are temporary or pay little are often hard to obtain. As Lucía, an activist in her twenties, insisted:

These days, at least what we see in all the neighborhoods to which we go, and where we live, is that people do not even get an odd job, every day it is more difficult, people do not get [even] off-the-books jobs, you can ask the majority of our fellows here, if they are not inside one of our cooperatives, it is almost impossible to get a job. (May 18, 2012)

Statistics confirm my respondents' concerns. Over the past three decades, the unemployment rate for Argentineans aged 18–29 living in Greater Buenos Aires has consistently been double that of people above 30 years old (Rubio and Salvia 2018). Workers in their teens and twenties are also more likely to be employed in informal and precarious jobs (MTEYSS 2017). Moreover, these problems are concentrated in the poorest segments of the population. The youth unemployment rate for the lowest income quintile is 2.7 times higher than that for the richest (SIEMPRO 2018). Young people in families with incomes below the poverty line are far more likely to work off the books than their nonpoor counterparts (MTEYSS 2017).

As bad as these numbers are, they capture economically active individuals and fail to cover the roughly one million Argentineans between the ages of 16 and 24 who neither study, work, nor search for employment. Around 82.3 percent of these people belong to the poorest 40 percent of households (MTEYSS 2017, also see OIT 2013; Feijoó 2015).[1] While most Latin American countries have reduced the incidence of this situation since the 1980s, in Argentina, it has actually increased (Cárdenas, De Hoyos, and Szekely 2015).

Participants describe in detail the different barriers to good employment. To begin with, the public education system is underfunded and cannot serve the needs of marginalized communities. Despite recent programs to increase high school graduation rates, obtaining a diploma no longer guarantees access to employment. In the words of Evangelina, a teacher in her twenties involved in a grassroots education program:

In the neighborhood, this one, that one, all neighborhoods, education is like, there is not a desire to study, because in this society there are no opportunities, today perhaps you do not see that the person who completed high school has secured

---

[1] While there is general consensus among scholars on the existence of structural barriers to high-quality education and jobs for underprivileged youth in Argentina and Latin America, there is substantial debate as to how to best conceptualize the issue. In particular, some authors criticize the notion of *Nini* ("*ni trabaja ni estudia*," Spanish for "neither works nor studies"), arguing that such a label is frequently used in ways that are simplistic, stigmatizing, and dismissive of gendered forms of unpaid labor. For an overview of this literature, see D'Alessandre (2013), Feijoó (2015), and Assusa (2018).

a job, I mean, you need to have so many other things to have some economic stability. (May 28, 2012)

Sadly, Evangelina's diagnosis is shared by activists in other districts and organizations. According to Abelardo, the director for education in one of the nation's largest piquetero groups, the perception that personal investments in education will not pay off acts as a major obstacle to his organization's initiatives:

People say, "[I]f a person who studied and did things is a fool who cannot find a job, who has to work giving out leaflets in the streets, me myself, who did not study, will not study and end up doing the same work [anyways]." (July 20, 2011)

In recent years, the opening of new public universities has expanded access to postsecondary education. However, disparities in the quality of high schools, coupled with costs, segregation, and discrimination, continue to act as important barriers for those living in underprivileged communities. For Alan, an activist in his twenties who is studying to become a teacher, this combination leads to the inaccurate but widespread perception that teenagers from working-class backgrounds (what many call *pibes de barrio* or "neighborhood kids") do not belong in institutions of higher learning:

In general, an idea shared by people is that neighborhood kids cannot go to the university, ever since I remember that was inculcated on us, that the university was for those who have more purchasing power, that if you were from a neighborhood you could suffer some form of discrimination. (April 11, 2014)

The lack of access to formal education is not the only reason why many working-class youth in Argentina cannot access steady employment. After all, very few of their parents ever finished high school. The problem is also that the quality of jobs available to those without extensive credentials has deteriorated over the years. Respondents in their twenties and thirties complain that their options for making ends meet are limited. Even the lucky ones who work in the formal economy frequently access only short-term contracts without benefits. Such was the case of Leila, whose only official employment was through a program that sought to give practical experience to high schoolers. She worked for a few months but was fired when she reached the maximum amount of months the internship allowed. The program did not lead to any permanent position:

I worked in a lot of places. I worked as a seamstress, as a housecleaner, and then I worked in a factory. I was in high school, and the school gave me an internship to work in a factory. Well, a certain month came and they fired you so they did not promote you ... they took us all out because they needed to replace the kids again, bring all new kids. (July 30, 2011)

Víctor had a similar situation. After he finished high school, his father got him a position in a small metallurgical factory. What looked like a promising apprenticeship rapidly turned into a problematic situation. Being off the books and lacking the support of a union, he was vulnerable to abuses and wage theft. Eventually, it became more profitable (and reliable) to sell pirated movies and CDs in an open-air market:

Víctor: I was a turnery apprentice. Then I began working on a manual lathe. And then I began using other machines. Then I left, I had problems with my pay.

Question: What do you mean?

V: Because I was off-the-books, and the owner wanted to swindle me out of some days' worth of pay. I mean, he paid us per week, and then per two weeks, or per ten days. And sometimes, the two weeks included fewer days. So he did not want to recognize a day, and the unpaid days were accumulating, and we demanded, we argued, and I stopped working. (May 31, 2013)

Iván, the district coordinator for the youth in his organization, describes a similar scenario of limited job opportunities. When word went around in his neighborhood that he had started helping with the administration of work cooperatives, young people began showing up at his house asking for help:

With regards to work, I think that in every neighborhood it is an elemental necessity. I notice every day more girls and boys who are looking for a job because they know me, they ask me, they go to my house to see if I know their situation, if a new project began, something to join the movement. An ever growing number, who go to my house due to a concrete necessity, or kids who come ask me to prepare a resume for them, to go look for jobs. I prepare it for them; we do that, some are lucky and get a job. Or they are hired as a trial period for a few weeks, they get a contract for three months, no more than that. (June 9, 2012)

Leila, Víctor, and Iván belong to different organizations and work in separate neighborhoods. However, their perspectives point to a similar root problem: The availability of high-quality jobs for young people has declined over the years, and the skills, credentials, and connections required to access the few remaining ones have increased. The negative consequences of these trends concentrate among the youth of underprivileged communities, with devastating effects. Iván is one of the many respondents who describe the aimlessness that afflicts countless boys and girls:

Lately, they cannot get anything. So every day the quantity of kids who walk around the neighborhood is larger. They end up, I do not know, doing nothing in their homes, they cannot even get an odd job for one or two days … They are on the street corner, they get together to play soccer, they end up gathering that way. (June 9, 2012)

According to Mariana, a youth leader in her district, this aimlessness makes people vulnerable to all sorts of self-destructive behaviors, such as addiction, crime, and interpersonal violence:

There are many kids on the streets. A lot of young people not taken care of, they have no jobs, they are on the streets. You see them doing drugs, stealing, hitting each other, because they kill each other, due to drugs, they kill each other. (July 30, 2011)

Luciana, a thirty-something teacher in the same project as Evangelina, describes the situation not just in terms of current aimlessness but also as the incapacity to plan ahead. In her opinion, the immediate necessities of young residents in her community are covered. It is the concern about the future, the long-term thinking, that is missing:

The basic need that I see these days in the neighborhoods is not so much food on the table, but forming a life project. Because you think of the basic necessities, having food, a roof over your head. But then there are other needs, like having a life project, having an idea of what am I going to do in the future, that is something that you see these days. At least in the neighborhoods, that is what I see. Because everyone has a meal each day. Or if they do not have it, they go and ask in a soup kitchen and have it. Those necessities are satisfied. The real issue is different, is having a project for your future, thinking that education will help, not just to work but also to know things you do not know. (May 18, 2012)

Alan describes a similar scenario. Most people on his block find a way to survive, but very few have a profession, and the handful of young people who study (like him and his sister) are like "little Martians" who differ from the rest:

Many people have small shops, some have their micro businesses, people sell food, people sell cleaning supplies, so they figure out a way. There are scavengers who find ways to live. But there are not professionals except for construction and things like that, there are no professionals. In my personal case, me and my sister are first-generation university students. Then around the corner there are kids who are studying too, there is a kindergarten teacher who graduated last year. But these are like little Martians, they are not many, [others] due to life circumstances or other things did not take the road of studying, they do not have an incentive, or they think that studying will not take them to a better place. ... Drugs, alcohol, are factors that take those kids to be there, drinking, hanging out, smoking, doing drugs, living practically in a state of constant partying, any day of the week. There is not much of an interest on their part about progressing, and in many cases they have a family. Many young fathers, many young mothers, in recent years that has increased, nowadays it is like normal. (April 11, 2014)

Lacking job opportunities and deprived of the social services that would allow them to successfully enter into the labor market, the marginalized youth of Argentina are highly vulnerable to exploitation, violence, and addiction. However, contrary to what stigmatizing narratives in the media and public discourse insist, a clear majority of young people in these areas continue to seek legitimate employment. They have been socialized, from their earliest days, into a whole series of expectations and ideals connected to traditional working-class morality. Their older relatives have taught them practical skills and instilled in them the value of hard work. Their tragedy is that socioeconomic transformations in the last few decades have eliminated the kind of jobs integral to the lifestyle they associate with respectability. In this context, participation in a piquetero organization allows them to engage in the routines that they were raised to see as honorable: getting up early, showing up to work, producing something valuable, and being, in short, a dependable and reliable worker.

5.2 DEVELOPING ROUTINES IN THE UNEMPLOYED WORKERS' MOVEMENT

Brian participated in his first piquetero protest during the worst moment of the 2001–2002 economic collapse. He was a seventeen-year-old high school dropout living in Almirante Brown, in the southern section of Greater Buenos Aires. The reason he joined was straightforward: He learned that during this specific roadblock, there would be an *olla popular*, an improvised soup kitchen, in the middle of a demonstration:

I was with my mom, and was going through a bad situation, the country was going backwards, there was no work, no food, no way to sustain yourself. And I went to my first assembly, my first roadblock, to see what I could get, to eat in the roadblock. (May 16, 2012)

Brian continued participating, and the organization rewarded his commitment by enrolling him in a workfare program. However, for many years, his involvement was irregular. His particular plan paid very little and was not enough to cover his expenses, so he took advantage of every opportunity to make additional income. He only joined full-time when a group of fellows from the nearby district of Lanús invited him to join a series of workshops that functioned at an abandoned factory:

Someone had offered me a job, and around that time I had to stop participating. It did not mean I did not hear, know where my fellows were, what they were doing. But when working for others, you cannot say to your boss, "che, I am going to mobilize with my fellows because we have a protest, or because we are struggling for this," so it was a bit difficult for me. By coming here, they invited me to a workshop, I had again the chance to participate, fight, with my fellows again. So that situation happened and it was truly great, here the fellas created a space for me, we knew each other from eight years of struggles, and well, I reentered the fight but now with the fellows here in Lanús. (May 16, 2012)

The organization's work is based on the model of horizontal decision-making. Through financing from the government, NGOs, and private contracts, the group has dozens of activists organized in a system of cooperatives. They produce cinder blocks, carry out small public works, and make improvements in the community. They also run a series of soup kitchens and offer different educational services, from a daycare to a high school for adults. The pay is only slightly higher than a social plan, yet Brian evidently enjoys the work. He is constantly making jokes, going from one project to another, and giving everyone a hand.

Brian's activism is also remarkable because at the time he joined the group, he was isolated, increasingly desperate, and by his own admission, had no interest in politics. When I asked him if he had any previous political experience, he responded:

Question: When you went to your first roadblock, did you have any experience as an activist?
Brian: No, no. I had just dropped out of high school twice the first year, and I did not have any activist mindset, nor the [idea] of struggling for something. I got out of my house, I had a shitty situation, and from one day to the other, I had a bunch of fellows, being able to share something, share a stew in a roadblock, being able to be with your fella, going out even to scrounge something for the stew, those things. And there I learned, today I feel very grateful with everything that has happened in what I learned in the organization and with many of my fellows. (May 16, 2012)

For Brian, in other words, the movement was a lifesaver. He joined to get food, yet to his surprise, he obtained much more: supportive fellows, learning opportunities, and eventually a job he enjoys. Being a piquetero gave him purpose by making him necessary: He is part of a cooperative with very limited resources, and any help counts. By showing up every day and doing his part, he contributes to the place's subsistence. Moreover, his daily practices confer a sense of respectability by matching his idea of what a hard-working person should do. His days begin very early: Shortly after I met him, he had a child and moved to the city of La Plata, more than 40 kilometers away from Lanús. This means he wakes up between four and five in the morning and returns to his house fifteen hours later. During the day, he is going from one activity to the other: I saw him participate in meetings, solve disputes between fellows, organize public events, and collaborate with several different productive projects, sometimes within the space of a few hours. The organization provides a motive to be busy and the resources necessary to engage in valuable routines.

FIGURE 5.2 Community improvement crew. Florencio Varela, January 2014. *"My relatives thought we would end up being thieves, addicts. None of that. We are hard workers. An odd job shows up, we go and do it. If we have to mow grass, or clean ditches, anything, we do it"* (Antonio).

Brian's story is very similar to those of other young people I interviewed. For them, participation in a piquetero group entails entering a heavily regulated space, where resources are connected to efforts and only those willing to work hard are entitled to benefits. Official control of the inner workings of organizations is very lax. Even though activists have to regularly submit paperwork about the attendance and performance of beneficiaries of workfare programs, only once in my entire fieldwork did I witness an inspection by state officials checking the accuracy of such documentation. However, conflicts about punctuality, absenteeism, and productivity were constant features of the organizations I worked with. Coordinators are usually strict about people showing up on time, doing their share of the tasks, and avoiding demeanors such as drinking and quarreling. This attitude is essential to the organizations' existence, as it enhances internal discipline and guarantees their main negotiation tool with the authorities: the capacity to mobilize large numbers of people.

Furthermore, the equation of efforts and benefits within piquetero organizations generates a major incentive for young people to participate: the opportunity to engage in the kind of everyday activities they see as respectable. In other words, activism allows these individuals to sustain themselves the way they have been socialized to see as decent: getting up early, arriving on time, and working hard. Daily engagement in the unemployed workers' movement also offers consistency, in the form of being necessary each day for the group to function. In an environment where most people struggle to make ends meet, piquetero activism provides (for some) an acceptable alternative, with predictable routines, a sense of meaning, and enough material support to get by.

A good example is provided by Kevin, who contributes extra time to the planning of events in his organization, even though he is not required to do so. For him, the most enjoyable aspect of his participation is his reputation (confirmed by his fellows) of being a reliable person. According to him, he enjoys "knowing that I do not fail others":

Failing others would be, "look, I need you today no matter what for a heavy demonstration," and you say, "no, I need to do this and this and this," because you can leave that for another day, the same with that and that. No, I would rather go to the organization and then, they know what you did, because you had more important things to do and instead of doing those things you went to the demonstration, that is to not fail people. (July 27, 2013)

In other words, Kevin cherishes being seen by others as someone that will not make excuses when work needs to be done. By showing up every time he is supposed to, he has achieved a particular status in the group, which in turn contributes to a positive sense of self. He compares his attitude toward the movement with the time during high school when he was involved in a sports team through a community program. Discipline, dependability, and camaraderie are attributes appreciated by both his past teammates and present fellows. A similar experience is described by Carolina, who felt useful and needed when older fellows asked her to join her organization's community radio program to do a special section on youth:

> *What I also liked, and this is personal, I liked to have, I felt like they needed me. I felt that if they called me to do a radio show, it was because they needed me to be there. So, I liked that, feeling useful.* (June 3, 2013)

By consistently fulfilling the tasks assigned to them, Kevin and Carolina develop an image as responsible workers. More importantly, this image supports a personal identity defined by virtue and integrity. Yet participation not only helps activists associate themselves with positive traits but also allows them to distance themselves from negative ones. For instance, Jonathan joined his organization after being fired from his work as a laborer in Buenos Aires' largest wholesale market. Despite originally having very negative views of the movement, with time he developed a strong attachment to his organization. For him, weekdays begin by signing in every morning at one of the group's cooperatives. After about six hours of work (which at different points involved helping with a printing project, mowing grass in a park, and painting public schools), he helps take tools and machinery to a storage unit owned by the organization. He often stays for a while, having meetings, helping others move goods, or fixing equipment. In addition, he is a member of the youth section of his organization and helps with logistics and security during demonstrations. For all this work, Jonathan receives a workfare plan and occasionally a bag of foodstuffs. This income is barely enough to sustain his family, but Jonathan connects it with his capacity to stay free from the drug epidemic ravaging his friends:

> *I am a guy that perhaps you might be doing drugs and I can be next to you, everything is ok. But I will not use drugs, you know? So for them, I am like anti-drugs, I am like a snitch. And I am just a healthy guy. I am not going to do drugs to be in good terms with those guys, to form a link with that group. No. With what I am earning here, I sustain myself and my daughter. When I entered this organization I did not even have a bicycle, I had nothing. With the 1200 pesos I make I was able to buy my motorcycle. When I worked in other places I could not buy*

anything. I got used to this. I know my limits, how much I can spend, how much I cannot spend. (June 1, 2012)

In other words, Jonathan links his activism with morally valuable features, such as restraint and diligence. He contrasts himself, "just a healthy guy" who makes money honestly, supports his family, and through financial planning is able to purchase valuable goods, with other youth who are wasting their life away on the street corners. Alan made a similar point when describing how he does not want to end up like the many addicted young parents on his block:

I see those guys and it is an example of how I do not want to end up ... I am learning good things that college does not teach you, like the culture of working, getting up early, see how people put up a fight, how the neighbor puts up a fight, does not give up, I think you learn that from the street and then there is the contrast, the guy that has tons of children and does not care, that generates a vicious circle because children are the reflection of their parents. (April 11, 2014)

In sum, engagement in the unemployed workers' movement offers young people an opportunity to engage in practices that reproduce the expectations and demands of blue-collar life and to separate themselves from habits seen as immoral. Given their situation of significant job instability, with short periods of intense employment in odd jobs followed by extended intervals of idleness, a workfare program offers regularity in daily life and appreciation for the kind of abilities that Argentina's marginalized and undereducated youth can offer.

Moreover, the expectations inculcated to young members also reflect the ideal proletarian family with a gendered division of labor. Boys and girls therefore tend to be assigned to different tasks, and while all young members are compelled to have discipline at work and self-control at home, the actual meaning of these ideals is gender-specific. For men, being a responsible worker is associated with refraining from crime and substance abuse. For women, it implies controlling their sexuality. In the piquetero movement, boys are taught to not be thieves, while girls are cautioned not to be promiscuous.

5.3 GENDERED EXPECTATIONS AND THE DEVELOPMENT OF WORKING-CLASS ROUTINES

Every week, coordinators from different neighborhoods in one of the organizations in my study get together in what they call "direction table." They spend a whole afternoon discussing current events, deciding future activities, and collectively solving the countless issues that emerge during the administration of thousands of workfare plans.

This day is different, though. The group just received some official documents demanding payment of back taxes. It is not a huge amount, but no one knows how this situation came to be, so some organizers meet separately to figure out a solution. This absence causes the meeting to be less structured, and activists talk more about problems in their communities. Their work is stressful: Dealing with a severely underprivileged population means that they face constant crises. In addition, many people rely on the organization's help to survive, and any paperwork mistake may mean a family going hungry. Today offers a chance to vent to others who understand both the complexity and the importance of everyone's work.

One of the big problems everyone highlights is the high rate of violence. Activists complain about the frequent robberies committed by poor, addicted young men. Guadalupe says she and others have been involved in an initiative to control crime in her neighborhood. Later that day, her husband, Mauro, explains to me what she meant: A few men in the area (himself included) threatened a group of boys who loitered on a street corner, doing drugs and drinking. If the boys kept letting people from outside the neighborhood steal from locals, the men would not call the cops but take care of the problem themselves. Apparently, the kids got the message:

I think the youth, with the end of military service [abolished in 1994] *many young men felt unprotected, without an education, their parents working odd-jobs, many factories closed, people who started projects but then ended up working odd jobs because they ran out of money, that generated that many young men today do not have social support or the possibility of studying. No, they are wandering around, they are marginalized because they do not get hired in different jobs. I live that every day, we had to organize to safeguard the neighborhood, we the neighbors. Kids from the neighborhood used to get together with some who were not from the neighborhood, there was a moment when fifteen used to gather on one corner, until one day we said enough, two or three of us got together and told them we did not want them to hang out there anymore, because women did not even want to go run errands. This happened recently, we organized, there was a meeting with more or less twenty neighbors, and today even though the kids are still around, they no longer gather liked they used to, on the corner.* (April 21, 2014)

When I asked Mauro to elaborate on what he and others had done to the boys, he used the expression *les pusimos los puntos*, which means imposing limits in a forceful manner. These young men were not only causing trouble but had also transgressed established norms involving taking care of their own community and respecting local women. Yet it is worth noting that Mauro also expresses empathy with the same boys he threatened: Their problem is that they cannot count on the institutions that organized the lives of previous generations, such as the factory, the school, or even the army. Their aimless and purposeless lives make them easy prey for drug dealers and criminal gangs.

Back in the meeting, after some time in which different people mention the specific ways in which interpersonal violence affects their communities, participants are ready to continue. Yet before anyone can discuss anything, a middle-aged woman begins loudly complaining about what she sees as a related issue: "[T]hose women who do not take care of their children but go out on weekends." Other activists nod in accordance as she describes how she tries to help young mothers take better care of their children: "I give food to the children of these people, because you see them barefoot, but they do not do anything, they wait for you to solve everything for them." In her view, the problem is the promiscuity of women who seek personal pleasure at the expense of their children:

I wash their clothes so their children do not go around all dirty, and the next day they complain if you do not do that. You give them used clothes and they throw it away. But yes, they do have money for makeup. They do not think about their children, they think about going out on the weekend to dance and make another baby. (Fieldnotes, April 21, 2014)

The woman ends by apologizing to others in the meeting for the digression, "I am sorry fellows, I had that poison inside me." Yet her remarks appear to be well received. Her complaint resonates with what many respondents frequently emphasize during conversations: the frustration they feel when they try to help people who are not willing to help themselves, and how little appreciation they receive from some of those they help the most. Furthermore, participants in the meeting also seem to agree with her portrayal of bad mothers. The image of the immature, undisciplined young woman who cannot defer gratification even to guarantee the well-being of her children is a common point among people in my fieldwork. The problem is not only the lack of sexual restraint but also their incapacity or unwillingness to make sacrifices on behalf of their offspring. These girls are seen as immoral because they ignore their "natural" instinct to nurture the young and defenseless. A responsible woman is thought to always give up her own comfort for that of those under her care. As the coordinator said, "They treat [their children] worse than their dogs, because my dogs, when I saw them hungry, I bought them food and I ceased to eat myself, because they are not guilty of my situation."

Although these comments took place in one organization, they are representative of a common thread in all the groups I worked in. Activists of all ages and ideologies insist that young people lack motivation, but the specific meanings of that diagnosis (and, consequently, the proposed solutions) vary by gender. When young people enter a piquetero organization, they are expected to behave in accordance with character traits seen as vanishing, such as discipline, hard work, and sacrifice. Yet these expectations also cover aspects of their lives beyond their time in the movement. Men are pressured not just to limit their alcohol and drug use during work but also to avoid "bad company" (*malas juntas*) that may get them in trouble. Women are admonished to control their sexuality in public and (when applicable) be good mothers at home.

These values and ideas reflect long-standing traditions prevalent in the culture of working-class communities. Piquetero organizations function as a place where the routines associated with those attitudes are possible and where young men and women can engage in the sort of activities they were raised to see as respectable. For men, this usually involves participation in infrastructure or productive projects, frequently under the tutelage of older activists. The opportunity to fill work days with demanding tasks makes participation very appealing. Jonathan's initial attitude toward the movement changed when he realized the amount of effort his fellows expected of him. He rapidly became involved in more and more projects:

At the beginning I went [to demonstrations] without enthusiasm, I mean, because before that I used to work in many places, and I always saw roadblocks and I always got to work late and I used to say, "These damn negros,[2] *they are blocking the road." Because I did not know their reasons. Until I started to integrate into the movement, and then I saw that it was a struggle, the necessity of people, why they did all that. And well, that's when I stayed.* (June 1, 2012)

For women, in contrast, the development of routines reflects a romanticized idea of their mothers' and grandmothers' lives. Consequently, they are more likely to enroll in projects involving direct social services (food assistance, health promotion, and early education), as well as paperwork and cleaning. For instance, Carolina participated in many different activities since she joined the movement. Yet she highlights

---

[2] In the Argentinean context, "negro" (black) is a frequently derogatory term referring to the urban working class or the undeserving poor. For more on the origins and implications of this term, see James (1988), Grimson (2007), and Sutton (2008).

the group of women who cooked meals in a soup kitchen as one of the projects that resonated the most with her:

[I saw] the line of people waiting for food, to eat. And I saw inside the kitchen and the people like crazy putting more pasta, taking the pots out, trying to make it last for everyone. Many times they themselves ended up not eating. And that began calling to me. I began to feel like an attraction towards what the women in the kitchen did and towards what people waiting for the food were suffering. (May 24, 2013)

In sum, just like the reconstruction of routines varies for older men and women, a similar process happens to younger participants. The idealized lifestyle they seek to develop is itself gendered, and consequently, entering a piquetero organization entails concurring with a set of gender-specific expectations. Although these groups have very progressive agendas in terms of women's rights and many operate as effective sanctuaries for LGBT people, participants of all ages also embrace traditional notions of masculinity and femininity.

5.4 HONEST, HARD-WORKING KIDS

The poor quality of law enforcement is a perennial problem in working-class communities of Argentina. State-level police forces are notoriously corrupt and incompetent. Federal forces such as the National Guard or *Gendarmería* are perceived as slightly cleaner but ruthless and prone to abuses of power. As a result, the implementation of community-based, effective solutions to interpersonal violence remains almost impossible.

Sabrina, an organizer for one neighborhood in the district of La Matanza, illustrates this issue with a recent experience she had. After countless complaints by residents about robberies, the *Gendarmería* had finally made a raid and detained a group of young people. However, neighbors were convinced the officers had made a mistake. One of them ran to Sabrina's house to ask her if she could do anything:

Last week I got home and the National Guard had for the first time come to our neighborhood. There were some kids on the corner, but those kids, some were addicts and others had just returned from work. They are hard-working kids. They have children and everything. They put them against the wall and began to undress them and hit them. So the neighbor who lived by that wall came and told me, "Sabrina, I do not know if you will be able to do something, but the Gendarmería *is there and they are going to take them, it is fine if they take the bad kids, but not to those who were coming from work."* (June 2, 2014)

Sabrina's husband told her to not confront the officers: "[T]he *Gendarmería* does not forgive you. If they have to put you in jail, they will put you in jail." Still, as a leader in her community (and a person who is not afraid to speak her mind), she went and challenged the only female officer present:

> I told her: "If they are working kids, why do you have to take them?" and she said, "who are you?" and I said, "I am nobody, but you are also nobody. Otherwise, arrest me. Afterwards you will face consequences, I can even get you fired from your job," I told her, "because I will demonstrate to you with proof that these kids come from work, they are not doing drugs on the corner. If you go to the other corner you will find kids who are doing drugs, who are stealing, who are taking cellphones from people. Go to the other corner, but not here, because I am telling you the truth." (June 2, 2014)

As more neighbors showed up, the officers began to question whether taking away the detainees was a good idea. According to Sabrina, they came up with a pragmatic solution: Those who could prove they were coming from work would not be arrested. Parents vouched for some of them, and in other cases, the suspects themselves called their employers:

> "Let's see, who are the ones who work?" Well, a father said, "he is my son, he needs to work, he has a child!" They began calling the companies, the bosses, and they said "yes, they work here, they work here, went home from here, went home from here." And well, they let them go. (June 2, 2014)

Eventually, even those who could not prove they were employed were released. The officers hit some of them but decided to not arrest anyone: "The problem was solved, and they left. They did give some good slaps to a few. The National Guard punches right away, they do not ask for permission."

This episode is remarkable for many reasons. It illustrates how abuse by security forces is so commonplace in the lives of marginalized communities that it has become naturalized. An incident described as relatively inconsequential included flagrant violations of due process, such as detaining people without probable cause, forcing individuals to prove their own innocence, threatening witnesses, and physically hurting detainees.

Moreover, the incident is significant because it highlights a moral equivalence, prevalent throughout my fieldwork, between work and honesty. Sabrina, her neighbors, and the officers all shared a common idea: There is a fundamental difference between young people who work and have families and kids who use drugs and steal. The problem with the

Gendarmería was not that they were mistreating people; it was that they were punishing those on the wrong side of the moral boundary between responsible workers and addicted thieves.

The appeal of piquetero organizations for many young people is related precisely to that distinction: These groups facilitate the engagement in routines associated with being a good worker. Faced with high unemployment, inadequate educational services, and discrimination, young men and women find it very difficult to access the kind of lifestyle their elders taught them was valuable. Steady employment is uncommon, and most rely on short-term gigs and precarious jobs. Compared to this situation, earning a workfare plan in a piquetero organization does not pay much but at least offers consistency and respectability. Instead of depending on others, you can earn your sustenance by showing up early, doing your part of the work, and making sacrifices when required. Moreover, there are always things that need to be done, and everyone welcomes an extra hand. In a context where exclusionary processes convey a sense of superfluousness to individuals, the recognition of your fellows and the association between efforts and benefits make young people feel needed and valued.

In addition, the contrast between honest laborers and immoral good-for-nothings points to another crucial reward of participation in the piquetero movement: The opportunity to belong to a group of trustworthy people. The expansion of unemployment undermined the material conditions for a number of established routines in working-class neighborhoods: Community institutions lost resources, drug use became rampant, and interpersonal violence skyrocketed. Hence, communal habits seen as wholesome (such as spending time in common spaces and sharing resources with neighbors) are perceived to be endangered. Surrounded as they are by individual and collective deprivation, organizations become oases of socialization, as the following chapter will show.

6

"We Drink Mate, Eat a Good Stew, Talk ... and That Way Time Flies"

Protection of Communal Activities

Bautista likes to say that for him, activism "comes from the inside," while pointing to his chest. He is a big, tall man in his fifties, with a soft voice and a patient demeanor. He was fired from his last formal job in 2001. Luckily for him, his elderly mother owned an apartment in a dilapidated housing project, and he avoided homelessness. Moreover, he had no children to feed. Yet daily survival became a challenge for a middle-aged, laid-off factory worker like him, and he was forced to become a scavenger. Every day, he would push a cart through the streets of his neighborhood, gathering discarded cardboard to sell at a nearby recycling business. One day in 2004, someone at the location told him about a piquetero organization in the area that was recruiting people. Bautista had already participated briefly in another piquetero group but left after four months when a promised position failed to materialize. Still, he decided there was no harm in trying again, especially given that he had already knocked on countless doors. "I told myself, 'well, let's do it, anyways, I have already signed up in a thousand places'." This time, his experience was different:

What happened is that I was doing badly, badly, badly. In 2001, I lost my job. Everything got together, the loss of my job, depression. Because losing your job, you know, all things combine, and I ended up a bit down. Then, since I realized that was not useful, I went out to scavenge. [One day] after going out to scavenge someone told me, "you know that in that place they are signing people up, they are giving, doing like soup kitchens." And you know, they started talking to me, and yes, so then I got hooked. I got hooked, because sometimes you say, "uy, they are blocking the road, uy they are doing this thing," but if you do not do those things, no one pays attention to you. (August 5, 2011)

Bautista is a friendly person who likes to discuss current events, enjoys American rock bands, and writes fiction in his spare moments. He happily speaks about the times he helped others sign up for social assistance and is adamant about the importance of grassroots development. However, he is also critical of central aspects of the organization in which he has participated for more than a decade. Years of exclusion from the job market, neglect by state officials, and unfulfilled promises of help have instilled in him a great deal of political skepticism, which he extends to the movement:

I learned a lot in the social movement, you learn the good and bad side of everything. In politics, like everything, you learn the good and bad things, because everywhere there are interests. There are always interests. The thing with this place is that there are a lot of politics involved. (June 14, 2013)

Bautista is not afraid to express his disagreements. He frequently criticizes his organization's strategy, in particular its alliances with middle-class progressive politicians who, in his view, do photo ops with poor people but never "come down to the neighborhood" to familiarize themselves with the needs of their constituencies. This puts him in a collision course with his fellows around election times when the group mobilizes to support candidates he sees as ineffective:

[Elections] are coming and my enthusiasm is gone … I do not like the candidates, I do not like any of the candidates. You know why? Because I feel they go against my ideas. I do not like the same thing, they are no longer clear. You know how the saying goes? To distinguish politicians from people you need to see how they act. Some of those who are in the coming election were already [elected] in the past. Some were already around, you can see how they act. Once, ok, but if I had to vote today, I would not vote for them. I already saw that they do not do much. It is like seeing some people, first time you do not notice, [but] you will not vote the same thing if you know they do nothing. That is why I already talked to someone and when the moment comes I will speak again if necessary with my coordinator, so I do not participate in the next election as a volunteer. (June 14, 2013)

Bautista also distances himself from what he calls "fanatic activism." He condemns leaders who demand too much from rank-and-file members, to the point of placing others at risk. From his perspective, it is wiser to pick your battles and avoid having others capitalize on your sacrifice:

I do not like fanatic activism. Fanatic activism would be, for example, to go out with a lot of people, I am the person in charge, I go out with you and others to put up posters or paint graffiti. And suddenly, another group, with different politics, comes and tries to cover our posters. We cover their posters, they cover ours, like that, you see. Sometimes, in those moments, people come with violence. They want to hit you so you do not cover their things. I have seen trouble; ten, twenty people come hit us. And I do not like violence. If I see there is going to be trouble, let us leave. We put posters somewhere else, we graffiti somewhere else. Because you are responsible for the fellows who are with you. Instead, the fanatic says, "no, let's fight." [But] the person for whom you are graffiting, the person who sent you to put up posters, they are in their homes. The one who is going to be hit is you. (August 5, 2011)

Another frequent complaint in my conversations with Bautista was what he saw as an overall lack of internal communication. In his view, coordinators use meetings to rubberstamp preexisting decisions taken unilaterally, do not effectively explain the ways workfare programs operate, and impose unrealistic expectations on those who earn resources through their participation:

If you stop participating here for a while you need to have a huge justification. Here, they immediately drop you from the workfare plan … Let me give you an example. The other day I was fucked, you know when you get one of those flus that knock you down? … I took medication, all the stuff, did not go out. I stayed home, and brought the [doctor's note], but they put "absent, absent, absent, absent." Here, for a given number of absences they can drop you from the cooperative. (June 14, 2013)

However, Bautista is emphatic about limiting his criticism to a few bad apples. He accuses particular leaders of failing to live up to their stated ideals. Despairing over the case of a conflictive activist who coordinators had refused to expel, he insisted:

Are we a movement that helps people, or are we a piece of shit? Common people in this district, in this movement, know that this person did this, and this, and this. But in the end, it is "hey, this person does this and keeps participating." People stop believing. They end up not believing in the movement anymore. They do not believe in the movement, and that concerns me. I do not want them to stop believing in the movement. So it is like [I said] at the beginning, the movement does not create the trouble, does not fuck up. It is those who are in charge, the leaders. (June 14, 2013)

This attitude is reflected in Bautista's actions. To my surprise given his frequent complaints about the organization's mismanagement, he regularly shows up when he is not required. His social program offers two weeks of vacation per year, but when I did fieldwork during that period, he was still present. His coordinator was in disbelief: "Bautista is the only idiot who comes here when he is on vacation." Furthermore, he continued participating in marches even though a combination of diabetes and leg inflammation made walking painful. As other activists told me, Bautista's health problems make him eligible for a pension, which would pay more than his workfare plan and not require him to do anything in return. However, he refuses to begin the paperwork.

Bautista's reluctance to take time off made more sense after our long conversations (and the opinions of his fellows) revealed two important aspects of his participation. First, a central part of being in the movement for him is the capacity to affect other people's lives for the better, not just in an abstract way but also in very concrete cases. His proudest achievements were the occasions in which the people he convinced to join obtained a workfare plan. Other activists corroborated in private the occasions on which Bautista had helped them. For instance, when Giugliana lost her newborn daughter (as described in Chapter 5), Bautista visited her, paid her cellphone bill, and helped arrange the funeral for the child. For her, it was a surprise, but for him, it was returning a favor:

When he was in the cooperative, we had not yet been paid. It was difficult for him to begin getting paid. And I had forgotten about it, I swear to you I had forgotten, I got the money for him to buy some medication. Bautista, you know him, the tall guy. I got the money so he could buy some medication that was very expensive. That was it, done. I forgot about it. When I ended up in the hospital, he came to see me. He said, "look, I do not go to the hospital to see anyone, Giu, eh." He had paid my cellphone bill, without me even asking. I told him, "why, Bautista, do you bother? quit joking." "No, because I do not forget, when I had nothing, not even to buy my medication, you were the only one that went out and got it." (Giugliana, February 26, 2014)

Second, daily engagement in the movement matters for Bautista because, as some of the activists in the organization told me, "he is lonely." Not only he is unemployed, single, and without children, but also he lives in one of the poorest areas of Buenos Aires, where decades of socioeconomic decay have undermined many of the institutions that used to get neighbors together. In his youth, Bautista developed relations with coworkers at the many factories that hired him. His routines as a manual worker sustained interpersonal connections that extended beyond each shift at the assembly line. Today, those spheres of socialization are gone for him. Therefore, for Bautista, activism serves as a link to other people. He describes participation as something that comes from his heart, a profound desire to help others and develop meaningful associations with people who, like him, are in constant need of assistance. Taking part in demonstrations and working in poorly paid workfare programs are consequently not a burden but an opportunity to be part of a group of supportive fellows, sharing resources, activities, and, most importantly, time. When I asked him whether he knew anyone in his organization prior to joining, he said:

Bautista: I did not know anyone. Then you begin making acquaintances, you begin making almost friends, and so on.

Question: And how was it that you made friends?
B: So, one time you go to a birthday. Or you go to their house, or they come to your house, and so on. Or you run into them on the streets. It is those little groups of people who you, every time you go to a demonstration, or a campout, you get together to drink mate, to chat to make the night pass faster. Or when food comes, you get together, everyone eats together, at night eating something warm. Because those campouts are always in the winter. In the winter, so cold! Between one thing and the other, you get together, everyone really close to each other, drinking mate, and so on. When you realize, it is six in the morning, the sun is coming up again. And so you pass the time in the campout. (June 14, 2013)

Bautista would repeat variations of these final sentences several times in our conversations, describing with a smile the physically unpleasant experience of spending winter nights protesting outside. Some activists referred to these events in terms of their outcomes, either positive ("we got the cooperatives," "the government had a good answer," and "we obtained our reward") or negative ("the news did not cover our campout" and "officials did not want to give in"). Yet Bautista highlighted another, more mundane aspect of these protests: the many pleasant routines involved in them. For him, campouts and roadblocks are a combination of socializing opportunities: Eat a nice, warm stew. Drink mate. Chat. Meet new people. Other respondents used similar terms to refer to the experience:

Claudia: I never in my life had been to a protest. In the first march, I said, "what am I doing here?" I wondered what was I doing. And those are experiences that afterwards, say, a campout. I never in my life [had been to] a campout. Me, sleeping there in the street? Never, I used to say to myself. But that time, I had a great time.

Question: Why, how was it?
C: Because we got all the fellows together, we ate, we even danced, they played soccer, it was a very nice experience. (January 13, 2014)

Victoria: For me, the nicest experience were the campouts.

Question: What did you like about the campouts?
V: *Because I met people from other organizations, which were cool like us, who liked to sing, sing to the politicians, sing to the cops. It was fun.* (June 10, 2014)

Kevin: *It was very fun to be there with all the people in the demonstration, because you know more people and learn how they are doing, how is the day-to-day life of that person. And you have fun, you walk around, even if you are all dirty, you are outside, in the middle of a square, we met people, we went where other people gathered, talked . . ..*

Question: And how was the day-to-day of that campout?
K: *The day-to-day was drinking mate, at noon eating, in the afternoon we had fun, played cards, we went for a walk a bit, and then at night when it got dark we went to the park to drink a coke or something, and then we were back at the campout, we sang, we made up songs. Then we had dinnertime, one hour for eating, some went to sleep after eating, others were up until the next day.* (June 27, 2013)

The following pages analyze the experiences of people like Bautista, Claudia, Victoria, and Kevin to argue that participation in a piquetero organization allows many activists not just to reconstruct or develop particular habits but also to protect communal routines once prevalent in their neighborhoods. The expansion of unemployment undermined the material conditions for a number of established practices in these areas. Conspicuous drug use, skyrocketing interpersonal violence, dilapidated basic infrastructure, and underfunded social services all conspire to lock fearful residents in their homes. Hence, wholesome habits associated with community life (such as spending time in common spaces and sharing resources with neighbors) are perceived to be threatened. In this context, organizations function as oases of socialization, where interpersonal trust and altruism are still possible. Respondents describe them as safe spaces where they "feel comfortable," engaging in all sorts of activities that are rendered increasingly difficult due to the lack of stable occupation and the deterioration of public life.

Moreover, just like reconstruction and development, protection of routines in the unemployed workers' movement is a gendered process. Men and women engage in particular communal practices considered to be "natural" to each of them and frame these activities using

FIGURE 6.1 Cooking pot, anti-riot fences, police cordon. Autonomous City of Buenos Aires, August 2014.
"When food comes, you get together, everyone eats together, at night eating something warm" (Bautista).

different narratives. That is, the sharing of time, duties, and resources frequently occurs in ways that are gender-specific. I explore this dynamic by analyzing two typical collective tasks within piquetero groups: the "milk cups," soup kitchens for minors where women predominate, and the "security teams" and self-defense groups where the majority of members are men.

6.1 COMMUNAL LIFE IN UNCERTAIN TIMES

The economic transformations described in Chapter 2 deeply affected public life in marginalized communities. In particular, mass layoffs and rising crime rates disrupted two particular social structures that organized daily routines in working-class neighborhoods: communal spaces and work shifts.

A large portion of my conversations with activists contain expressions of despair about the undermining of public spaces. Respondents describe a past in which families spent time together in playgrounds and sidewalks, when local institutions such as improvement associations and small sports centers served as regular venues for collective activities, and when people felt relatively safe in the streets. In contrast, today a central grievance of almost all interviewees is being forced to lock themselves inside their homes, especially when it is dark outside. Communal areas are no longer seen as places of kinship and cooperation, but instead locations to be avoided.

I used to organize meals, and people do not want to participate anymore, because they do not want to leave their homes due to insecurity ... Because of the drug addicts, which at any time go around, run over, assault, ask for things, in the streets, they are walking, on a bike, on a motorcycle, in a car, however. Due to the insecurity people practically do not want to go out much, I do meetings on Saturdays from 3pm to 4pm, 4:30pm, [because] they already have to go home, they do not want to get home around sunset. (Julia, July 14, 2011)

We used to have the right to be seated there outside drinking mate at whatever hour, late at night, we left bicycles out there and nothing ever went missing. Now we cannot be seated there because suddenly a bullet comes your way and you do not know where it came from. (Camila, April 25, 2014)

Respondents describe the rise in interpersonal violence, drug use, and criminality as major motives for why it is more difficult to hang out with neighbors and meet new people. However, those are not the only reasons they highlight. Just as important is the fact that the decline of manufacturing jobs undermined a crucial source of commonality: the structuration of time generated by work shifts. Not only did some neighborhoods grow because of nearby factories, but the fact that a substantial proportion of residents worked in a similar field also imposed a regularity to life in these communities. Days were predictable because at given hours workers would leave their homes, and at others, they would return. The routine of walking to and from public transportation, waiting for and riding the bus or the train, and in some cases, being employed by the same industry or affiliated to the same union brought people together and generated links between families. Today, when unemployment is higher, jobs are less secure, and occupations are more diverse, the camaraderie generated by a less segmented labor market is seen as gone:

Those of us who have memory, who are sixty years old, know that unemployment is a phenomenon that in the past practically did not exist. We remember rivers of human beings leaving at factory shifts, I lived in a place where at ten in the evening, I sold newspapers, walked the streets, the traffic stopped because of the factories, it was impressive, it was a river of people reaching the avenue to take the buses to go to the neighborhoods. But you know, all that disappeared. (Elías, June 18, 2014)

The main effect of the weakening of communal routines is that people have fewer options to interact with strangers, developing meaningful connections in which they can expect positive reciprocation. In other words, when public space becomes frightening and professional life does not impose shared time, residents of poor communities retreat from each other, secluding themselves in their houses and assuming the worst of their neighbors. As Luis said sadly of the community he loves, "This neighborhood always shows up in the crime section of the newspapers." Others made similar points:

Not long ago a guy pretended to be the postman, got close to my dad, and snatched his gold chain. You understand? Now you cannot even trust the postman anymore, if he is the postman or not. Business owners lock themselves more now, that did not use to happen. During siesta *time, you cannot leave the door, the fence, unlocked. You have to lock it.* (Giugliana, February 26, 2014)

My neighbors across the street built like three stories high, quite the house. Rumor has it that they are involved in strange things ... There are a lot of strange people in my neighborhood. And the kids, I do not know, the kids that grew up with me, who are about my age, the reality is that one is addicted to cocaine, another is addicted to crack, another one is stealing. (Maitén, June 9, 2013)

Regardless of the accuracy of past accounts, the truth is that many activists in my study express a profound need for spaces where people can be trusted, resources shared, and time spent in the company of others. Consequently, it is not surprising that many value the movement not only as a source of material support but also as an opportunity to engage in communal activities that were an integral part of an idealized yet endangered working-class lifestyle.

6.2 OASES OF SOCIALIZATION

It is a stormy January morning in the district of Florencio Varela. Half a dozen people are preparing to work on a community improvement project. However, the weather prevents us from going out, so to pass the time, we start a round of mate and chat. Celeste complains that it is the third Tuesday in a row that it rains, and Tito jokes that I must be responsible because every time I visit, it pours. People talk about the frequent blackouts affecting the city and share tips for making sure food does not go bad. During a break in the rain, Vanesa shows up. She does not need to come to the organization today, but as she says, "I finished cleaning at home and had nothing to do, so I came to bother you here." Adelia vents about a problem in her family: Her sister "is acting like an idiot," having an affair with a bus driver downtown while dating a man in the neighborhood. In the past, her romantic entanglements ended in violence. Adelia is worried, and half-jokingly wonders whether someone cast a spell on her sister. Celeste responds loudly: "[W]hat spell? She's horny." Everyone laughs. Vanesa shares some of her domestic problems too. People listen attentively and offer words of comfort.

Two days later, at another organization in the district of La Matanza, a group of activists are doing paperwork. Tomás, a member in his twenties, just returned from vacation: He visited some family members who live in the countryside. Since it is still January, many projects are on break, and thus, administrative duties are less demanding than usual. We sit down and take advantage of the downtime to talk. Miguel Ángel, a man in his fifties, arrives and begins teasing Tomás about sheep. I do not understand much until they explain that Tomás helped a cousin shear some animals, and Miguel Ángel has been joking that instead, he had sex with them. We all laugh. Iván, the coordinator for the organization's youth, comes and asks Tomás for some help with flags for a demonstration. Later in the day, we all have lunch together. As we clean the dishes, Norma arrives. She is not supposed to be here, as it is her vacation period. However, she says, "I was bored at home." She serves mate to other people and helps when needed.

FIGURE 6.2 Sharing a mate cup during an out-of-town demonstration. Córdoba, May 2014.
"Drinking mate at whatever hour" (Camila).

During my fieldwork, I saw numerous instances of activists showing up at the organization in their free time. Many times, this was to help with a special activity, but in several other cases, there was not a particular reason for their presence. In addition, downtimes were rarely spent alone: people got together for meals, to share mate, or simply to chat in between tasks. Moreover, it is not uncommon to see nonmembers in buildings belonging to organizations: Relatives stop by, children use the space to play, and neighbors ask questions about particular issues. In sum, piquetero groups seem to be spaces of intense socialization, where people gather for much more than politics.

Participants highlight the opportunity to develop meaningful connections as one of the most pleasant aspects of their participation. Many refer to activism as "therapy" or describe their groups as "family." For instance, Victoria suffered a stroke that, to this day, limits her capacity to work. However, one of the first things she resumed after partially recovering was participating in a cooperative:

You have problems at home, [but then] come here, listen to others, and you clear your head, you laugh. Here we crack up laughing with the girls every morning. When I was sick it was a thing that I could not come here and I felt even worse. I wanted to come to work, I wanted to be with my fellows. (June 10, 2014)

Valentina uses similar terms. She joined reluctantly during the 2001–2002 economic collapse but with time developed a strong attachment to her organization. Today, she works full-time doing paperwork and managing a cultural center, even though her workfare plan only requires four hours of work a day. For her, the organization was an escape from a deteriorating domestic situation, in which her estranged husband refused to leave her home. Despite the stress of managing complex administrative duties, she is a constant presence in the group:

To me, it is therapy and to me this is a family ... I said in a meeting the other day that here I learned to laugh, here I began to laugh again. I used to not laugh anymore, because I had so much bitterness in me. And you here are busy with other things, you feel useful. (February 14, 2014)

Mauro contrasts his blood relatives, who were around him when he was a well-paid autoworker, with his "real family," the fellows who hang out together even though they do not have much to share. Describing how he overcame his initial hesitance to participate, he said:

I got hooked, because of the quality of fellows that we made. Perhaps when I had a job, perhaps I had more pesos but I did not have the friends I have today, sometimes we share a stew in the streets, a pastry, and that hooked me. (April 21, 2014)

This engagement in communal routines takes place in different ways. First, dead time between tasks or during breaks creates opportunities for people to socialize. Gabriel, a man in his sixties who is estranged from his children, found that the maintenance cooperative to which he was assigned was a great source of companionship, allowing him to "not be encompassed by solitude":

[We did the] maintenance of the building. We made a very nice group of twenty-five people, who came from Monday to Friday. We swept the patio, swept the rooms, cleaned bathrooms, cleaned the sidewalk, [and] did general maintenance.

It was a very nice experience with the people I was with, I would go and buy pastries, because I always had coins in the pocket, they came and prepared the hot water to drink mate, we sat down as a group there. (July 23, 2014)

Even on busy days, when there is not much free time, the very fact of sharing responsibilities forces people to be in touch with one another. Norma laughs that "if I do not come here, perhaps I get sick." Her organization allows her to carve spaces of autonomy and "leave that world of the home, always the home, the home, the home." She describes as enjoyable something that others would find annoying (for instance, having to stay until late in a meeting):

I have a good relationship with all the fellows. Perhaps you talk about one thing, another, and the hours pass. Yesterday I think we left at seven, because there was a meeting with a neighborhood, we came to the meeting, when we left outside was already getting dark, around seven. I got home at half past seven, we went with Olivia and Marisa. And time passes, you get in here with the problems that there are and time passes, the hours pass. (April 1, 2014)

Claudia makes a similar point, even though she is a member of another organization and her duties as part of a health commission are very different from Norma's. The very complexity of the problems her group addresses helps her put her own personal troubles into perspective:

I also like being with the fellows. Because it is like doing therapy. You see that one comes and talks about one thing, another comes and talks about something else. And you kind of leave the routine of your home by being here and say, well, others have more problems than I do. Wow, my problem is nothing compared to other people's. We talk about our children, those things. (January 22, 2014)

Another crucial aspect of socialization in piquetero groups is the opportunity to share resources and find solutions to the constant problems that plague the lives of marginalized communities. Not only does this bond people together (such as Bautista and Giugliana when each took care of the other during health crises), but it also attracts potential participants and brings nonmembers into contact with the movement. Organizations function as spaces where altruism is still possible, where people (even strangers) can expect help from others when needed. As Carlos, a district coordinator, told me:

People see our place like a community service center, where they can go and say "Hey, I have this problem." It is not that we feel we are anyone's saviors, it is more like "ok, come in, let us organize and look for a solution." And I think that tends to become like a family, because then people come to drink mate, see what's going on, what problems, brings someone else's problems. And we move forward with that. Why? Because we are just another neighbor. (Carlos, July 20, 2011)

Laura, the leader of a small organization, constantly offers advice to neighbors looking for solutions. In a context where public services are substandard and accessing help is a very convoluted process (see Auyero 2012), the experience of activists managing welfare programs makes them experts in the challenging art of getting the authorities to fulfill their role:

Extract from fieldnotes, January 10, 2014
After cleaning, we sat down to drink mate again, chatting in a good mood. A few things worthy of mention happened. First, many people stopped to ask questions, generally to Laura, from the fence on the corner's gate (which was closed without a lock). One of them was a woman of about fifty years, who said, "Laura, I have to ask you a favor." She wanted to know how to get the municipality to install the sewage drain in her house. She said she went to two government offices, and that in the second they told her to write a letter to the mayor ... She said "if I write to the mayor it is going to take a year," so she is going to places to ask. I was surprised that she told Laura she had been to the building of [an adversarial organization]. Despite that, Laura gave her advice. First she told her to go to "there, where the cooperatives are." Then she told her to go to [a neighborhood], to a specific government office, and ask for García. The woman asked Laura to write the instructions down, which she did.

The fact that piquetero organizations serve as safe spaces, where resource sharing and problem-solving are possible means they are particularly important for people suffering from violence and discrimination. Victims of domestic assault are particularly common in the movement. To them, everyday engagement in activist routines, even if for only a few hours a day, provides an escape from an unsafe environment at home. In addition, organizations allow many participants to process past episodes of abuse via engagement with others who had similar experiences. In the words of Candela:

In this organization I found the family I never had. I found fellowship, I learned to release myself, to defend myself. Here I learned to not be humiliated by men, a man cannot treat you however he wants. I learned my rights as a woman, to express myself and fight for what is mine. To say enough is enough. I also have rights, I also have to defend my rights as a woman and go to work and make myself seen, made myself valued as a woman. Not that a man humiliates me and subdues me in any way. (June 16, 2014)

This component of refuge is particularly important for sexual minorities. A crucial (yet largely understudied) aspect of the piquetero movement is the way in which many organizations have served as informal shelters for

LGBT individuals. Ornella, a trans woman, recalls the importance of having her coordinator (Josefa, a woman in her sixties) insist that people address her with her chosen name:

Ornella: I used to think that the life I have was not correct. Because for society we are kind of, like sick people. It is as if instead of opening doors, they close one after another.

Question: Do you still feel that?
O: No, nowadays I do not, since I started in the movement I do not.

Q: Why, how is that?
O: Because you see, well, in the places where I have been you realize how they look at you, how they treat you. I do not feel that here. I feel they respect me for who I am, they accept me for who I am.

Q: Can you give me an example of this respect?
O: For instance, my name, the name on my ID, some people here know it and others do not. One day I came here and introduced myself as Ornella. And here they said Ornella and since then, all the fellows call me Ornella …

Q: And how was that?
O: It was because of Josefa. [She said] "She is a person who is like this and that, and I want her to be respected here, that people treat her the way she feels, no matter who she is." (June 24, 2014)

As the previous pages have shown, the intense socialization within piquetero groups takes place in different forms. However, respondents present all of them as dependent on labor, making a clear distinction between the healthy relationships emerging from working together and the immoral connotations of being lazy freeloaders. Few situations cause as much conflict as participants being asked to show up, only to have nothing to do. Political disputes, bureaucratic inefficiencies, and logistical difficulties cause frequent delays in the assignment of projects and the distribution of materials necessary to implement them. Situations such as soup kitchens closing due to local authorities halting the distribution of food, productive cooperatives hindered by paper-work backlogs, or cleaning projects that cannot start because officials fail to release tools frequently generate loud complaints. Camila recalled to me how much she enjoyed the group of friends she made in a cooperative involved in community improvement initiatives. Yet she despaired when they had to end one project due to government neglect. Even though she still got paid, she hated the experience of being involuntarily idle until her coordinator found a new assignment of cleaning schools:

What we wanted was to w-o-r-k [highlighting each syllable, tra-ba-jar], *not just being there drinking mate. To do that, I stay at home, we wanted to w-o-r-k. Work, clean, and well, until Carlos found us a place to work ... it was a waste of time, a waste of time.* (April 25, 2014)

In sum, people in the piquetero movement protect routines associated with communal life in different ways: by hanging out during free time, helping each other, and sharing responsibilities. The outcome is an experience of belonging that provides refuge from the decline in public life. Deprived of institutions and spaces that used to bring people together, activism offers a chance to hang out with others in relative safety and expect positive reciprocation even from strangers.

Nevertheless, this process is not experienced equally by everyone. In particular, the tasks that bring participants together frequently vary for different genders. In addition, the meanings associated with socialization reflect established notions of proper behavior for men and women. In other words, just like reconstruction and development, protection of routines is a gendered process. Few examples show this as clearly as two common occupations in piquetero groups: milk cups and security teams.

6.3 "THEY HAVE SOMETHING IN THEIR LITTLE BELLIES": MILK CUPS AND MORALLY SANCTIONED FEMININITY

Milagros says that helping children is her "weakness": "Doing things for the kids, I love it, I love it." She is a woman in her fifties who runs a "milk cup" (*copa de leche,* also called *merendero*): a soup kitchen for minors. Every afternoon, children from the community receive a cup of milk and a bit of homemade bread at the location. The place is also busy in the mornings when activists make clothes and crafts using donated materials, which they sell to help buy ingredients. All in all, about half a dozen women, from their twenties to their sixties, work at the place.

Milagros joined the organization in 2000 after a vertebral injury made her lose her job at an elderly care facility. Following a complicated recovery, she regained the capacity to walk but was unable to lift heavy weights or bend over regularly. This situation made it impossible for her to return

to her occupation. Faced with this conundrum, she approached the head-
quarters of a piquetero organization, located a few blocks from her house.
She had heard of the place but had never been involved in it.

It was a difficult time in the country, and it took Milagros a year to
finally get a position in a workfare program. Yet she recalls the experience
in a positive way. She had anticipated a charitable organization and
instead found a place where she was expected to make sacrifices to earn
a benefit:

This is not like Caritas [the largest Catholic relief association], *where you enter
and they already give you things. Here everything is through the struggle. We get
plans in the streets, I remember that to obtain a plan we had to go sleep in the 9 de
Julio* [Downtown Buenos Aires' main avenue] *all night on the pavement.*
(January 2, 2014)

In other words, participation in the movement not only provided Milagros
with much-needed material support but also fit her self-image (threatened
by disability) as a hard-working person. She credits her mother with
instilling a never-give-up attitude in her: "[I]t is like I was breastfed into
the struggle. I learned the struggle, I always say, I learned it. I was always
aware of my mother's struggle." In her organization, she insists, "[N]o
one is going to gift you anything. Here you earn things, with your effort,
you earn things."

The affinity Milagros felt became even more entrenched when a few
years ago, her youngest son became addicted to crack cocaine. Milagros
felt responsible for the situation: unlike all her other children, she had
been forced to work outside the home during the boy's childhood. Her
workfare plan, coupled with her husband's small mechanic workshop,
was not enough to pay for rehab. It was in this context that her fellows
stepped in. They signed her son up for a cooperative and told her to use the
money to finance the treatment. She asked to work for two: "I said, double
shift. I do my hours, then my son's hours so I do not take money from
anyone." However, the organization refused: "[M]y fellows, very solid-
ary, said no, because I went to them with the truth." After two difficult
years, the young man recovered. Milagros' face beams as she describes his
condition: he has a wife, a baby, and is building a home for the new family.

Since she joined the movement, Milagros has fulfilled all sorts of
functions and participated in several different projects. Yet the one she
talks about the most is her current one. The organization has a soup
kitchen nearby, but it is open only for lunch. Concerned about the

possibility that some children go hungry at night, she approached her coordinator:

We saw the need in the neighborhood. In the organization there is a soup kitchen, kids go there at eleven in the morning, they form a line with a tupperware to pick up food. But that is at noon, at night those kids have nothing to eat. And I say, if they have nothing to eat at night, at least let them have some afternoon snack. . . . So I told my coordinator, why don't we set up a project so we have children there, so women also have a place to work, a milk cup so children can have something warm to drink in the afternoon and at least have that in their little bellies before going to sleep, milk and a piece of bread. (March 10, 2014)

The organization approved Milagros' proposal, and with the help of her husband, she set out to do it. Her mother-in-law offered her the use of a half-built room in front of her house, where she had planned to install a small store. Coordinators arranged to have building materials delivered; she found a neighbor willing to do the construction work at a reduced price and bought a used front door she could use. The result is a small but clean space, where women sew in the morning and cook in the afternoon and where children stop for a warm meal after they leave school.

The members of the project appear to have a good relationship with each other. Some are related by family ties (usually older women who bring their daughters or granddaughters to work with them), and they tend to hang out together in events outside the milk cup, such as meetings and demonstrations. They frequently gossip, make jokes, and talk about their families. They also help each other, both every day and during moments of crisis.

This last dynamic became evident with the case of Renata, a short woman in her sixties with strong opinions, a skill for needlework, and a passion for old movies. Shortly before I met the group, her husband had passed away after battling a painful disease. The situation took a very heavy toll on her. As she told me once, "[N]o offense to you, but he was the best man who ever lived." The people at the milk cup gathered around her, collecting money for funeral expenses and allowing her to take time off. When she returned, they worked hard to distract her. It was a slow process, but they made progress. As weeks passed, it became evident that Renata's mood was improving. She laughed more, as when someone put medicinal weeds in the mate we were sharing, and others joked that Renata had put a "love weed" (*yuyito del amor*) to cast a spell on those who drank it. She acknowledged the effect of participation on her well-being:

This is therapy, you may not believe me, but this is therapy. It is therapy that you come here, I get home relaxed, happy for what I did, happy because there is a little child for whom I could make a bread, I could give it to that child, a glass of milk, this is therapy. (January 20, 2014)

Milk cups have been one of the most prevalent services provided by piquetero organizations since the movement's emergence. Relatively easy to set up and cheaper to operate than a soup kitchen serving full meals, they have the additional advantage of being an established tradition in working-class communities of Argentina. Milk cups are also a largely feminine space: the people doing the most time-intensive work (cooking, serving food, and cleaning) are mostly women (see Ramos Ávila 2003; Cross and Freytes Frey 2007; Partenio 2008; Colabella 2012). Some men do participate in these projects, but they usually engage in logistical tasks: gathering fuel, moving heavy foodstuffs, and occasionally doing construction and repairs.

These projects operate in all sorts of locations, from improvised buildings and activists' homes to places shared with other activities (such as workshops, depots, or meeting areas). Most are small, and many lack a full kitchen, relying on firewood to cook. Almost all seek to complement the work of local schools, which frequently provide meals to students. It is also common for milk cups to offer additional social services, such as *roperitos* (gathering, fixing, and distributing used clothes), vaccination drives, maternal health initiatives, and homework assistance.

Milk cups can be very challenging. First, like soup kitchens, they usually depend on state resources (mostly foodstuffs but in some instances equipment), which can be unsteady. Bureaucratic and logistical problems frequently cause substantial delivery delays. In other cases, the amount and variety of ingredients provided by the government is insufficient (a recurrent problem is the lack of perishable items such as fruits, which are more expensive and difficult to distribute). Activists try and get the resources from somewhere else, through a combination of donations, buying in bulk, or selling homemade goods (like Milagros and her fellows do). However, those strategies have limitations, and sometimes, organizations are forced to cut hours or, in extreme cases, close down. Dante recalls the intense efforts involved in keeping a milk cup open every day:

This soup kitchen functioned in the house of some fellows, we did the milk cup. We did the soup kitchen two days a week, Saturday and Sunday, and the milk cup every day. Well, besides the foodstuffs we got from the government, we wrote letters asking for donations at stores, we went with the fellows to the wholesale market to get vegetables, all that. [It took] a lot of sacrifice. (July 24, 2014)

FIGURE 6.3 Milk cup. Florencio Varela, June 2014.
"You see the smile of a child when they eat a pastry or a piece of bread and laughs and tells you 'oh, how good it is!' I feel proud of being able to serve the children" (Victoria).

Luisa, an activist in the district of Esteban Echeverría, complains that disputes between levels of government means that she is not receiving fresh ingredients:

The organization sends us what they get. They are all non-perishables. All non-perishables. Since last December the municipality does not participate anymore, does not send anything. And I cannot go talk to that system because there is a problem there in the municipality with the national and the provincial governments. (June 12, 2012)

Aurora's organization's departure from a particular political coalition meant that the resources she obtained through the alliance were cut, leaving her with an impossible choice:

We started to have problems, and I did not want to, for example, do the soup kitchen once a week. What is the use of doing it once a week when children have to eat every day, drink milk every day? … That is when we stopped. Other fellows continued. Other fellows kept doing the soup kitchen once a week, the milk cup once a week. (May 19, 2012)

These challenges are compounded by the ambivalence that milk cups generate among officials and activists themselves. No one would say that feeding the hungry is wrong, yet all agree that the solution is far from ideal and that the end goal is for families to eat at home:

I would not like to go to a neighborhood and say, "I see the need to open a milk cup." To me the milk cup and the soup kitchen do not have to exist. Because everyone should have a dignified job so that person can put food on the table at home. (Néstor, June 11, 2012)

We always say, we would like to not have soup kitchens, to not have the need to have meal centers and milk cups in the neighborhoods, we would be happy, it is not something we do because we are glad we have kitchens. It is because people have to eat. (Salvador, May 16, 2012)

These challenges are even more salient due to the crucial role of these projects. As many activists insist, food assistance works for many as a last line of defense against hunger, and as a result, milk cups and soup kitchens serve as "thermometers" of social strain. As Facundo says, "When the soup kitchens are empty, the situation is improving. When you see that they begin to fill, it means the situation is bad." Clarisa describes how the organization's office in her neighborhood, which offers warm meals and milk to children, has varying numbers of beneficiaries depending on the community's short-term economic conditions:

There was a moment when attendance had gone down. Through that you can realize whether things have improved or not improved, because it was not that a kid stopped going for three days and we paid no attention. No, we went to the house. And perhaps the mother went out and told you, "no, you know, we do not need anymore, go see this other kid that needs more than us." But later it reverted because they came back. They come and the quantity of children who participate increases. (July 25, 2011)

Still, despite all the challenges and the enormous responsibility of feeding the most vulnerable, people who participate in milk cups describe it as a deeply meaningful and enjoyable activity. For Analía, a mother of three in the process of separating, it was a way to escape depression:

I had arrived at the neighborhood, I was new, I did not have much relationship with the neighbors … I found other women who also went to participate, because they also participated in cleaning, they made the bread for the children, another one made the milk, the tea for the children, we distributed it, and like it did me good to meet other people and be with them. (January 9, 2014)

For Tatiana, the opportunity to help children was key to regain a sense of self-worth after an abusive relationship:

I learned to value myself, because it was so much listening to "you are useless, you are worthless, the only thing you know how to do is to have children" … my partner at the time was, "who could like you, who could look at you, look what you are," awful things, that are repeated so much that you believe them. When I entered here no, I began to value myself, because I could do many things, offer many things. That did much good to me, I saw kids in the movement with shoes or clothes I had given them. A cookie, you know what it was to give them a cookie and see their happiness? We lived many things like that. And to me it was good, the one who told me that I am useless, I do not know why he said it, because at least I see the happiness in a child. (February 27, 2014)

Virginia's attachment to the activity was such that even though her organization has a location much closer to her home, she still chooses to take two buses and cross the entire district to go work every morning to the same kitchen:

There is an [allied] movement that is near my home. But I already got used to here. It is as if this was my home, I come, put the kettles [on the fire] for the fellows, prepare some mates, because I come here without having had breakfast. And then, when the other woman comes, we being cooking. It is as if this was my home. I feel comfortable here. (June 14, 2012)

Gisela is another example. As a former youth coordinator for her organization, she and her fellows first helped in a large soup kitchen and later set up an improvised room to address the food needs of children during the years immediately following the 2001–2002 crisis when economic recovery had barely reached their community. As she showed me photographs of the location, she recalled the way the whole project made her feel comfortable and included:

A neighbor lent us a place and we, what did we do? The kids, all those who worked in youth went out looking for corrugated metal sheets, I took sheets from my house, we had a lot that had no use, we all looked for things to set up the place. So a structure, like, to do a milk cup. Every afternoon we made pastries for kids, it got full of children! Because that is an area where there are many children, that zone, full of little children. We made an afternoon snack, and then three times a week we did a soup kitchen. (June 9, 2013)

A central component of these experiences is the possibility to engage in morally sanctioned forms of public femininity. In other words, milk cups (and, to a similar extent, soup kitchens) serve as spaces where women of different ages can perform shared practices seen as appropriate to their

FIGURE 6.4 Gisela's improvised milk cup. Lomas de Zamora, circa 2003.
"A structure, like, to do a milk cup. Every afternoon we made pastries for kids"
(Gisela).

gender, like cooking, cleaning, and caring for the young. This dynamic is
linked to a broader narrative prevalent throughout the organizations
I worked with, which frames women's involvement in the movement in
terms of motherhood. According to this discourse, the enthusiasm and
dedication of female activists has to do with their "natural" tendency to
defend their children, especially when their husbands lost their jobs. As the
argument goes, confronted with the collapse of their traditional lifestyle,
women took to the streets: "A woman is like that, she defends her children,
faces everything"; "80% of the movement are women, we were housewives,
but had to leave that and learn on the streets"; "my family was at risk, my
children had to grow up, my children had to study, my children had to eat."
As Isabel explained:

*We all came here due to necessity. You asked me why I am in this organization, why
women are in this organization. I will tell you why. … We took the banner of
hunger, of desperation and with all our strength we went to the roads, because our
husbands stayed at home, the husbands of fellows stayed at home. Many fellows
were even hit for coming to this organization. Until we made our husbands*

understand, the men got depressed, and I have many fellows who went to the protests after being hit. But we took the banner of hunger and we went out, like we did all our lives. All our lives the women took care of things, we are responsible for our homes. (June 9, 2014)

These routines not only entail embracing modes of conduct seen as wholesome but also allow activists to separate themselves from stigmatized characters. Few figures command more contempt among participants in milk cups than the "bad mothers" who seem unconcerned about their children. Given that maternal care is perceived to be a natural instinct, then failing to exhibit it brands a woman as immature or corrupt. Tita, Angelina, and Patricia, three women in their seventies, fifties, and twenties, respectively, who worked together helping milk cups, made the argument to me:

We have the milk cup and the soup kitchen. There we try to get mothers involved, that is not easy. Because they send the kids to eat and drink the milk. But sometimes do not even care to accompany them. We make a meeting and we tell them, we send a note so they come. Because the truth is that these days the youth are very stagnant. Let's say the truth. (Tita, July 28, 2011)

They leave [their children] locked at home without leaving them food. I do not know how they can leave them that way, alone. A little girl nine years old left alone with all the little ones. She has to take care of the siblings. It is in many places, it is not only in one house, in many places this happened. (Angelina, July 28, 2011)

We are trying, for instance, to make sure young girls know how to take care of themselves. Because it cannot be that adolescent kids have children. The other day I found a girl who told me, "I had my son at fifteen. For me, it is a doll, it is a little doll," she told me. Because of course, she was just playing with dolls, and after a bit has a baby, then she is not living her adolescence well. (Patricia, July 28, 2011)

In sum, by cooking and providing a safe space for the neighborhood's kids, women participate in a type of motherhood-associated femininity seen as praiseworthy. Milk cups constitute a safe communal space where they can pool resources and care for those seen as most vulnerable, fulfilling what they refer to as their "natural instinct" toward child-rearing. Some men do participate in these spaces, but the majority fulfill auxiliary roles. Moreover, men rarely refer to childcare as a "natural" vocation and much less frequently mention helping children as a particularly important aspect of their participation in the movement. For a male-dominated space, the next section explores the example of security teams.

6.4 "IF THEY LOOK FOR US, THEY WILL FIND US": PUBLIC MASCULINITY IN SECURITY TEAMS

It is a cloudy August afternoon, and a few thousand activists gather at Buenos Aires' iconic *Obelisco* (the city's busiest intersection) to march. It is the eve of Saint Cajetan's Day, a date with important religious and political implications in Argentina. As the patron of the unemployed, people ask the Saint for "bread and work" or thank him for having found a job. The religious festivities have also traditionally served as an opportunity to protest joblessness and demand assistance for those excluded from the labor market. For that reason, today's march is a bit different than usual: a statue of the Saint has been added to the front of the column.

There is, however, a more discrete goal for today's demonstration. Several hundred plan to spend the night in *Plaza de Mayo*, right in front of the presidential palace, which is the destination of today's march. This goal has not been advertised because if the authorities learned about it, they may use fences to block access to the intended destination. People discreetly carry tents, food, and even portable kitchens.

When we reach the square, everyone rapidly sets up the campout. The police do not intervene, preferring to keep a distance of a few meters. They set up a cordon and remain vigilant but for the most part do not interfere with the protest. Activists organize their own security and ask participants in the march to contribute their time in a series of shifts. As the sun sets, different groups being cooking stews, and everyone tries to pass the time by chatting, playing soccer, or listening to music. People make rounds of mate as they bundle up.

It is an unpleasantly cold night. Protesters take turns doing shared tasks and then return to some spot to try to sleep. If they are lucky, they find a space in a tent. Otherwise, they lay down on the ground. However, there are some activists who barely sleep. The streets are empty at this hour, and the cops a few steps from us seem more annoyed than violent, but you can never tell. A particular problem is the use by law enforcement of plain-clothes officers, who gather intelligence and assist with detentions. It is also not uncommon for these people to start trouble so the authorities have an excuse to disperse demonstrators. I see Alejandro walking around as if looking for something. He coordinates the organization's security and tells me he has been following a possible police infiltrator. He does not seem worried: the suspect has left the area, and like most of the move-ment's protests, this one is taking place peacefully. After the sun rises, the activists decamp, taking Saint Cajetan's statue with them.

FIGURE 6.5 Campout in front of the presidential palace. Autonomous City of Buenos Aires, August 2014.
"People feel safe that you are going to take care of them" (Alejandro).

Another day, Alejandro and others share anecdotes about their inter-actions with cops. After a few stories, he says with a smile, "[B]eing in security is nice." He is in his fifties and suffers from poor health. Recently, a doctor told him his spine is in very bad shape, the result of a lifetime of hard manual labor. Yet he continues to lead the team. He boasts that younger participants are in better shape than he is but only due to their age. In an encouraging way, he insists that if he, with his years, can do the things he does, "a young kid, like you" can do much more.

Security teams (or "self-defense," as some activists refer to them) are a common feature of piquetero organizations. They are groups of people who organize crowds during demonstrations, separate activists from the cops, and guard both the organization's buildings and public figures. Chronic police abuse and corruption mean that almost no one in the movement expects law enforcement to fully respect their rights. Experience has taught organizers that it is better to have your own safety measures, especially if your work frequently puts you at odds with the authorities.

From my observations, security teams tend to be male-dominated spaces. While women participate in self-defense lines and crowd management during demonstrations, almost all coordinators in these areas are men. Women are also less common in components of the work that are not as visible – such as physical training and meetings – or perceived as particularly dangerous – such as guarding locations or engaging in physical conflict (see Bidaseca 2006; Maneiro 2012; also see Massetti 2004; Corsiglia 2012).

For as long as Alejandro's organization has existed, there have been people in charge of security. He joined the team many years ago, shortly after he entered the movement. Back then, he says they had few materials and no one with experience in combat sports. As a result, the first few times they had to struggle physically against cops or counterprotesters they received more blows than the ones they gave. Many members were woefully unprepared: among laughs, Alejandro tells of the time the group went for a jog and a young man who underestimated the task ended up almost unable to breathe.

These days, the team is in much better shape. Alejandro brags about the equipment the group accumulated over the years: weights, benches, and punching bags. They also are far more experienced in dealing with conflictive situations, asserting their presence when necessary, and keeping other activists safe. Still, the work is demanding. Not only do they have to spend extra time and effort during demonstrations and political events, being alert to any potential trouble, but they also have to meet regularly after they complete their workfare duties for meetings and exercise. As Alejandro insists, "[Y]ou have to be ready. If you are not ready physically and mentally you cannot be standing for five hours in a place." He elaborates:

For instance, when we mobilize a march, when we move, say, the mass we move is 1200, 1300 people, all the people you see in the front, with the vests of the movement, those are from the organization. On the sides, all that people you see on the sides with the vests so people do not leave the line, so they are not hit by any motorcycle or truck, those are fellows from the organization. Behind, closing, so that a car does not enter where people are walking, those are all from the organization. (July 15, 2014)

Standing in a line and checking that people do not wander off might seem like a relatively simple responsibility. Yet demonstrations involve much more than that. Coordinating the dozens of people doing the job, making sure there is no foul play from the police or adversarial groups, and managing the inevitable conflicts that emerge when thousands of people block a road are all complex duties that require preparation and experience. Mauro explained to me how he and others gradually accumulated the necessary practice and skills:

Question: Regarding marches, political participation, what were the different things you did through the years?
Mauro: First it was participating in the neighborhood, in the many marches we made with demands. Then we organized a bit what was self-defense by neighborhood, organize marches, roadblocks, the shifts of the fellows. It was a whole thing, you had to guarantee that vehicles do not enter in the roadblock, that the fellows are safe, therefore we took turns with the fellows from self-defense. We learned, we organized, by trial and error but it was a commitment one had and a responsibility we had to carry out.

Q: And how do you organize the work with people?
M: That is why I tell you, we have meetings, in self-defense you do not have to be the most badass or the most anything, instead you have to give a commitment. Organize, organize the first line, where the leaders go, the rearguard, if possible the sides of the marches so the fellows are safe. Because otherwise it is a chaos if every person goes on the sidewalk. Then we try that people go as organized as possible. Then of course, there are moments in which you have to confront, or react, when they try to kick you out, that is another issue, for that we have a vanguard group, we are in charge of trying that nothing unusual happens. (May 5, 2014)

In addition to the complex logistics of demonstrations, security teams perform other crucial but far less visible roles. First, they offer security to leaders during private and public events. Not only is there the possibility of police violence, but also rival groups and local politicians may want to disturb demonstrations or gatherings. The situation becomes particularly acute around the time of elections. Many of Alejandro's tensest moments have happened then:

Politicians, the government, use cheap hands, people from soccer gangs, hooligans. So our leader goes to, say, one location, you have your fellows ready physically and mentally, mentally means you are with your eyes looking, not the candidate, but around and you notice, because you have been on the streets, who has a good intention and who does not ... You put your body, on an equal ground. If you can fight the National Guard, you can fight the riot police, are you not going to have a fight with a pair of assholes who want to ruin things for you and the candidate? (July 15, 2014)

Members of security teams also guard strategic locations and assets of their organization. Many times, the goal is to ensure the safety of participants. As Damián says:

I am in the role of security on this floor … you have to be very careful, the problem with social movements today is that if they grow too much, or they have too much success, lots of activism, lots of activists, it can affect someone else. So, from there it emerges that someone can come and do something, put something in the building, so well, we take care of fellows like our leader and the rest. (July 26, 2011)

In other cases, the objective is to prevent the stealing of materials or hinder evictions from occupied locations. Elías lives in an abandoned governmental building that his organization repurposed more than a decade ago:

I close my eyes at night and I am in the movement, and the next morning when I open them I am in the movement. It could be said that I am an activist the twenty-four hours, because when I sleep I also dream about the movement. (June 18, 2014)

Security teams, in sum, rely on volunteers to provide crucial roles for their organizations. Their members not only make extra efforts but also face additional risks. Although the vast majority of piquetero protests take place without incident, occasionally, there are clashes that lead to injuries, arrests, and on a few tragic occasions, even deaths.[1] Axel, who participated for many years in a security team, remembers vividly the time he witnessed an activist die:

[The victim] was there, on the floor. There was one of our fellows, Irene, she no longer participates with us, Irene was there and told him, "do not leave us, do not leave us, open your eyes, do not leave us." And you could already see, they had raised his shirt and he had a wound, but blood did not come out. And he was, he was already cold. (March 26, 2014)

Nevertheless, despite its demands and dangers, most current or former participants in these teams highlight their involvement as particularly meaningful. The practices associated with keeping others safe grant a set of crucial rewards. Through working together in certain tasks, engaging in specific forms of physical training, and carefully cultivating a specific collective image, people in these groups are able to draw

---

[1] Despite remarkable improvements since the end of the last dictatorship, collective action in Argentina can be dangerous: Between 1995 and 2017, eighty-eight people lost their lives during different types of protests (CELS 2017).

boundaries between themselves and those who engage in forms of public masculinity that are seen as shameful, such as crime, drug use, or idleness.

Participants engage in this moral boundary work in many ways. First, there is a discourse of sacrifice, especially on behalf of people seen as less powerful, such as women, children, and the elderly:

When we go to the marches, we guarantee that no matter what happens, if the police repress us, it is preferable that we put our bodies, that we get hit instead of the women, the children, the old people ... One has struggled a lot for the movement to grow and be as big as it is, and you know that you go anywhere and people see you, and people are happy ... they feel safe that you are going to take care of them. (Alejandro, July 15, 2014)

Security is what you do when you mobilize, when you mobilize you have to take the troops forward, you have to put yourself in the role of preventing people from doing trouble, manage the people walking with you, make sure they are in order. Security is that we have to be at the front and if something happens we have to be there, those of us in security have to be there. (Lázaro, June 27, 2014)

Participants also frequently refer to the public recognition and authority that being in charge of other people's safety entails. For example, Kevin highlights the "respect" he began to feel once he joined the team:

Kevin: I joined the security one day that we were in a general reunion of all organizations in the district, and Fabián comes, to the group we have, and told us all to join the security. There was the godfather of my little sister, two other boys, one a bit fat, big, and then a boy that was taller, and then it was me. He told us four.

Question: What did he say?
K: If we wanted to join the security. The other three said yes right away, but only for the demonstrations. To me it was more difficult.

Q: Why?
K: Because, what if I got injured, if there was repression they could harm me, but then I realized it was what I wanted, go to the front and defend the people who are behind ...

Q: And when you joined the security, how did things change?
K: It changed a lot, because I felt much more respect than what I felt when I was not in security. Respect because people came, asked you if they could do something or not, and instead if you were not in the security they pushed you, they cursed at you ... They come and say "excuse me, are you in security?" "yes," they

ask you if they can go somewhere, if you can accompany them, they treat you much better than they treated me before, and I like that, because they never gave me so much respect as they are giving me now. (June 27, 2013)

For Kevin, a young man with a strong work ethic but limited opportunities to exercise it, being commended for making efforts and taking risks is very gratifying. The only other activity that gave him comparable levels of what he calls "respect" was the few years as a teenager when he received a fellowship to play rugby, a sport perceived as masculine and tough.

The recognition granted to people like Kevin for their public role is a major source of pride. By allowing demonstrations to happen (and, consequently, generating concessions from the authorities), security teams receive credit for the effectiveness of piquetero organizations. However, the less visible aspects of these teams also offer attractions. In particular, activists underscore the value of regular preparation, meetings, and exercise. Devoting extra hours of one's time to these communal activities is seen as a healthy (and manly) way of contributing to the cause. Just as Alejandro points to the importance of "being ready physically and mentally," Elías, who participates in another organization, emphasizes that physical training is as important as ideological preparation:

Ideologically, I prepare by strengthening my ideology, my political objectives. Through literature. I prepare physically doing exercise, so I can have a strong arm and withstand a fight of forty minutes, that is how I prepare. (June 18, 2014)

Finally, security teams convey a sense of collective respectability by banning stigmatized practices such as alcohol and drugs. Members take pride not only in being sober during public events but also in their role ensuring that others do not transgress this rule. Participants in almost every organization I worked with accused other groups of allowing these behaviors. Gabriel, who guards a community service center most days and participates in security lines during demonstrations, recalled the repeated conflicts he had with members of an allied group:

We have had many problems with people who have been with us. People from [organization]. They are insolent people. Because they drink and smoke trash. Then they think they can push around anyone. So they have clashed with me a few times. (July 23, 2014)

The enforcement of this prohibition is difficult, time-consuming, and frequently generates conflict. Heavy drinking is a habitual practice among men in Argentina, and many participants in piquetero organizations struggle with different forms of addiction. However, the presence of intoxicated members is very problematic, as it both undermines the safety of the group and generates bad publicity. Organizers hence have limited options. More than once I witnessed people being expelled from an event due to drinking. On other occasions, people were allowed to drink only once an event had finished or after they had completed their duties. As Gabriel frequently explains to those who stir trouble, a good worker never gets drunk in public or before his shift is over:

I tell them, take care of yourself, behave well, if you do not behave well it is your problem, not mine. I buy a beer and put it in the fridge. A little plate of food, and a little glass while eating. I drink my little glass, pour myself another, no one knows, no one has to see it. Or sometimes there in the kitchen, we eat a plate of food and share a beer between two people, no one can tell us anything because the kitchen is closed, they already distributed food, my shift ended at one. I eat and then leave. (July 23, 2014)

Participation in a security team, thus, comes with specific demands, risks, and expectations. However, these costs are precisely what makes involvement so appealing for some activists. Working with others to make sure people are safe offers validation for notions of manliness that are at the core of working-class culture in Argentina: protecting your community, sacrificing your well-being for those who are weaker than you, and keeping your body strong and healthy. It is a way of embracing the kind of public masculinity that many in marginalized neighborhoods see as vanishing.

6.5 PEOPLE YOU CAN TRUST

Miranda, an experienced tailor, joined her organization about a decade ago. Money was tight, and the prospect of a small workfare program to supplement her income was very appealing. After participating for a year, however, a problem with paperwork meant that her plan was canceled. Feeling hurt for having lost what she considered a job through no fault of her own, she signed up with another organization. Her original coordinator, who lived close to her house, tried to convince her to return, promising to solve the issue. Miranda hesitated for some time but eventually agreed. When I asked her what made her change her mind, she said:

I missed my fellows, that is, the routine, you know, like a routine, that you say "well, I am going" ... getting up, going, being with my fellows, we covered different topics or we did the jobs that we needed to do, that, you know, that routine, I missed that. (July 15, 2014)

Miranda now belongs to a group of half a dozen women who sew clothes and make stuffed toys to distribute to children. Originally, they met three times a week, but as the organization obtained additional resources, they were assigned a more generous program that required them to attend every weekday.

In addition to the movement, Miranda is also involved in an Evangelical church. She speaks about her faith to anyone who will listen, causing other activists to jokingly refer to her as "the nun":

Extract from fieldnotes, June 24, 2014.
I went to the mezzanine, where all the sewing team was working. Sara was with them. They were in a good mood, and showed me what they were doing: small bags for children's day, with that plastic-like cloth they use to make stuffed animals. The idea is to fill the bags with candy and distribute them. Some women cut the cloth, while Sara and Miranda were cutting the excess with a special machine. Sara was teaching Miranda how to use the machine, apparently Miranda did not know. Sara gave her orders with jokes: "if the Lord comes to pick you up, ask Him to give you thirty more days so you finish this task first."

The backgrounds and perspectives of the people in the sewing group could hardly be more diverse: a deeply religious social conservative like Miranda coexists with a transgender woman like Sara who constantly jokes about sex. Yet it is evident from their interactions that they enjoy each other's presence, are committed to their shared task of producing goods for kids in the community, and are pleased with the quality of the product they make with limited resources. Of all the clusters of activists I saw over the years, Miranda and her fellows are among the most stable in terms of membership. They spend their mornings drinking mate while working on their benches and are usually together during demonstrations and assemblies.

Cases like Miranda are very common within piquetero groups. As research has pointed out (see Wolford 2010; Corrigall-Brown 2011; Blee 2012; Viterna 2013), small networks and localized contexts are crucial for the trajectories of individuals within a social movement organization. The way participants interpret their mobilization experiences is influenced by who they interact with on a daily basis and in which ways. In my case of study, the opportunity to spend time with others is a crucial reason why people develop attachment to their participation. In an environment where socioeconomic transformations undermine communal routines that were once prevalent, piquetero groups serve as oases of socialization. In them, people can still expect the best of each other and feel validated in their self-image as moral individuals. As Dante explained while reflecting on his years in the movement:

I was always an honest person, so I was lucky to have an organization where the majority of fellows who are part of this are honest people, people you can trust, even though afterwards you may obviously have differences in more personal issues. (July 24, 2014)

The communal practices that people engage in vary. As the Examples of milk cups and security teams indicate, women and men in the piquetero movement tend to socialize in gender-normative ways. For the former, communal routines are suffused in a discourse of motherhood and loving care for the young. For the latter, they entail an emphasis on keeping your body healthy and your mind sober in order to defend the community.

Together with reconstruction and development, protection of routines is thus one of the three mechanisms in which activists in the unemployed workers' movement engage in daily practices that convey respectability and consistency. However, not all participants share this perception. Many people who join a piquetero organization never come to see their involvement as more than a survival strategy. In addition, others who do find participation appealing face insurmountable barriers to remaining engaged. The following chapter therefore explores the complexities of potential, voluntary, and reluctant dropouts.

7

"A Small Thing to Get By"

Potential, Voluntary, and Reluctant Dropouts

June 26 is one of the most important dates for piquetero organizations. On that day in 2002, police forces killed two young activists during an attempted roadblock. The event came to be known as the "massacre of Avellaneda," after the district where the assassinations took place. Every year since then, protesters gather at the location of the murders to demand justice. For the tenth anniversary, commemorations are bigger than usual: a twenty-four-hour-long event including an evening festival on the 25th, a vigil over night, and a demonstration on the 26th. Thousands of people occupy several blocks, listening to live music, participating in cultural activities, or just gathering around the many fires set up to fight the cold.

The next morning, a tall man in his forties tells me his story. His name is Nelson, he is married with children, and participated in the movement during "the worst years, 2001, 2002." He was laid off in 1999 and spent two years seeking a new job without luck. Piquetero groups were becoming increasingly prevalent in his neighborhood around that time, but he did not trust them. Only after repeated failures at gaining employment did he accept the invitation of an activist who was also a childhood friend. Nelson was lucky: The group had just obtained some spots in a workfare program, and he received one of them: "That is how I went to my first march."

At the time Nelson joined, the organization was new; resources were limited; and the social emergency deepened every day. Tensions in the group were high, and arguments happened frequently. However, he formed a friendship with many other members, including one of the victims of the massacre we are commemorating today. Nelson remembers

160

FIGURE 7.1 Overnight vigil. Avellaneda, June 2012.
"I wish we did not need to be at the front of this march" (Nelson).

him as a young man full of energy and good intentions. Once, for instance, he helped a neighbor move construction materials even though he had just taken a shower and was ready to go out. Another time, he invited Nelson to have a beer and chat after a loud discussion.

On the date of the massacre, Nelson was right behind him. They expected repression but not a manhunt. The police infiltrated the protest, using undercover officers to stir trouble. He recalls the details of that terrible day with sadness: armed strangers pretending to be demonstrators, the beginning of incidents, frantically running away from the cops, the shock of losing a friend, politicians blaming the deaths on the protesters, and the complicity of many journalists with the official narrative.

The massacre was traumatizing but only deepened Nelson's resolve to continue participating. Yet months later, as the economy began to recover, he was offered a job out of town which would pay substantially more than the amount he received through his organization. Under pressure to support his kids, he decided to leave with a heavy heart.

Nelson insists he wants to return to work in the group, but in the decade between his disengagement and our conversation, he has only participated occasionally in special events like today. As we walk toward the point where the demonstration will begin, he greets some of his past fellows and points to the first line in the demonstration, reserved for the relatives and friends of the fallen. He says, with a sad voice, "I wish we did not need to be at the front of this march. But that is what we got."

This chapter explores the reasons why individuals like Nelson disengage from the movement. The ways in which participants exit piquetero organizations are varied. Some drop out for good, while others merely suspend their involvement temporarily. Some keep in touch with their former fellows, while others lose all contact. Some depart willingly, while others do so forced by the circumstances. This diversity is consistent with a broader literature on collective action, which emphasizes the complexity and variability of individual activist experiences (Passy and Giugni 2000; Fillieule 2010; Corrigall-Brown 2011). The relation between a person's biography and his or her engagement in mobilization is constantly evolving, and consequently, the characteristics and the intensity of each individual's participation vary over time.

Therefore, understanding disengagement from the piquetero movement entails not only comparing those who continue to participate with those who have left but also exploring the diversity of motivations behind the decision to withdraw. In particular, it is crucial to distinguish individuals whose reasons for leaving are mostly external (i.e., they face insurmountable obstacles to continued involvement), from people whose motives are largely internal (i.e., they do not find participation appealing enough). By doing so, we can treat dropouts not as a monolithic category but as a set of experiences roughly divided into three main groups: potential, reluctant, and voluntary.

Potential dropouts are those who are not particularly attracted to activism but stay involved because they lack a better alternative to make ends meet. The following pages illustrate this trajectory with two cases. The first is Melina, a woman in her thirties who complains that participation is too demanding but whose capacity to find a stable job is limited due to a series of medical conditions. The second case is Angelina, a woman in her fifties who despite openly disliking her work in the movement keeps participating because of bureaucratic delays in her application for a government pension.

In contrast, voluntary dropouts are those who are able to leave the movement for a more convenient source of income. I show this dynamic by following two respondents before and after they withdrew. Ernesto participated for three years but never developed an attachment to his organization due to repeated conflicts and left when offered a position as a janitor. Luis, a lifelong street vendor, returned to his former job when his dream of using the movement to obtain an occupation with higher status and reliability became unattainable.

Finally, while voluntary dropouts disengage willingly, reluctant dropouts do so only when forced by special circumstances. As examples of this process, I use Axel, a young man, and Tita, an elderly woman. I met Axel when he was an enthusiastic member of the security team in his organization, yet by the time we sat down for a series of interviews, he had dropped out. The need to feed his family led him to take a construction job that paid several times more than any workfare plan. In the case of Tita, even though at the beginning of my fieldwork she volunteered her time in several milk cups, a health issue that emerged in the subsequent years made such involvement impossible.

Comparing the experiences of respondents in these three groups with those of long-term participants allows us to identify the crucial mechanisms that make sustained activism possible. The one thing potential and voluntary dropouts have in common is that, for them, collective action does not become an end in itself but instead is just "a helping hand" to get through tough times. In contrast, reluctant dropouts share with long-term participants what I term "resistance to quitting": a strong tendency to overcome obstacles to participation. For them, mobilization has specific features that make it a particularly meaningful way of accessing resources. However, this attitude has its limits, as even enthusiastic activists (like Nelson) are not immune from life events that impede participation. Therefore, understanding long-term attachment to a social movement entails exploring the ways in which individuals' practices while mobilized resonate positively with other aspects of their lives, leading to dispositions that sustain involvement.

7.1 "FEW PEOPLE HERE VALUE YOUR WORK": POTENTIAL DROPOUTS

Despite only being in her early thirties, Melina is affected by serious health issues. She is a cancer survivor, has celiac disease, and has once suffered a mild stroke. Consequently, she frequently needs to take time off for medical reasons. This situation has caused delays in her formal education (she finished high school as an adult) and, most importantly, substantial barriers to stable employment.

Melina also comes from a politically active family. Her late uncle, a municipal employee, was a lifelong member of the local branch of the Peronist party and brought her to events from an early age. For twelve years, she participated, and thanks to her uncle's contacts, she secured a coveted job as a cleaner in a health post. However, she was fired a month before the position was to be made permanent. Disillusioned and feeling betrayed, she left the party. Not long afterward, a friend who ran a milk cup in a piquetero organization invited her to join. Melina knew some people in the group and had occasionally helped her friend buy ingredients. However, she only joined reluctantly:

> *I got here through a friend, I was looking for work ... My uncle used to give me vouchers I used to help her, because the organization did not always have sugar for all the milk cups, she sometimes did not have any, I sometimes went and bought it for her. She told me, "give me photocopies of your documents," [I said] "fine, but I am not going to any roadblocks, ok?"* (June 20, 2013)

Melina's refusal to participate in demonstrations did not last long. In fact, she gradually began accumulating duties. By the time I met her, she helped with administrative paperwork, coordinated a group of workfare beneficiaries, and served as interim youth leader in her neighborhood. Yet, even though she agreed with the work her organization does and highlighted the group's transparency, during our conversations she also voiced grievances. She felt that coordinators did not allow her to take time off, imposed erratic schedules, and prevented her from spending time with loved ones:

> *It is a holiday weekend and we should not be working. Like any normal person ... I do not have children, but [want] to see my family, have my own time with the people I want to be with, not pay attention all the time to my cell phone.* (June 20, 2013)

In addition to having unreasonable expectations, Melina also felt that other activists took advantage of her goodwill and placed unfair demands on her time because she was single and childless. "I hear a lot 'you can do it because you are single,' the other day I said, 'I hate being single'":

> *Older people have a way of thinking, they want to be with their family, want to work, want this, but when there is an activity, if it is in the morning everything is fine, but if it is in the afternoon, "no, I cannot do it, no because my husband complains," "no, because ... " "send her, she can do it" and that is not how things should be.* (June 20, 2013).

In other words, Melina sees the time demands of activism not as a personal choice or enjoyable activity but instead as an imposition. She does not mind working long, irregular hours but feels that others skew such efforts. To make things worse, the reason her fellows assign her onerous tasks has little to do with her skills and diligence but instead with the fact that she has no children. From her perspective, others see her time (and, consequently, her work) as less important just because of who she is. Hence, activities that others would value as a way to socialize and contribute to a worthy cause are a waste of effort for her:

Few people value your work here, the things you do, they are very few, you can count them with the fingers of one hand. I am one of those people, I am correct in my work, very orderly. If I am going to have a meeting, I do not think the meeting needs to take more than an hour. One hour, two hours, explain things. And sometimes the meeting takes longer, in stupidities, they talk more about their personal issues than about other things. (June 20, 2013)

Given her complaints, it is not surprising that Melina has considered leaving. However, she has not done so. When I asked her why, she responded:

Why don't I leave? Because I do not know if I will be able to find something, with so many medical procedures. Because if I have to do a treatment in the mornings and need to go to the doctor, a stable job would not respect that, the health insurance. It happened to me already once, I had a good job and had to quit after a month . . . they told me, "you did not tell us that you had this disease, and it could suddenly flare up." (June 20, 2013)

It is probable that a registered job would allow Melina to take time off for medical purposes, but private employers are reluctant to legally hire a person with health issues. An informal occupation would be easier to find because it would likely not include such protections, but without them, Melina is not able to make a living. A solution would be employment by the government, yet finding a position like that usually requires connections with local politicians, especially for a person without post-secondary education. A former fellow of her uncle recently invited Melina to sign up for a job but offered no guarantees and demanded that she prove her commitment by working without pay for a while:

I was told, "we will give you a permanent position." "If you are going to give it to me, give it to me tomorrow, on Monday I meet with you, we go to human resources, you sign the papers, only then I will believe you." "No, you need to do some politics with us." "No, I will stay where I am, I know I will be paid each month." (June 20, 2013)

Thus, Melina is stuck in her organization. Activism entails unreasonable demands and makes her feel undervalued, but at least it allows her to take time off for medical reasons. Given her situation, it is unlikely she will find a job with all benefits and protections mandated by law. Her only real alternative would be through her old political party, but that involves abandoning her current source of income and trusting people who already betrayed her in the past. Consequently, she remains involved in a place that is far from great but at least is safe:

I would not like to cross to the other side, I was there once . . . For me to cross over, as I say, it has to be a job that I know is secure. I better stay where I am which is secure. (June 20, 2013)

Melina is among the many in the piquetero movement whose involvement is largely motivated by the absence of a better option. While her wish is to get a stable job with the flexibility she needs, others hope for a pension or subsidy. Such is the case of Angelina, a woman in her fifties who has waited for a long time to have her common-law marriage recognized by the authorities so she can access a widow's pension. Despite substantial efforts in recent years to universalize access to retirement and disability benefits, people like her frequently have to wait extended periods of time to either become eligible or get their paperwork approved.

Angelina worked all her life. When she was fourteen, she dropped out of school and was hired in a children's clothing store: "[M]y dad told me, either you study or work." At age 20, she found a job at a garment factory, which she quit six years later when her son was born. Wanting to be around the child more, she became self-employed. First, she sold textiles door to door and later ran a small *quiniela* operation, a clandestine form of lottery popular in working-class neighborhoods.

By the time Angelina began working independently, however, her community was already struggling with increasing levels of unemployment. For several years, her husband's work as a painter, combined with her small business, kept the family afloat. Yet the situation in the area was deteriorating rapidly:

It was a disaster, a disaster, a disaster. . . . I remember they fired people and did not give them any severance, I have friends who worked for twenty years and did not get any severance. It is a thing that I cannot believe, that period in Argentina, I cannot. (February 19, 2014)

This vulnerability hit home when Angelina's husband had a series of debilitating strokes: "[E]verything went down." Not only did the family lose its main source of income, but also her own capacity to make money was reduced by the need to take care of her disabled spouse:

He was a painter, made good money, he painted in constructions, was a good painter, one of those you cannot find anymore. That is how he got sick, he inhaled paint and that caused a stroke. Besides he smoked, ate with a lot of salt, all that caused a health problem. He had four strokes. The third one left him paralyzed on one side and stuck in a wheelchair. (February 19, 2014)

It was in this context that Angelina approached the local authorities seeking help. She received a small subsidy, which together with an off-the-books job in an elderly day center allowed her to support the family. However, eventually, the municipality canceled this assistance. The mother of a close friend, who ran a soup kitchen for a piquetero organization, offered to sign her up. She accepted and soon afterward received a part-time workfare plan. A few years later, when she was let go from her job, the organization awarded her a spot in a better-paid cooperative program, leading to her full-time involvement:

Those of us who worked in soup kitchens, we belonged to this organization and did our hours, because you had to comply with the hours they gave you, if you did not go to the soup kitchen they assigned you, of course they would never give you anything. And since we were doing our work in the soup kitchen, we were working, to all the people who worked they gave us a cooperative. (February 21, 2014)

Over the years, Angelina also contributed to health promotion initiatives, becoming friends with some of her fellows. However, she rarely spent more time than required with the group and complained loudly when leaders announced upcoming demonstrations or special events. What seemed to irritate her the most were the inconsistencies of the work: the irregular distribution of supplies, administrative problems, and official neglect caused some days to be hectic with activity and others completely idle. Having to show up with nothing to do was not only boring but also led to hurtful accusations of laziness by participants in other projects.

Despite her differences with the organization, Angelina's most bitter complaints did not go toward it. Instead, the issue that concentrated her irritation was the slowness with which the authorities processed her claims to a pension. After her husband of thirty years passed away, she became eligible for state support. However, the fact that the couple was not formally married meant that the social security office kept asking for additional proof that the relationship had existed:

I am doing the paperwork, and at the beginning they tell you, do not hire lawyers, come personally. Do the paperwork in person. Let me tell you, since the month of December I have been going to the social security office, and there is always something missing, a paper, another paper. Fine, I did not do the official cohabitation paperwork, that you need to take. But I went with witnesses and proved it. I told them, if I have to bring more witnesses, I will. No, they said, with two witnesses it is enough. I went, did everything, and there is always something missing: Why didn't we buy a home? Why didn't we buy a car? Why didn't we buy this and that? Well, because we could not! (February 19, 2014)

The pension was incompatible with her workfare program. Yet while the latter had substantial work requirements, the former had none, freeing Angelina to use her time in other lucrative activities. Consequently, this scenario would be a net gain for her. Participation in the movement had been essential during the difficult years that followed her husband's disability and the loss of her job at the elderly center. Now a better choice had emerged but was blocked by red tape:

They still cannot give me the pension. Can you believe it? With the proof, I swear I want to go on television and talk about it, so the president knows, because it cannot be that they, with the proof they have, everyone writes letters for me, you can write a letter and present it. And they still tell me "no" at the social security office. (February 19, 2014)

It took almost an entire additional year for Angelina's request to be finally granted. When I last saw her, she had just received her first payments. She still went to the organization because there was the possibility of informally working on some projects but insisted that "if it does not work out I will stop coming, I am not going to come here for free."

Melina and Angelina differ in many aspects, such as their age, previous political experience, and activities while mobilized. Moreover, their particular reasons for remaining involved vary. For Melina, participation is one of the few earning opportunities compatible with her health issues. For Angelina, it is a way to sustain herself while waiting for the authorities to recognize her claim. However, both share a crucial characteristic: their activism has not acquired any special meaning beyond being a way to obtain resources. The lack of stable jobs, coupled with the insufficiency of social welfare, means that for people like them, life is a succession of temporary schemes to make ends meet (Lomnitz 1975; González de la

Rocha 1986, 2006). Melina and Angelina never developed the perception that their practices in the movement could provide consistency and respectability. They were assigned to erratic tasks (either due to mismanagement by coordinators or bureaucratic inefficiencies leading to shortages in supplies), and they felt their time and efforts were not respected by other members. Hence, they do not see activism as qualitatively different from other options for addressing material deprivation, such as government assistance, participation in political parties, informal occupations, or selling on the streets. It is just the most convenient option for the time being.

Other activists point to a similar dynamic. Some emphasize their dislike of participation as a major reason for their desire to leave. Paloma, a young woman tired of the frequent conflicts and low pay in her organization, was actively looking for jobs when I interviewed her:

This reaches a point when you want to look for some other gig. I see my friends, all of them go out, I have friends outside of here, they work somewhere else, and sometimes the salary we have here is not enough. Two thousand pesos are not enough to buy anything. And you say, I finished high school, I studied computers, I want to search for something else. Sometimes you reach a point when you are tired of having fights all the time. (March 14, 2014)

In other cases, even participants who enjoy their involvement acknowledge that if they wanted to get another job, they would not be able to. For instance, despite being a skilled seamstress, Priscila's chronic leg swelling prevents her from finding the kind of work she had in the past:

The truth is that for me, the time of good jobs is over. . . . I cannot find any because there are not any left. We always ask for jobs, but that is beyond my reach. I cannot work in a factory anymore, I cannot work twelve hours. That is why I tell you, I am satisfied with this organization. (May 19, 2014)

The experiences of these activists highlight an important point: many people in the unemployed workers' movement sustain their involvement because they do not have a better alternative. The vast majority of new members join a piquetero organization as a way to access social assistance. If participants fail to develop attachment to the specific practices associated with mobilization, that is, if collective action never becomes more than a component in a larger strategy of survival, these individuals are more likely to drop out when they find a better way of obtaining resources. In that situation, these potential dropouts become voluntary ones.

7.2 "THE PIQUETEROS ARE A CLOSED STAGE": VOLUNTARY DROPOUTS

I met Ernesto when he was a member of the security team in his organization. He is a short man in his forties who describes his life as a righteous struggle for survival. He only finished elementary school, and his last formal employment was in the 1980s. Ever since then, he has taken all sorts of odd jobs, from polishing pots in a small workshop to selling pastries door to door. For him, it is a source of pride that he never ceased to "fight for each coin" to sustain his family:

The only thing I never did in my life was stealing. Never, never. Thanks to my stepfather, who told me "you, when you go out, stand tall. Do not let anyone ever point at you." (May 17, 2013)

When other jobs were unavailable, Ernesto resorted to scavenging and selling recyclables. That was his situation in 2010 when a neighbor invited him to sign up for a piquetero organization. Participating in exchange for foodstuffs helped complement his meager income. A few months later, he obtained a position in a workfare program and was assigned by the group to help in different projects: cleaning a community center, cutting grass in a park, and building a shrine for a religious icon.

Ernesto's hard work gave him a reputation of being a trustworthy fellow, and as a result, he was invited to contribute to the organization's security team. He enjoyed the position. In particular, he loved being in front of police lines and teasing the cops: "I told them everything, 'hey, *cornudo* [cuckold], *boludo* [idiot], you are here and your wife is with someone else. I am going to grab you and kick your ass'." During the demonstrations we shared, he volunteered frequently to carry heavy drums and constantly made jokes to help pass the hours.

However, when I saw him again a year later, he had left the security team. He still spoke well of other members but said he had "seen something I did not like." Later at his home, he explained what had happened: The team's coordinator had scolded him for fighting with another member during a rally. Even though witnesses supported his point of view, he told me, the coordinator did not care to listen. Within a few days, Ernesto asked to be assigned to other tasks.

Following this incident, Ernesto's time in the organization became increasingly conflictive. After a heated argument during a meeting, he tried to leave for a rival political group. His brother, a member of the Peronist party, suggested he moved his workfare position: the party's local office was trying to attract into its ranks disenchanted piquetero activists. Ernesto worked in the new place for two months. However, the transfer was not authorized, leaving him in limbo.

Eventually, one of the local leaders in the piquetero organization convinced Ernesto to give the group a second try. He agreed, but other activists were resentful of his attempt to move and accused him of betrayal:

One day we were in the square and Mariana started "I do not know why they take back people who went with the Peronist Party, why don't they kick them out." I stood up: "you are very wrong. No one kicked me out. I left voluntarily. And I left for this and this reason, you do not know my reasons. I am tired of you. I am out of here." (June 20, 2013)

To avoid conflicts, Ernesto was assigned to work in a warehouse where the organization kept foodstuffs, tools, and other goods. But the bitterness remained. He complained that many people in the group did not do their share of work, showed up late, and still got paid as much as he did. Other members told me in private that they saw Ernesto as hostile and unreasonable. The final straw took place during a solidarity event for the victims of local floods. After working for a whole day under the rain, Ernesto asked if he could change into some donated dry clothes. When his request was denied, he decided he had had enough with the organization's leaders:

They do not take care of people. And when they demand something, they truly demand it. There are people that go every year, we do not miss even one day. And if you miss one day, leaders complain a lot. But there are others that never go, and you see them at the ATM getting paid. That is unfair. (June 20, 2013)

Ernesto's decision to leave coincided with an opportunity to do so. In 2013, he was offered a position at a cleaning company. His work as a janitor in a downtown office building would be the first time in decades that he had a job with all benefits mandated by law. In addition, the pay would be much better. He worked several months in an off-the-books "trial period" until he was officially hired in early 2014. Given that his workfare assistance was automatically canceled after being registered as formally employed, he stopped going to the organization. Months later, I ran into him on the streets, and he invited me to his house. He happily told me: "[T]he piqueteros are a closed stage. Now a new stage opens in my life."

Despite his complaints, when I interviewed Ernesto before and after he had left the movement, he always claimed to be proud of being a piquetero: it was an example of his relentless pursuit of "each coin" to support his loved ones. To him, the movement was simply another link in the long chain of odd jobs he held since his childhood. Some aspects of being a piquetero were more enjoyable than others, but they constituted neither a break with his unstable work history nor a connection with a lifestyle offering consistency and respectability. Activism, from his perspective, was just another way to make ends meet until something better showed up:

I told the people in the organization that the plan was a small thing to get by, but it does not get you by for long. I cannot spend three, five years making 1200 pesos. If I have the chance to take another job, I will choose that job. I will make 3500 pesos in a job that is much more convenient. It is more money, and it will be stable, and tomorrow I will have a retirement plan. With the workfare plan, what do I have? I have none of that! (June 6, 2014)

Ernesto is not the only activist with this type of trajectory. Luis joined a piquetero organization in 2009 through a vocational course. Over the years, he became increasingly involved, re-enrolled in high school, and even took a short course at a local university. His motivation was clear: a lifelong vendor on public transportation, as he aged, he became increasingly concerned about his capacity to continue working and his lack of retirement options:

It got stuck in my head that I do not want to sell on the buses anymore. I do not want to end up like many people I know, many fellows who died, they were old, I was young, I was beginning to sell, they were grown men, who ended dying with nothing. Not being able to talk, barely able to get on the bus ... A moment comes when you cannot walk and you have to get on the bus because it is the only thing you have to survive. I helped those people, and it got into my head that I do not want to end up like that. (June 27, 2013)

The organization fit his goals very well: in addition to managing social assistance programs and cooperatives, the group also offers training opportunities and adult education for approximately a thousand people each year. Luis became a regular participant. He received a workfare plan, which, combined with his involvement in different productive projects, allowed him to leave his old profession and gradually develop new skills. He knew that although three decades of selling on buses had given him valuable experience, street smarts alone would not be enough to secure a living:

The university of the streets, what do the streets teach you? They teach you nothing, to be rogue, to see how many drinks you can get others to pay for you in a bar, to think you are smarter than the rest. The university is a building, and you have to study, read, and learn. See how my head changed? Perhaps many years in the streets allowed me to be outspoken and able to talk in a room. But to speak you need to learn, about economics, politics, society, culture. The streets do not teach you what a social economy is, the streets did not teach me math, they taught me to count bills. The university of the streets does not exist, it is a lie. And I tell you that as a guy who worked for thirty years in the streets. (June 27, 2013)

Luis's hope was to become a teacher. His plan was to take advantage of the many tuition-free, high-quality public universities in Greater Buenos Aires, signing up for an associate's degree and eventually leading classes in the organization. The long-term goal was to obtain a reliable, decent job with financial stability:

I want to get into teaching. That is why I am making efforts, I am studying. I am 46, by the time I finish the associate's degree, I will be fifty. With a bit of experience, because I will become a remedial high school teacher. A bit of experience teaching, and having other expectations, this is very personal, very personal. I need my personal comfort, I want to get home and be comfortable. So I do not need to run from one place to another, without money to buy even a sandwich. Get home and relax, dedicate myself to that, prepare myself to teach classes. My expectation is that. (June 27, 2013)

This enthusiasm seemed genuine. Luis boasted about the college course he was taking, talked about content from his high school classes, and obtained good grades. Yet other activists were skeptical of his plans, citing his history of drinking problems and disorderly family life. For example, Ezequiel, Luis's coordinator, commended him for trying to learn new skills but was privately concerned about whether his expectations were realistic:

Luis is only now studying, I knew him young, he was a street sweeper. A drunkard and womanizer, which are things that are fine in their moment. ... Luis found ways, street vending, and with that he survived. He invested 25, 30 years in that, and the moment came when his body responded differently, and besides he had tons of kids. He was a product of all that. Now it is not super late but he is in a hurry, he wants things, he is studying and when he finishes he hopes to have a good job, with a good salary. It will not be like that, you will graduate, you will have a spot here, but it will be very basic if you just started ... because it is precisely that, you took too long to begin studying, took too long, your life went away. (March 28, 2014)

Luis's disagreements with his fellows became more consequential due to money issues. His decision to stop selling on the buses meant that he was more reliant than ever on material support from the organization. Yet the group depended on contacts with local politicians to obtain funding for productive projects. Budget cuts and red tape frequently caused delays and cancellations, which hit Luis particularly hard: other activists were already teachers and could rely on a regular paycheck, but his income was far less stable. He felt his work was not only paid little and late but also unappreciated. The conflict with his fellows gradually became a dispute over who was the real worker. Luis complained that the same people who criticized him were unwilling to do difficult manual tasks: "[A]nyone can work in front of a computer." He particularly resented having to run errands for others who "would not grab a shovel even if a judge ordered them to."

In other words, Luis found himself in a difficult position. As an aging street vendor without a high school degree, his income and security were deteriorating rapidly. The organization offered him the possibility of becoming a skilled professional, but that dream also highlighted the vulnerability of his situation and the low social status associated with his profession of thirty years. Consequently, from his perspective, the organization's recurrent money troubles were far harsher than they were for his fellows, not only in practical terms but also (and primarily) as instances of disrespect.

As my fieldwork progressed, I saw these tensions escalate. The situation became painfully visible at an end-of-year celebration I witnessed. While many activists were busy distributing diplomas to people who had finished courses, Luis was in a corner grilling for everyone. He had just finished the course at the university and was making progress toward his high school diploma but still felt stuck:

Extract from fieldnotes, December 20, 2013
I asked how Luis was doing, and they told me he was cooking the chicken. I went there and found him . . .. The first thing he told me was, "I finishhhhhed the university" [marking the word, terrrrrrrrmine]. And he told me about his plans to give classes. He said something that captured my attention a lot, "I do not want to be a drudge anymore, that is my issue." He was heating the chicken on the grill, there was a pile of chicken ready to serve. He said he did not mind doing that, but that he did not want to be a "drudge" anymore (he said this with strength).

The situation became unsustainable a few months later when a series of planned projects were canceled due to lack of funds. Apparently, a politician with strong links to the group had promised to finance this work, but the money kept being delayed, testing Luis's patience:

Extract from fieldnotes, March 27, 2014
As soon as I arrived, I greeted Luis and we sat down to talk. I asked him how he was doing, and he said, "I am a bit exhausted. I have a lot of work, but do not see

a single coin." That is when I realized he was in a bad mood, very angry with Ezequiel. Apparently, Luis and his son did some foundation work but were not paid, so they stopped the work. [An allied politician] ("that idiot") has to send some money, but has not. . . . Later, when we went to buy some soft drinks, Luis told me "I want to talk to Mario [the organization's leader], things cannot go on like this."

Luis insisted that he did not want to leave the organization entirely, but after a few months, he ceased going. He obtained his high school degree but did not attend the graduation ceremony. Other activists told me he had returned to working on the buses and was also selling empanadas in a street stall. Eventually, I was able to track him down, and he invited me to talk during a lunch break at a bar. After introducing me to other vendors, he began outlining his many grievances: "I had two months when I almost could not pay rent." The problem was not just material deprivation (something he has experienced many times in his life) but also being repeatedly told to be patient: "I cannot wait for you to finally get the money from [a politician], I need to go out to work." He felt his fellows had abused his generosity: "I still go once in a while, when they call me to do something I go. But only if they pay me."

Despite his soured relationship with the group and his insistence that he would never work "for free" again, Luis still defended the organization's agenda, to the point of getting in an argument with his friends at the bar. In this respect, he was similar to Ernesto, whose political opinions had not changed after leaving. Both saw the movement in general as worthy but felt they were in a situation where others took advantage of them, where their hard work had been unrecognized and their contributions misunderstood.

Other activists shared similar experiences. Pilar made no effort to stay involved after retiring (as some of her closest friends did) because leaders did not acknowledge what she sees as personal sacrifices. As a result, she gradually came to think of activism as just another gig:

I did a lot of things for the movement but the movement never did anything for me. I am thankful anyway because it allowed me to work and earn a salary of 2000 pesos. But that was because I worked, they never gave me anything for free. I earned my salary, and well-earned it was! (March 12, 2014)

Juan Pablo participated between 2000 and 2003 but left as soon as construction jobs became more available. He saw activism as an emergency measure, "to gather a few pesos" but not a wholesome way of life.

In fact, with time, he came to see the demanding routines of mobilization as an obstacle to obtaining good employment:

I signed up because there were few jobs and there was not much money coming into my house. So it was a bit useful. [But] I went out to find another job, and they demanded that you participate, and when they demanded a lot, I had no way to find another job! [The leaders] force you to be there, they need people to be there. As soon as I found a stable job, I left. (June 7, 2014)

David also saw his involvement as a temporary solution. He knew from experience that social programs may be terminated with short notice and hence used part of his plan to build a small store in front of his house. When time constraints made it impossible for him to keep both the plan and his store, he decidedly chose the latter:

The cooperatives [his workfare program] are not a law, so today they exist, but tomorrow maybe not. And I do not want to go back, go through what I already went through, my economic problems. Then I thought about my future, and I said "Ok, I will buy the materials to build my own store." So when I saw that I had more or less what I wanted to have, I went to the organization and thanked them for all their help and all the support they gave me, and told them that I was leaving the cooperative. (June 13, 2013)

The experiences while mobilized of Ernesto, Luis, Pilar, Juan Pablo, and David vary substantially, as do the aspects they liked and disliked about their participation. Their specific reasons for leaving the movement also diverge considerably. However, they all share the commonality of seeing collective action not as an end in itself but instead as one source of support among many. Unlike potential dropouts, however, at some point, they accessed an alternative to make ends meet, which from their perspective was better than collective action: a formal job (Ernesto, Juan Pablo), self-employment (Luis, David), or retiree benefits (Pilar). Consequently, they did not hesitate to leave. Nevertheless, for other participants, the decision to drop out is much harder.

7.3 "IT MAKES ME FEEL GOOD TO TALK ABOUT THE MOVEMENT": RELUCTANT DROPOUTS

As we finish the second of our interviews, Axel says, "[I]t makes me feel good to talk about the movement." He is a tall, skinny young man who participated for a decade but left after parental responsibilities forced him to take a job that paid better than a workfare program. He began working as a teenager helping his father, a construction worker specializing in plastering.

After a few years of apprenticeship, however, the 2001–2002 economic crisis left everyone in his family unemployed, and the whole group resorted to a piquetero organization that was active in his community:

[My father] became unemployed, he knew about the movement, bah, I do not know, a neighbor told him, "look, over there they are signing people up for plans." Then my old man, since I was not working, told me "give me your documents, your papers, I will sign you up, perhaps there is some plan." (March 26, 2014)

It was in the organization that Axel met his wife, with whom he has a daughter. As years passed and the economic conditions in the country improved, his relatives left the movement one by one. However, he was different. Many aspects of mobilization appealed to him: the friends he made, the opportunity to collaborate in a community radio station, and most importantly, his involvement in the group's security. When I met him, even though he had recently experienced two instances of violent repression, he was one of the most skilled and enthusiastic members of the team. For him, the movement had distanced him from bad habits and idleness, allowing him to become a better person:

[The movement] changed me a lot. Before, when I was younger, I did not care about anything. Anything or anyone. I went to the street corner, every day to the corner. I drank every day, almost every day we drank there on the corner. It was always the corner. The corner, the corner, the corner . . .. Now it is like I worry more about my life, my life and the life of other people, how they are, if they need anything. (March 31, 2014)

However, sustaining a family with the resources the organization could give him (a workfare plan and occasionally foodstuffs) was extremely difficult. A few times during his ten years in the movement, Axel had to take time off to exploit temporary lucrative opportunities. He also worked long hours to accommodate both his activism and a side gig as a bouncer. Yet these were provisional solutions. Through his father's contacts, he was frequently offered better-paying jobs in construction, which his relatives increasingly compelled him to take:

My old man told me to drop out, to go work, go work, go work. That I was being lazy, work, go to work. Always, "go to work." And I always told him, "but you made me know the movement," with those things he got very angry. And I always told him, "if you showed me this, now let me be, I like it and here I am." It was always that, always like that. (March 26, 2014)

Eventually, the pressure became too much. Having to opt between his passion and his family, he chose the latter and accepted a construction job in a downtown building. The guilt he felt was so strong that instead of announcing he was leaving, he simply ceased to participate and did not return his fellows' many calls:

When I left, it was from one day to the next. This was a weekend, I had worked in the cooperative on Friday, I do not remember well what I did that Friday, but I know I went working in the cooperative, and the next Monday I did not go anymore. I did not warn them of anything. My fellows sent me messages, "what is going on, Axel, tell me," and I did not answer. I did not know how to tell them that I was leaving the movement. It cost me a lot. Bah, it hurt me. More than anything, it hurt me a lot. (March 21, 2014)

Many activists in the organization expressed to me their disappointment and annoyance at having a highly regarded participant drop out without a trace. Eventually, one of them managed to contact Axel via social media and invited him for dinner. They made amends, but Axel decided against returning: "If it was up to me, if I did not have a family, I would still be there in the movement. I do it for my daughter; I left it all for my daughter."

Like Axel, Tita was also forced to withdraw from the movement. I was introduced to her during a solidarity event organized by her organization. She was the leader of a group of women working with children in several milk cups. A retired woman in her seventies, she migrated from Paraguay in her youth and worked for decades in the leather industry, first in a factory and later in a small workshop at her home. When nineties-era policies led to the closing of many factories, she and her husband opened a small grocery store. However, the economic crisis around the turn of the century caused substantial trouble for the business, not only due to the decline of customers but also the increase in violent crime. The couple looked for other ways to make ends meet but was not able to do so until 2005 when almost by chance they signed up at a piquetero group:

A client came and told me, "Tita, there they are signing people up, in that street."
"What for?" "I do not know, for a movement." I went and signed up. We had the store, it was a lot of work, I continued participating, already got hooked. My husband stayed alone, and told me, "[W]hy don't we close this and continue in the movement?" So it was that we closed, because it was risky. They robbed us a lot of times, four, five times. So it was tiring. I entered the movement first, then I signed him up, and we stayed there. (March 11, 2014)

At the moment of joining, Tita had limited political experience and was not very familiar with the movement: "I went to sign up, I did not know what for." Yet she gradually developed attachment to some of the projects in her organization:

We had a meeting and they said, "we have many areas, you can enter the area of health, gender, communication." And I said, "what is health?" "Well, it is to be with children, weigh children." So I signed up in health. And there I got hooked and hooked, and I am until now. I retired and keep struggling. As long as God gives me strength, I will continue. (July 30, 2011)

In other words, for Tita, participation became more than a way to access resources. Two years after joining, she was able to retire yet continued participating despite no longer being eligible for the type of help her organization distributed. She interpreted her engagement in collective action as a way to fulfill a long-delayed personal goal and also compensate for the deprivations of her childhood:

I worked all my life, but I always thought; "one day I will do something for the kids," because I like to be around children. Because I had a childhood that ... I was never hungry, but I never had a nice pair of shoes for school, I never had a dress. And now I have the opportunity to give something to kids. And I participate. I go, weigh the kids, take candy, or ice cream in the summer. And I love doing that. (July 30, 2011)

Tita's passion for her work was evident in her actions. She worked without pay for many years, offered her own house for different projects, and donated several machines from her workshop. However, in 2012, she was diagnosed with cancer. Facing a difficult and exhausting treatment, she left the movement. Her coordinator offered to support her work with additional resources, but she simply did not have the energy:

I had health issues, and left the milk cup, I had three surgeries, breast cancer. I left work, left the milk cup, they wanted to send me people so I could do it, but people are difficult, they are not responsible, and I am demanding. I said no, I do not want to have anything else to do with it, given my treatment .... The tumor stayed in place, did not ramify, that saved me. One day I saw Carlos and told him, "I want you to drop me, I am not working anymore." "No, Tita, we are going to send people so they prepare the milk." I said "no, I will continue the treatment, someday God will decide what happens, now I cannot continue with the milk cup, it is much work, you have to give three times a week food and milk and the children come eat, you have to prepare, have to make bread, it is a lot of work." (March 11, 2014)

Fortunately, a combination of surgery, radiation therapy, and chemotherapy saved Tita's life. She recovered, but other age-related health conditions remained a barrier to her return to the movement. She has many friends in the organization, and opening a milk cup would be nice, but her experience with illness has left her with little capacity to do the kind of demanding tasks she did until recently.

Axel and Tita are not the only activists who leave the movement compelled by the circumstances. Stories like theirs were common among the former participants I interviewed. For instance, Pedro was involved for many years but had to drop out when a combination of out-of-town job opportunities and adult education left him without time for the movement. He tried to remain involved, but his responsibilities were too much:

I had to go work, I got a good opportunity, and it was an improvement, the opportunity to have a job and you know, you can get to something, slowly build your home . . .. I wanted to also participate in the movement but the times did not fit. I more or less studied, I got back from work, took a quick shower, or took a shower at work, came back on the train, got home, left the bag from work, took the backpack and went to school. I came back, slept until the next day I had to go work again. (June 22, 2014)

Soledad was one of the earliest members of her organization and participated for a decade and a half until chronic joint pain, exacerbated by a domestic accident, made it almost impossible for her to walk. For a while, the organization accommodated her by opening a soup kitchen at her home, but eventually even that became unsustainable. Today, she laments that her condition prevents her from doing the two social activities most central to her sense of self, activism and religion:

I cannot walk. More than once I wanted to go thank [the organization], see them. But I cannot. As I told you, to go there I need someone who takes me and afterward brings me back, and that is very difficult . . .. It is like, I left the Church, and regret that I do not go to Mass, well, the same with this, they are two things that were very important to me. (July 25, 2014)

Néstor was a member of his organization's press team, in charge of getting journalists to cover the events he and his fellows organized. He enjoyed the activity but had to stop to take care of his sick mother:

I stopped working for personal reasons, more than anything because my mother is sick and I had no time to continue the responsibilities that I had, and for that, I preferred to stay more time with my mom, than with other things. (June 11, 2012)

In sum, even activists for whom collective action is a meaningful activity are occasionally forced to withdraw. They enjoy their practices while mobilized and consequently make efforts to remain involved, but their capacity to overcome obstacles to participation has limits. Pressured by relatives, compelled by material needs, and/or affected by health crises, some of them have no choice but to drop out.

By all accounts, Elías is a committed activist. He dedicates extra time to the movement, participates in his organization's security, and even lives in a building occupied by the group to ensure no one steals anything. A few times over the years, he has had to scare away burglars with the firecrackers he uses for demonstrations: "I do not want to use a weapon, because I do not want to kill anyone. But you know how they run away when I throw at them with that?"

Despite his limited formal education, Elías is also a well-informed man who spends his downtime reading political books. He loves to engage in debates and has contributed to a radio station run by his organization. He is also strongly optimistic: despite suffering many defeats throughout his activist career, he is convinced of the justice of his cause and the value of the movement's struggle:

We have a great ally, which is this very system, its contradictions will kill it, and we will push so that happens. We will not kill it ourselves, it is going to be killed by its own contradictions, like all empires were killed, its own contradictions and the peoples that struggle to liberate themselves from it. (June 18, 2014)

However, neither commitment nor optimism prevented Elías from suspending his participation for almost half a year following a family crisis. The demands and difficulties associated with collective action became unbearable when he felt he was needed somewhere else:

I have a younger son with addiction problems, with drugs, I have my oldest daughter who started to have problems with domestic violence, by then I saw that I was not doing well here and then there was the possibility for me to do what I needed to do. Late or not, but I needed to pay attention to those two situations with my children, I had to move, pum, I left the movement. I went to live with my daughter, who had separated, after very strong domestic violence. My kids are very good kids, you see, they did not deserve that situation. (June 18, 2014)

Elías only returned to his organization once he felt the problems were under control and after other activists insisted:

There were fellows who went to look for me. Hipólito, Úrsula, Carolina, we met, we got together, shared things, I have a very good relationship with them, we shared things, music, going out, holidays, birthdays .... They made me come back ... "come with us, we invite you, we miss you, you are important, we have something that is strong, we are friends, fellows." (June 18, 2014)

Elías' example shows the multiplicity of ways in which people leave the piquetero movement: temporarily and permanently, willingly and reluctantly, gradually and suddenly. The previous pages explored this diversity by differentiating between three main groups of dropouts: potential, voluntary, and reluctant. The importance of this tripartite distinction lies not in any moral valuation of different types of participants, nor in a potential discussion of which trajectory is more "authentically" activist. As other scholars have argued (Quirós 2006, 2011; Corrigall-Brown 2011; Viterna 2013), the sheer diversity of political participation makes such a debate pointless. The crucial task instead is the identification of the mechanisms that make a person perceive collective action as intrinsically valuable.

As I argued in the introduction, addressing this question entails focusing on the daily practices of activists. The positive resonance between the background of each participant and his or her experiences while mobilized (Bourdieu 1977; Desmond 2007; Shapira 2013), the learning of new ways of appreciating activist routines (Becker 1963; Wacquant 2004), and the recurrent affirmation of these perceptions through interaction with others (Benzecry 2011; Tavory 2016) contribute to what I term "resistance to quitting," a deep-seated disposition to overcome obstacles to participation. Potential and voluntary dropouts have in common the absence of this attitude: the only thing separating them is that the latter obtain a more effective alternative to participation. Both groups fail to develop attachment to their organizations and rarely see their practices while mobilized as ends in themselves. For them, the movement is just "a helping hand," a way to survive until a better option materializes. On the contrary, reluctant dropouts are much more attached to mobilization. Like other committed participants, they tend to see their activist routines as meaningful sources of consistency and respectability. The difference is that specific life events make it impossible for them to continue participating. Resistance to quitting, in other words, is not immunity.

In sum, the ever-changing relation between a person's biography and his or her experiences while mobilized generates specific dispositions, which in turn influence their subsequent activist trajectories. For some, this increases the likelihood of dropping out when a more convenient way of accessing resources emerges. For others, it makes them more resilient to barriers that may interfere with their participation. The implications of this argument for our understanding of collective action are the subject of the following (and final) chapter.

8

Conclusion

Throughout his life, Elías has known many challenges. However, he insists that the biggest one was finding his footing after he and countless others were laid off. Compared to a past in which factory labor offered material sustenance, facilitated collective organizing, and structured daily life, over the past four decades, his community has suffered from an ever-worsening spiral of anomie and exclusion:

This is a movement of the unemployed, the last cookies in the jar, the most impoverished sectors, pushed to marginality, with all the social evils, with the drugs, with the prostitution, with the alcohol, all those issues, that is our people, the most marginal, the last cookies in the jar. That is who we are, there is a substantial difference with the past, we used to be an organized working-class movement, we were all workers, you understand? (June 18, 2014)

This quote vividly outlines the consequences that neoliberal reforms and deindustrialization have had on working-class Argentineans. In forty years, the country transformed from being one of the most egalitarian in Latin America, with low levels of unemployment and relatively generous welfare policies, to one in which vast segments of the population lack access to opportunities for upward mobility. For millions of families, the present has become more difficult and the future more uncertain.

However, Elías' words also describe an influential case of resistance to these challenges. Since the 1990s, piquetero organizations have incorporated and given a voice to innumerable people who continue to claim their rights as citizens of a once more inclusive nation. Through the development of extensive grassroots networks, the strategic use of disruptive tactics, and the efficient administration of resources, these groups have played a crucial role in numerous underprivileged communities.

The previous chapters explored the complex motivations and diverse experiences of activists in this movement. My goal has been to study the emergence of commitment despite substantial obstacles. How is it that people who join as a way to access resources gradually come to see their involvement as an end in itself rather than a means to other ends? Why do members who remain skeptical or indifferent toward central aspects of an organization's ideology still develop a strong attachment to it? I argue that participants use their practices while mobilized to partake in a respectable working-class lifestyle that is increasingly uncommon for poor Argentineans. Activism allows individuals to embrace the kind of routines they see as best fitting to them, providing their daily experiences with a reassuring sense of order and worthiness in a context of pronounced socioeconomic decline.

This process varies by age and gender. Concerning the former, while middle-aged activists reconstruct routines from an idealized past, younger members develop habits that they never got the chance to engage in. In addition, all participants regardless of age protect communal routines endangered by the decline of public life. With regard to the latter, whereas men engage in practices associated with blue-collar labor, women predominate in activities related to domesticity and childcare. In other words, the organizations in my study reproduce traditional notions of masculinity and femininity ingrained in the ideal proletarian life that they seek to save from extinction. Hence, people in the movement reconstruct, develop, and protect routines in gender-specific ways.

There are many reasons why the richness of experiences within the piquetero movement is relevant for our understanding of collective action. This conclusion elaborates what I consider are the most important. First, I outline the overarching lesson from this book: the importance of everyday experiences and concrete motivations for political participation. Second, I develop this general point into four specific principles that can be applied to research on other instances of social mobilization. Finally, I argue that studying grassroots experiences like the piqueteros can teach us a lot about current challenges to democracy in Latin America and the world.

8.1 EVERYDAY STRUGGLES AND THE MEANING OF WORTHINESS

Malena insists that dignity is "being able to buy a hair dye." She is a woman in her sixties who participates in a small textile cooperative within a piquetero organization. Although she has strong opinions, she avoids talking about politics with her fellows ("It is like I disagree, I try to not touch that topic"). However, she appreciates the opportunity to work. In spite of her skill with industrial sewing machines, her age and a walking disability make it almost impossible for her to obtain a formal job. Her children have offered to support her, but she declines to stay home:

Malena: I always say that even if what we make is little, because we cannot subsist on it, you know? I always say that it is earning dignity, it is getting our dignity back.

Question: How is that?
M: Because the fact that I can use hair dye, buy hair dye, is through the effort that I make coming from home to work here. By sitting here, I buy that dye with my own effort, I am not asking my son if he can buy a dye, I am not taking that from my son's budget, from the home. That is why I say we are earning dignity, receiving my dignity again, I feel very dignified.

Q: What does your son think of you coming here?
M: He is angry.

Q: Why?
M: Because he thinks I should stay at home, he feels strong and capable of supporting me. In buying my medicines, in supporting a home, in buying food. But I have been a woman of struggle, of always working, and I say no, they will not defeat me, I will continue, at least what I buy I do not take from the family's budget, I take it from what I am earning. (April 3, 2014)

Malena is not the only respondent who linked the resources obtained through the movement with dignity. Priscila made a similar point:

From this place I get my plate of warm food. I take the money from here, I cook, and I eat a warm meal. It is not like I wait for another person to give me a cold meal or yesterday's food. Because I want food from today. (May 19, 2014)

Nevertheless, for Malena and Priscila, dignity is not just associated with the satisfaction of needs ("hair dye" or "a warm meal") but also related to the way in which those needs are met. As Jennifer Sherman (2009) and Ariel Wilkis (2018) argue, low-income individuals use different sources of money to establish moral hierarchies in their communities.[1] Within piquetero organizations, the semantic and practical link between effort

---

[1] For a discussion of the social processes conveying particular meanings to money, see Zelizer (1994).

and benefits allows recipients to claim membership in the valued category of those who work hard, setting themselves apart from the "lazy ones" who expect "good things to fall from the sky." By showing up regularly at an organization and engaging in demanding tasks, participants move from being passive receptors of charity to active laborers in control of their situation. Activism endows their daily lives with two crucial aspects threatened by mass unemployment: respectability and consistency.

This dynamic explains the significance of "genuine jobs" as the central demand of the movement. Throughout my fieldwork, respondents repeatedly expressed frustration at government policies centered on unconditional direct assistance. Their desire is to earn their living doing the kind of jobs they see as proper for them. In the words of Tatiana, a mother in her forties:

Why doesn't the government open factories? That would give us work, but good work, so we can make ends meet, earn a good salary, and give my children a good meal, because that is something we cannot do, I cannot do it, I cannot sit down on Sunday and tell my children, "let's eat a good milanesa[2] *with mashed potatoes," because I cannot afford it, I cannot do it.* (February 27, 2014)

Tatiana does not just want to treat her children to a good meal over the weekends. She wants to earn the resources necessary to do that with her labor, instead of depending on the goodwill (and arbitrariness) of others. Donations are good to solve emergencies, but they deny the respect that comes from being able to make your own decisions. Tito made a similar point:

When I do not need to ask for foodstuffs anymore, when I do not have to ask for a plan, that would be because things are going the way they should. Tito and any other resident of the neighborhood sits down at the table and eats whatever he wants. Whenever he wants, he wants to eat a milanesa *he eats it, he wants to eat a soup he eats it. Whatever it is. But what HE wants. Not what we have to give him.* (May 14, 2012)

In other words, participants in the piquetero movement interpret their efforts in terms of solving the material and symbolic deficits caused by exclusion from the labor market. The overall agenda of their organizations expresses itself in the day-to-day experiences of activists through the struggle to support themselves in a way consistent with what they were

[2] *Milanesa* is a typical dish in Argentinean cuisine: a meat fillet breaded, usually fried, and served with mashed potatoes, french fries, or a side salad.

raised to see as respectable. The fact that dignity acquires such specific, even mundane meanings does not imply that these individuals are simplistic or uninformed. Instead, it indicates that for them, as for countless activists throughout history, the personal is political. As Lourdes emphasized during a meeting:

Extract from fieldnotes, June 6, 2014
At one moment Lourdes said, "this is a political movement," marking the syllables of political, "po-li-ti-cal." To reinforce her point, she said, "when you go to the butcher, ask for half a kilo of beef and the guy gives you four hundred grams, you say "no, I am sorry, I paid for five hundred, give me five hundred," you are doing politics. When you go to the health post, they say they will take in five patients, you stay because you are the fifth person in line, and they close after the fourth person, you complain and demand to be seen, you are doing politics. When you get on the bus and the driver says you cannot get on because you do not have money for the ticket, and you complain, you are doing politics." What Lourdes was trying to do was to convince those who listened that they had to "fight" for what they had, in other words, she was trying to justify the demands that the organization makes of those who got a plan or foodstuffs through it. With that objective, she said the usual phrase of "what we obtained we obtained through the struggle."

Lourdes' insistence on the political nature of everyday struggles illustrates an essential point: For the vast majority of participants in a social movement, politics are not confined to abstract ideas but embedded in concrete aspects of everyday life. Consequently, if we aim to understand the emergence of activist dispositions, we need to avoid the reification of collective action as a special endeavor, qualitatively different from other aspects of a person's experiences. The following section elaborates on specific ways in which this principle can be implemented in the development of new scholarship on social movements.

8.2 TOWARD A BETTER UNDERSTANDING OF ACTIVIST DISPOSITIONS

In recent decades, there has been increasing concern over the limitations of the paradigms that have dominated social movement research since the 1970s. Scholars have pointed to problems such as overreliance on structural explanations, exceedingly schematic models, and limited engagement with other areas of knowledge (see Goodwin and Jasper 1999; Walder 2009; McAdam and Boudet 2012). Studies on activism have not been an exception to this trend. Several authors have questioned prevalent conceptions of political participation as overly rationalistic and negligent of the role of affectual and emotional dynamics (see Goodwin, Jasper, and

Polletta 2001; Gould 2009). Much of the criticism has also centered on the field's lack of attention to the diversity of experiences, perspectives, and trajectories of activists within movements (see Wolford 2010; Corrigal-Brown 2011; Viterna 2013). Researchers have also cautioned against the literature's excessive focus on the recruitment phase and the consequent misinterpretation of the processes leading to the sustainment or decline of political participation (see Passy and Giugni 2000; Fillieule 2010; Corrigal-Brown 2011).

Cases like the piqueteros have much to contribute to this debate by illuminating how the intricate relation between people's backgrounds and their experiences while mobilized generates dispositions which in turn affect their postrecruitment trajectories. In particular, my analysis of why some participants develop a strong attachment to their organizations while others in a similar situation do not suggests four interrelated lessons.

First, the connection between an individual's personal beliefs and activist routines might be as important for long-term participation as their alignment with the official ideology of organizations. Literature on social movements has tended to conceptualize activism as the outcome of ideological conversion. However, the development of commitment does not necessarily require that a person agree with his or her organization's views. Instead, long-term participation may result from a positive re-signification of activist routines, a process of "learning to enjoy" that is ratified through interaction with other participants (Becker 1963; Benzecry 2011; Tavory 2016).

In other words, we must not forget that collective action is first and foremost a practice. That is, individuals do certain things and engage in particular behaviors when they participate in contention. Thus, whether these activities are enjoyable and meaningful is crucial to people's commitment to the social institutions that make them possible. Unveiling the mechanisms that lead some participants to see mobilization as intrinsically valuable is essential to understanding the diverse postrecruitment trajectories of participants.

Second, if mobilization becomes enjoyable due to its resonance with the backgrounds of activists, then our models of collective action must assign to their experiences outside of the movement the same explanatory value as those inside it. Given that participants usually see activism as inseparable from other life spheres (Mische 2008; Litcherman and Eliasoph 2015), we should not compartmentalize in theory domains that are united in real life. In particular, the strength of a person's attachment to his or her practices while mobilized is influenced by the relation between these practices and other sources of gratification and meaning. That is, sustained participation depends on the degree of connection between mobilization and valued identities associated with other aspects of activists' lives. If the activities associated with being in a movement help a person define him- or herself as part of positive categories, they will provoke pride and validation. However, if these activities conflict with those categories, if they are perceived as something that members of an esteemed reference group would not do, then they will be seen with either indifference or shame.

Third, since the mechanisms that influence people's attachment to social movements are also present in other instances of collective life, it is imperative to expand our toolkits by borrowing concepts from outside the limits of our field. The capacity of new frameworks to explain contentious events worldwide will depend on our willingness to engage in broader debates and learn from parallels between people's practices while mobilized and other social activities. We need to engage in what Dianne Vaughan (2004, 2014) calls "analogical theorizing": the development of concepts by comparing phenomena that apply to diverse cases. Despite the uniqueness of any social phenomenon, the processes that influence the experiences of individual participants are rarely exclusive to it. As Vaughan argues:

> Regardless of differences in size, complexity, and function, all organizational forms have characteristics in common. They share basic aspects of structure: hierarchy, division of labor, goals, normative standards, patterns of coming and going. Further, they share common processes: socialization, conflict, competition, cooperation, power, culture. This means we can compare them, generating theory based on analogies and differences that we find. (2014: 64)

In sum, understanding collective action requires going beyond the limits of social movement theory in search of broader insight. The growing insularity of the literature on protest and insurgency (shared by many other areas of sociology) not only means a reduced audience but also entails a threat to the explanatory power of our frameworks.

Fourth, social movement theory should be careful not to overestimate the importance of extraordinary events for mobilization. While collective action can break with people's customs and expose them to new lifestyles, we must not discount the possibility that its appeal can also lie in its ordinary, everyday aspects. The fact that protest frequently emerges as a defense against perceived threats to quotidian life (Thompson 1971;

Jasper 1997; Snow et al. 1998) suggests that both divergence and conformity with convention can promote activism.

What is most important, the desire among the rank and file to protect traditional ways of life does not necessarily preclude a movement from pursuing progressive agendas. The process of translation between grassroots narratives and organizational goals (Robnett 1997; Wolford 2010) means that the demands of members can be effectively addressed in multiple ways. In the case of the piqueteros, for instance, adherence to old-style views of working-class labor and family has led to support for redistributive policies such as state-funded cooperatives, universal pensions, and guaranteed basic income for mothers and children. Scholars of culture and social psychologists have long argued that people's attitudes and behaviors are far less consistent than we frequently assume (Gross and Niman 1975; Schusman and Johnson 1976; Swidler 2001; Jerolmack and Khan 2014). Consequently, allies who portray activists as free of contradictions make the same mistake, albeit with different motivations, as opponents who belittle organizers for failing to live up to an unrealistic standard of coherence.

This coexistence of seemingly opposite views within a poor people's movement has important connotations for analyzing the political consequences of working-class decline around the world. As Pablo Lapegna (2016) argues in his book on peasant mobilization in Argentina, our sympathy for those who resist the effects of growing inequality should not lead us to ignore the dilemmas and ambiguities of their work. Put another way, it is crucial to avoid sanitizing the politics of subordinate groups. Escaping rigid binaries like "resistance/consent" or "innovation/ tradition" allows us to identify the potential contributions of grassroots groups to democratic consolidation and wealth redistribution in different societies.

8.3 ECONOMIC VULNERABILITY, SOCIAL ANXIETY, AND PROGRESSIVE ORGANIZING

Since their origins, organizations in the unemployed workers' movement have been part of a distinct regional and global context. Over the last few decades, the combination of economic and political liberalization in many areas of the developing world has led to the emergence of diverse forms of collective organizing. This dynamic has been particularly pronounced in Latin America, where drastic neoliberal reforms have coincided with an unprecedented period of democratic expansion. On the one hand, widespread joblessness and the undermining of social safety nets have pushed large segments of the population deeper into marginality. Yet on the other, there has been an overall reduction in political violence and a consequent expansion of opportunities for dissent. The result has been a mobilized society that has been vital for the consolidation of existing civil liberties, the recognition of new social rights, and the demands for solutions to long-standing grievances.

The wave of grassroots mobilization that expanded through Latin America since the last few decades of the twentieth century has received substantial attention (see Roberts 2008; Silva 2009 for a review). However, this literature has frequently overemphasized the novel aspects of these movements, in detriment to their connections to already existing forms of collective action. Observers tend to portray contemporary examples of activism in the region as attempts at creating new forms of social organization, downplaying their adherence to traditional repertoires and agendas. However, cases like the piqueteros are a complex synthesis of new and old. As Federico Rossi (2017) argues, the demands of the unemployed workers' movement for the distribution of social assistance are better understood as a "struggle for (re)incorporation" of sectors whose rights as citizens and workers were repudiated by pro-market reforms. Despite their innovative features, piquetero organizations have from the beginning framed their goals as the reconstitution, in a new environment, of past relations between vulnerable populations and the state. Over the years, this creative adaptation of established conventions has been a major reason why activists have been able to advance their goals and strengthen networks of committed participants, remaining a visible and influential force in Argentina's popular politics.

This complex relation between tradition and innovation in my case of study raises important points for our understanding of popular politics globally. Around the world, neoliberal policies have disarticulated forms of social integration which provided material support and symbolic meaning to vulnerable populations. Facing a diminished sense of self-worth, frustrated by the lack of political responses, and worried about their sources of livelihood, a growing number of people worldwide seem to have embraced authoritarian and xenophobic agendas. Nevertheless, as the previous chapters have shown, this is far from an inevitable reaction to the anxiety produced by rising inequality. The desire by marginalized groups to return to a romanticized past has also fueled movements advocating for political and economic inclusion.

Analyzing the appeal of grassroots experiences like the piqueteros can thus provide crucial insight for understanding the future of democracy worldwide. If movements pushing for the rebuilding of past links between the state and excluded populations continue to represent large portions of the citizenry, a scenario in which the authorities are forced to redistribute wealth becomes more likely. In contrast, if these experiences fail to attract a significant segment of those who feel politically and economically disenfranchised, then the outcome can be much more negative.

8.4 MAKING THE REVOLUTION DAILY

As we wrap up the second of our interviews, Gisela brings a bag filled with old pictures from her many years in the movement. She smiles as she describes each one in detail. Some show important events: camping with other activists, a trip to a distant city, and large demonstrations. Others display more commonplace activities shared with her fellows: eating together, listening to a local band, and cooking for children.

The pictures provide an overview of the many things Gisela has done for the movement. She was a youth coordinator, operated a milk cup, and taught remedial elementary and high school classes. A quiet person with a reserved personality, Gisela initially struggled with adopting responsibilities, but gradually became comfortable working with others and managing groups. Over time, almost without realizing, she got increasingly involved: "[S]ome of us were a bit more interested than others, and we began to stay."

One of the last pictures shows her on a stage with three other people. She is wearing a vest with the organization's name, and unlike the rest of the photographs, in this one she is not smiling. She tells me it is from the first time she spoke in front of a crowd, during an event in downtown Buenos Aires: "I was already a youth leader. Imagine, my face had changed. I was more serious."

At the time, Gisela did not even realize she was being photographed. Her coordinator snapped the picture and later gave it to her as a keepsake. On the back, he wrote a short poem, which Gisela shares with pride. The poem reads:

For a revolutionary man or woman there is nothing impossible. Everything can be reached, all is needed is perseverance, patience, work, discipline and trust in the people.

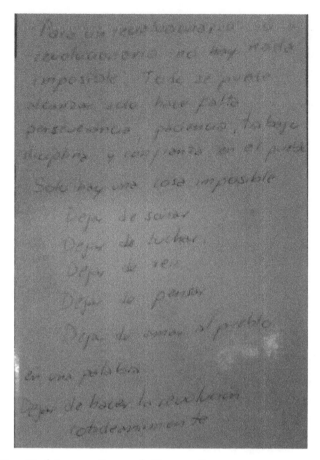

FIGURE 8.1 Gisela's poem. Lomas de Zamora, June 2013.
"I did not know he had taken this picture. Afterwards he gave it to me and wrote a message" (Gisela).

> *There is only one impossible thing*
>
> > *Quit dreaming.*
> > *Quit struggling.*
> > *Quit laughing.*
> > *Quit thinking.*
> > *Quit loving the people.*
>
> *In one word*
> *Quit making the revolution daily*

The poem illustrates much about the daily experiences of activists like Gisela. For more than two decades, they have worked in Argentina's poorest neighborhoods, seeking to organize those excluded from a changing labor market. Despite the far-reaching consequences of deindustrialization, they have refused to accept the relegation of those who Elías calls "the last cookies in the jar." Through their everyday practices, they continue to defend their dignity as workers and demand the authorities recognize what they see as their rights. Thanks to their challenging, complex, and sometimes contradictory work, they have compelled the Argentinean state to implement policies that address the worst effects of neoliberalism. At first sight, their struggle to solve the endless problems that plague the day-to-day life of their communities may seem banal. However, the future of democracy and equality worldwide depends largely on the efforts of people like them.

An Ethnography of a Poor People's Movement in the Global South

Field research for this project took place in July–August 2011, May–June 2012, May–July 2013, and December 2013–September 2014, in six districts of the Metropolitan Area of Buenos Aires (see Map 1). In all, I spent fourteen months gathering different forms of data: 950 pages of fieldnotes, 133 recorded interviews with current and former activists from nine piquetero organizations, and more than 4,000 photographs and videos.

When the project began, my goal was to analyze what I saw as the decline of the piqueteros after the economic collapse of 2001–2002. This topic had developed out of my dissatisfaction with the tendency of social movement theory to focus much more on the emergence of contention than on its sustainment or downfall. In addition, I wanted to understand how organizations had adapted to their apparent weakening.

However, as I immersed myself in the fieldwork, talking with activists and witnessing their work, it dawned on me that the question was far more complex than I had anticipated. An interpretation of the movement's recent history based on a narrative of decline simply did not stand up to scrutiny. While it was clear that the membership and street presence of piquetero organizations had dwindled, this was only one aspect, the most visible one, of their situation. Fieldwork at the grassroots level revealed a different story, one in which most groups had managed to maintain their core structures, had developed networks of committed activists, and were recognized as legitimate actors in the management of state resources. In sum, I was witnessing not a story of decline but one of permanence and, in some aspects, strengthening.

Hence, as I accumulated data, my main empirical puzzle became why most organizations were still active more than ten years after their last peak of contention. The key to answer this question laid in explaining the trajectories of activists. I realized that a crucial aspect of the resilience of many piquetero groups was the cementing of core networks of committed members. However, this development seemed to challenge the explanations suggested by the literature on political participation. At the moment of joining, the profile of my interviewees did not match the one that theoretically should lead to sustained involvement: Most of them were destitute, with low levels of formal education and limited feelings of efficacy. The vast majority had approached their organization not due to ideological affinity but rather as a way to obtain resources needed for survival. What was more interesting, many of the most enthusiastic participants I talked to remained indifferent or antagonistic to central aspects of their organizations' agenda, even after years of participation.

Understanding both the movement's trajectory since 2003 and how some of its members developed long-term attachment thus became two aspects of the same question, the answer to which required an emphasis on the relation between activism and its broader context. As a result, as the fieldwork progressed, I began to center more on the resonance between the personal histories of participants and their practices while mobilized, as well as on the relation between piquetero groups and other experiences of collective life in their communities. In other words, I broadened my empirical focus, both at the individual and organizational levels. This appendix explains in more detail the steps I took to do so.

COMPONENTS OF RESEARCH

Empirical evidence for the book was collected in three ways: interviews, participant observation, and contextual information.

Interviews

I used 133 in-depth interviews to explore the interrelation between biography and activism for the whole life of each respondent. Besides ten meetings with national leaders in the movement, the bulk of my recorded conversations were life-story interviews (Atkinson 1998; also see Weiss 1994; Becker 2002) with current and former rank-and-file members. My goal was to illuminate three aspects of each respondent's life: (a) How did his or her background contribute to being recruited to a piquetero organization? (b) How did the experience of mobilization relate to other spheres of his or her life? (c) How did this connection influence their trajectories after recruitment? Interviews followed the life of subjects chronologically, letting them elaborate relevant points in their own terms and leaving interpretative questions for the end.

My experience with this methodology reinforced my belief in the value, for research on political participation, of extensive interviews that center on the past and present practices of activists. Focusing on an individual's biography allows the incorporation into the analysis of findings that may be otherwise dismissed as "noise." As Javier Auyero and Debora Swistun (2009) have shown in their study of environmental suffering in Buenos Aires, statements of doubt, incomplete recollections, and contradictory findings may be key to understand people's experiences and decisions. In the case of the piqueteros, using interviews to reconstruct the personal history of activists allowed me to discover their frequent ideological disagreements with their organizations, as well as the centrality that working-class routines played in their appreciation of mobilization.

Think for instance of Giugliana, of whom I write in Chapter 5. Having a long conversation about her past and present, giving her time to develop on issues she found relevant, was extremely informative about her reasons for participating. I learned of her struggles with domestic violence, her concern about the effects of neighborhood decline on her children, and her deep gratitude to fellows who lent a helping hand during her worst moments. She elaborated extensively on her work history and her desire to make a living honorably and explained in detail how a workfare plan, while demanding in time and poorly paid, also meant community recognition, personal validation, and freedom from abuse. By going back to the interview transcript, supplementing it with other sources of evidence, I was able to understand why she enthusiastically supported an organization with whose ideology she mostly disagreed.

Furthermore, life history interviews helped me address two particular challenges. First, an individual's recollection of his or her experiences is inevitably imperfect, especially for episodes farther back in time. Structuring interviews as chronological reconstructions of the respondent's history reduces the probability that relevant facts are forgotten, by providing a mental map to identify issues in need of elaboration (Weiss 1994). Second, impression management creates an additional difficulty, because individuals are less likely to accurately describe aspects of their lives that they see as affecting other people's perceptions of them (Goffman 1959; also see Jerolmack and Khan

2014). This issue was particularly salient for me given the polarized views on the piqueteros prevalent in Argentina's public opinion. Starting the conversation with direct inquiries about the subject's reasons to participate may have biased some of them into providing answers perceived as more socially desirable. Consequently, prioritizing elaborate descriptions of past and current events over questions about personal standpoints was essential in creating trust and eliciting more informative responses (for examples of a similar methodology, see Wood 2003; Munson 2008; Viterna 2013; also see Katz 2001, 2002).

Interviews took an average of one hour twenty minutes and frequently required multiple meetings.[1] I recruited subjects by asking people during participant observation. If they said yes, we would set up a time and location, at the discretion of the respondent. Most meetings took place in an organization's building, the respondent's house, or a public space. In addition, I used snowball sampling to recruit dropouts and other activists who were not regularly present at the sites where I did research. I took particular care in asking for referrals from different people in each organization, to ensure a more diverse sample.[2]

Interviewing dropouts was an important research goal from the beginning.[3] This task was more difficult than expected. Identifying, contacting, and meeting former participants turned out to be very time-consuming, demanding the sacrifice of many hours that could be devoted to participant observation. In addition, as time in the field accumulated, I noticed that the experiences of activists were far more diverse and complex than I had anticipated. Consequently, I decided to interview only a subsample of dropouts and focused on recruiting a broader range of current participants. To compensate, I used the extended period of

---

[1] Around 83 percent of interviews were individual. Whenever possible, I tried to talk with respondents one-on-one, but sometimes, they invited other people to participate, or joined meetings that had already started. Consequently, 17 percent of subjects were interviewed as part of a group. The average number of people in these conversations was 2.8.

[2] In terms of gender, age, time of recruitment, and national origin, the sample was divided as follows: Seventy-six respondents identify as female, fifty-five as male, and two as trans-gender. Twenty-three are in their twenties, thirteen in their thirties, twenty-eight in their forties, forty-one in their fifties, and twenty-eight are older than sixty. Thirty-seven joined their organization in the 1990s, sixty-nine in the 2000s, and twenty-four after 2010. Three respondents were unclear about the time of their recruitment. 121 were born in different provinces of Argentina, while 12 are immigrants from neighboring countries. Appendix B includes a complete list of recorded interviews, with some basic information. As in the rest of this book, names of people and organizations have been replaced by pseudonyms.

[3] For studies that compare current and former activists, see Klandermans (1997), Passy and Giugni (2000), White (2010), and Corrigall-Brown (2011).

fieldwork to my advantage, following the same individuals at different stages of their involvement in their organizations. In particular, I was able to interview people before and after they left the movement. I also had recorded conversations with some activists while they were in the process of disengaging.

Participant Observation

The second component of my fieldwork was participant observation of activities carried out by the organizations I worked with. I observed special events such as demonstrations and large assemblies, but the majority of my visits to the locations[4] of these groups took place during regular days.

My involvement in the daily life of organizations helped me generate trust with my respondents and get to know informants. It was also a crucial source of evidence in two specific ways. First, it was the context for valuable informal conversations. I soon realized that in many cases, skipping the formality of an in-depth interview and keeping the recorder off was a great way to learn about the experiences of my respondents. It happened quite often that in the middle of an event, different activists started to tell me their history, sometimes without me even asking anything. The disadvantage was obvious: I had to wait until later to write down what the person had told me. Nevertheless, the benefits were also important. Exchanges felt more natural, and the lack of a defined format made it easier for some people to participate.

Second, while interviews were a window into the background and experiences of activists, participant observation gave me an opportunity to witness their everyday routines. Therefore, I centered my attention on what some respondents call "those days when nothing happens," that is, the unremarkable tasks that constitute the vast majority of their time in the movement. This methodological choice yielded substantial benefits.

---

[4] The word used by members of the movement to refer to the places where they meet is *local* (plural: *locales*). Throughout the book, I have translated this term as "locale," "center," "office," "location," and "building" interchangeably, since each of these words captures aspects of it. A *local* is a building or room, usually improvised, where social movements and political parties in Argentina carry out their activities. They have different purposes: storage of foodstuffs and tools, soup kitchens, education centers, and meeting spaces. Many of them are located in the house of a local coordinator; others are squatted buildings; and a few are rented or owned by the organization. Generally, for each neighborhood in which an organization is present, there is a *local*.

Students of social movements are (unsurprisingly) drawn toward visible contentious events that break with established routines. However, in most grassroots organizations, such occasions are the tip of the iceberg: For each protest, there are countless hours spent in more mundane activities. Moreover, these activities are frequently deeply meaningful to people in a movement (McAdam 1988; Robnett 1997; Wolford 2010; Blee 2012).

A good example is Mauro, whose story I share in Chapter 4. Had I focused mostly on protests and public events, I may have missed a crucial component of his activist experiences: the varied tasks that fill his time in the movement, fixing equipment, moving stuff, and helping others. Considered separately, each of these activities would seem inconsequential. Yet together, they allow Mauro to reconstruct routines from an idealized past and embody the kind of person he aims to be. I doubt I would have been able to identify the combined effect of these chores without spending a great deal of time observing the seemingly trivial aspects of daily life in his organization.

In addition to notes, other products of my fieldwork were photographs and videos. I have used a small selection of them throughout the book to illustrate particular dynamics. Photography had two unexpected advantages. First, many activists were delighted that I was capturing their work, insisting that I take pictures of them. I distributed dozens of copies in digital and print format. A few times, I was even scolded for not bringing the equipment with me to a particular activity. Second, holding a camera gave me remarkable freedom of movement during protests because law enforcement frequently perceived me as a journalist and therefore was more hesitant to restrict my movements.

My interviews and observations therefore complemented each other and took place at the same time. I wrote detailed fieldnotes at the end of each day, compiling a comprehensive story of what I had seen, experienced, and done. As Robert Emerson, Rachel Fretz, and Linda Shaw (1995) argue, writing fieldnotes is a process of interpretation and sensemaking, in which "findings" cannot be separated from the way they are observed and documented. Consequently, I included my actions, perceptions, and feelings in the notes.

Once the fieldwork was complete, I processed transcripts and fieldnotes in three steps. First, I read them thoroughly, using a system of small cards to write relevant trends and information. Second, I used these cards to categorize patterns in the evidence, developing a tree of nodes. Third, I used NVivo software to code the data based on these nodes.

Context Information

Finally, I complemented the data from interviews and participant observation by using databases of contentious events and reviewing existing studies on the movement.

I relied on three databases to explore variations in the movement's trajectory since its beginning. The first one was created by the Study Group on Social Protest and Collective Action (GEPSAC in Spanish) of the University of Buenos Aires (see Schuster et al. 2006). It includes all protests registered between 1983 and 2006 in Argentina's two most widely read newspapers, *Clarín* and *La Nación*, classified by variables such as the actors involved, the repertoire used, and the demands expressed. It provides a unique perspective on the importance (compared to other instances of mobilization) of piquetero organizations during the key years that surrounded Argentina's 2001–2002 economic collapse. The second database was created by Nueva Mayoría, a think tank located in Buenos Aires. It registers all roadblocks that took place in Argentina since 1997, distinguishing by province and protesters (Nueva 2008, 2009, and 2016). The third database was generated by Diagnóstico Político, another think tank in Buenos Aires that has compiled data on the number, location, and organizers of all roadblocks in the country from 2009 to 2016 (Giusto 2016).

I also relied on the extensive literature on the piquetero movement, written both by academics (Barbetta and Lapegna 2001; Svampa and Pereyra 2003; Delamata 2004; Massetti 2004, 2006; Svampa 2005, 2008; Epstein 2006, 2009; Quirós 2006, 2011; Torres 2006; Battistini 2007; Garay 2007; Wolff 2007; Pereyra 2008; Pereyra, Pérez, and Schuster 2008; Ferraudi Curto 2009; Frederic 2009; Gómez 2009; Ramos 2009; Grimson, Ferraudi Curto, and Segura 2009, Benclowicz 2011, 2013; Manzano 2013; Pozzi and Nigra 2015; Rossi 2015, 2017; Kaese and Wolff 2016), journalists (Schneider Mansilla and Conti 2003; Young 2008; Boyanovski Bazán 2010; Hendler, Pacheco, and Rey 2012; Wainfeld 2019), and activists (Colectivo Situaciones and MTD Solano 2002; Kohan 2002; FPDS 2003; Mazzeo 2004; Oviedo 2004; Flores 2005, 2007; Gómez and Massetti 2009; Pacheco 2010).

The combination of different methodologies, case studies, and agendas provided a multifaceted account of the history of the movement. Databases and literature allowed me to contextualize the information gathered through interviews and participant observation, helping me observe relevant events from different perspectives. Such methodological triangulation (Denzin 1978) allowed for checking the robustness of hypotheses and addressing the limitations of each specific source of evidence.

SAMPLING

The piquetero movement consists of dozens of organizations. How did I choose which ones to focus on? On the one hand, I wanted to know the experiences of as many groups as possible. But on the other, I also wanted to have time to study each in detail. Consequently, I followed a two-stage plan. During the first three phases of fieldwork (in the summers of 2011, 2012, and 2013), I focused on a larger sample of organizations, which gave me a general sense of the movement's characteristics and allowed me to identify relevant processes and questions. I used the information collected in this first stage to guide the final (and longest) period of fieldwork.

My original goal between 2011 and 2013 was to focus on eight organizations. The criteria for choosing them were:

(i) Geographical location: The Greater Buenos Aires area, where most organizations are based, is divided into 24 municipalities, with diverse social and political conditions. I decided I would focus on groups based on different districts. I worked on five of them (La Matanza, Lomas de Zamora, Lanús, Esteban Echeverría, and Florencio Varela), plus the city of Buenos Aires itself (see Map 1).

(ii) Ideology and alliances: The most important division that separated organizations during the time I was doing fieldwork was whether they were supporters or opponents of the presidencies of Néstor Kirchner (2003–2007) and Cristina Fernández de Kirchner (2007–2015). Therefore, I contacted groups on both sides of this dispute. I also included organizations that had switched sides.

(iii) Trajectory: I included organizations with different trajectories, from some that sustained a large portion of their membership to others that were reduced to little more than their most committed members.

In addition to these guidelines, I followed the principle of always taking advantage of a research opportunity. This happened when I first contacted different leaders from an organization in my sample. One of them

answered that his faction had formed a separate group due to disagreements over the political situation of the country. This was a great chance
to study a division from the two sides, so my sample increased to nine, to
include this new organization.

For the final stage of my fieldwork (December 2013–September 2014),
I centered on four of these organizations, following the same criteria.
Their main locations were in La Matanza, Lomas de Zamora, and
Florencio Varela. Two were anti-government; one was pro-government;
and another had switched from allied to opponent. Two of them were
large in size (membership in the thousands), and two were smaller (in the
hundreds). I remained in contact with members of the other five groups
but decided that concentrating on a subsample would help me delve
deeper into their internal dynamics.

When I first approached organizations, I expected some resistance and
distrust. Consequently, I decided I would contact leaders and activists
prior to any visit. I created a list with the emails and/or phone numbers of
public figures associated with each of the groups I wanted to study. The
information came from two sources: a friend from college who had
interviewed some leaders for his thesis, as well as newsletters and official
statements posted on the Internet. About a month prior to my first trip,
I sent emails to the contacts on my list describing my study and asking for
authorization to participate in the events of the organization and
interview some of its members. I did not expect many replies, and I was
right (only a few wrote back). A week later, I started calling the people
who had not responded to the email. The results were very good: almost
everyone I contacted said they had no problem with me doing research
and visiting them.

For each organization I studied, I sought to develop a strong
relationship with an internal sponsor, that is, someone who trusted me
and put me in contact with other activists. In some cases (especially in
small organizations), the main leaders fulfilled this role. But in bigger
groups, it usually was the case that after a short meeting with a national
figure, I was directed to someone of lower rank. That is why the majority
of my informants ended up being neighborhood coordinators. For
instance, take the case of Josefa. Shortly after arriving in Buenos Aires in
mid-2011, I arranged to meet with the head of her organization at a coffee
shop in downtown Buenos Aires. He only stayed for five minutes, but he
was accompanied by one of his assistants, Carlos, whom I interviewed.
Carlos invited me to an upcoming community service event, where he
introduced me to many people from the district, among them Josefa, who

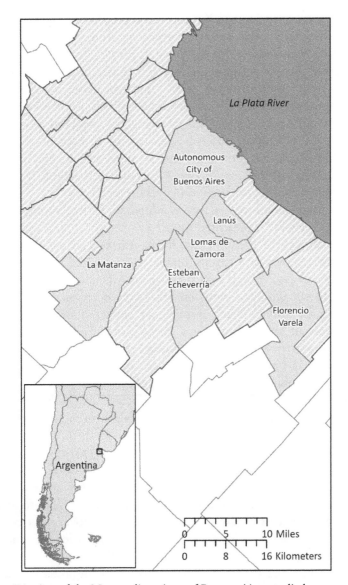

MAP 1 Districts of the Metropolitan Area of Buenos Aires studied.
Argentina – Subnational Administrative Boundaries, Instituto Geografico
Nacional and UNHCR, https://data.humdata.org/dataset/argentina-
administrative-level-0-boundaries, CC BY 4.0 (http://creativecommons.org/licen
ses/by/4.0/).
U.S. Department of State, Office of the Geographer. (2013). Detailed World
Polygons (LSIB), South America, 2013. U.S. Department of State. Humanitarian
Information Unit. Available at: http://purl.stanford.edu/vc965bq8111.

ran the organization in a specific neighborhood. She rapidly grew fond of me and became a great contact, inviting me to every event the group organized and introducing me to countless people.

Covering diverse perspectives and trajectories was essential to my project, yet it confronted me with a dilemma. Over the years, I did research on many different organizations with various ideologies. How could I adopt a role that elicited openness and cooperation while also being seen as a "neutral" observer? I needed my respondents to trust me and be open to me, but at the same time, I wanted them to understand that I was working with different groups. My challenge, therefore, was finding equilibrium between insiderness and outsiderness.

I sought to maintain this balance by adopting a particular role, one I call "allied sociologist." I presented myself as a scholar who is sympathetic with the struggle of the piquetero movement as a whole regardless of disagreements between organizations and emphasized my belief in the importance of poor people's movements for Argentinean society. Just as artists, social workers, and lawyers usually participate in these organizations without being members, I portrayed myself as an ally rather than an activist, an *amigo de la casa* ("friend of the house") instead of a *compañero* (fellow activist). And I made clear from the beginning that I was working with several different organizations. If asked, I always said the list of other groups I had contacted.

Achieving the intended balance was a difficult task. On the one hand, it frequently happened that my respondents began to see me more as an activist than a sociologist. I was sharing time with them, showing lots of interest in their struggle, and attending almost every event to which I was invited. That led to being called a *compañero* on several occasions, especially later in the fieldwork. In addition, semantics complicated my role even further. In Argentinean Spanish, many words used to describe a likeable and trustworthy person are the same to express common political allegiance. For instance, the word *cumpa* (friend or buddy) is short for *compañero*.

On the other hand, there were times when the opposite problem happened: I was perceived as an outsider, not because of lack of trust but largely because of the way I look. To my surprise, some people thought I was not Argentinean. First, these groups are accustomed to people who come from developed countries to visit the movement. As a tall, "white-looking" Argentinean that came from the United States to do research, I was sometimes confused for an American. Second, even when people knew I was Argentinean, when asked about where I was from, they assumed it was *Capital*, that is, downtown Buenos Aires, a much wealthier area. As a result of both confusions, I frequently had to clarify that not only was I Argentinean, but that I was born and lived for 25 years in Greater Buenos Aires. This is not a minor thing. Coming from the *Conurbano* (the outskirts of the metropolitan area) is very different from being a *Porteño* (from the city itself). There is considerable discrimination against the former and, as a result, a lot of resentment toward the latter.

In sum, I made constant efforts to move from a role of *compañero* to one of "allied sociologist." This implied making sure my respondents understood that although I was supportive of their cause and enthusiastic about participating in demonstrations and events, I also did the same with other organizations. In general, I was successful. There were several occasions when I was even encouraged to go talk to other groups. Of course, the merits for this situation lie mostly in the goodwill of my respondents. However, there were a number of decisions I made during my fieldwork that helped me achieve the intended role. First, I was always willing to do anything my respondents were doing at the time. I offered to help clean curbs, cook a meal, keep a fire alive, or carry loads. Most times, the offer was welcomed. I never pretended this would eliminate all barriers between my subjects and me, but I wanted to avoid being seen as "someone from the Ministry," that is, a specialized outsider who comes and sees how everyone is working but does not work himself. Second, I got to my field sites by myself, using public transportation. Only a few times did I accept the offer of having an activist guide me to the closest bus stop or train station, and this was due to concrete safety concerns. The benefits of doing this were twofold. I demonstrated to my respondents that I was not a complete foreigner because it is hard to move around Greater Buenos Aires without native knowledge of the transportation system, and I gathered first-hand evidence on one of the main problems of these neighborhoods: their physical segregation due to very bad buses and trains. Third, I pointed out that I have a history of participating in demonstrations since very young, although I never did it as part of an organization. Finally, although I shared the list of organizations I had contacted, I never gave the name of any interviewee. This was not only an Institutional Review Board (IRB) requirement but also a way of letting everyone know that people from other groups would not learn about their personal participation.

Although I found much better access than expected, that does not mean I had no problems at all. In some of the groups I studied, there were people who did not trust me, especially because I live in the United States.

For example, one day, I was going to a demonstration on a bus when a middle-aged activist told me half-jokingly, "[Y]ou must be a spy, you get information about us and then you take it up [North]." For a few seconds, I did not know what to say until I listed all the documents I had to carry when traveling abroad and concluded in a jovial tone, saying, "even if I wanted to sell them information, they would not trust me." The interesting thing is that this person is a close friend of one of my main informants in that organization, another activist who invited me to her house, openly talked about her life (in our first interview, she described a very traumatic episode), and never asked me for any proof of who I was. This incident showed me that having respected sponsors within an organization would not eliminate distrust completely.

Another problem was the potential for gatekeeping. My reliance on informants, plus the fact that I always asked for permission to participate in events, helped me generate trust with the organizations I studied. Nevertheless, that potentially allowed them to exclude me from things they did not want me to see. However, I do not think this has been a major problem. First, it assumes that my informants actually wanted to hide facts about themselves. Second, even if someone tried to conceal something, my experiences in the field suggest that it is hard to do. Many of the people recommended by coordinators for interviewing were open about negative aspects of the organizations. On many occasions, I witnessed fights, but only twice in the entire fieldwork was I asked to leave a meeting. Most times people laughed, saying, "you see, this is a *quilombo* (mess)." Other times, I was actually invited to stay during intense arguments, as one leader said, "[S]o you know the internal *despelotes* (conflicts) we have."

Only once, though, did I lose access to a field site. It took place as I was nearing the end of my research, and it occurred unexpectedly. I was convinced I had an excellent rapport with the members of the group, but one morning, as I asked them if they knew people who had left the organization, one of the leaders suddenly told me that he no longer trusted me. Many of my behaviors that I thought conveyed respect were interpreted as suspicious; perhaps I was spying on them? For instance, I always called before visiting. However, what I intended as a polite act was interpreted as an attempt at gathering information.

I never knew if other members of the group shared this person's views. He suggested having a general meeting to decide whether I would still be granted access to the organization's events, but when I tried to call to arrange that, I received no response. I decided to respect what seemed to be reluctance to meet me and not insist.

I always knew that losing access to some of the organizations I worked with was possible, especially given that my fieldwork extended over a period of several years. However, cutting links to a group that I honestly liked and cared about was more distressing than I had envisioned. In the following weeks, I tried to make sense of such an abrupt change: What had I missed? I remembered events occurring over the years that seemed minor at the time, such as when in a meeting someone described the profile of a "typical" undercover cop, which seemed to fit me very well. To this day, I am still unsure what caused the loss of access. Perhaps I had unwittingly offended someone in the group? But the relationships were very cordial until then. Had I stumbled upon a shameful secret? I would be surprised if any of this had happened because the group had been very open to me until then.

After much thinking, I concluded that the probable explanation was some combination of all of the above. From my perspective, the organization was a group of very honest people going through hard times. In the last few years, some members had been arrested after a protest; the group had gone through a succession of bitter divisions; and despite their best intentions, conflicts with other community figures had intensified. In that context, perhaps my behavior aroused suspicions, and what for a long time was perceived as innocent interest became progressively seen as treacherous.

Regardless of the reasons for it, this specific incident was a painful example of the ethical and practical issues involved in the work of an ethnographer. Engaging with the field, "being there in the neighborhood," allowed me to learn about the experiences of hundreds of people who struggle each day to give their families a better future. At the same time, it showed me the intricate dilemmas that are inherent to any human being. Losing access to a group of nice people reminded me what my research was about: surpassing the futile and patronizing debate on whether the piqueteros are evil or heroic and understanding them as individuals inserted in a specific context, with a particular history and complex motivations.

EPISTEMOLOGICAL ASSUMPTIONS, ETHICAL ISSUES, AND LOGISTICAL CHALLENGES

From the beginning, my project drew heavily on the principles of reflexive sociology (see Bourdieu 1988; Wacquant 1992). This epistemological stance became stronger with time, as my research focus shifted toward the interrelation between social action and its context. In particular, I relied on Bourdieu's notion of habitus to both formulate and tackle my research question. For Bourdieu, every aspect of social life is the result of a "relation of true ontological complicity" (1988: 783) between the field, "a set of objective, historical relations between positions anchored in certain forms of power" (Wacquant 1992: 16), and the habitus, the embodiment of those relations "in the form of mental and corporeal schemata of perception, appreciation, and action" (Wacquant 1992: 16). The field–habitus relationship allowed me to understand the behavior of activists in more complex terms than the simple agency/structure dichotomy:

> The habitus, being the product of the incorporation of objective necessity, of necessity turned into virtue, produces strategies which are objectively adjusted to the objective situation even though these strategies are neither the outcome of the explicit aiming at consciously pursued goals, nor the result of some mechanical determination by external causes. (Bourdieu 1988: 782)

Applied to the specific case of the piqueteros, this approach entails exploring how the interaction between people's history and their experiences in a social movement leads them to appreciate participation as an end in itself. In other words, the interplay between biography and activism generates enduring dispositions that sustain involvement despite the existence of obstacles (what I term "resistance to quitting").

Furthermore, adopting a reflexive approach also implies that the very presence of the researcher influences the processes he or she studies. In my case, this situation was particularly salient with regard to three dimensions.

First, as I mentioned earlier, my race, gender, and class influenced my interaction with participants. Some of my physical features (a tall, fair-skinned young person) are markers of privilege that placed me in a position of authority from the beginning, something that was reinforced by my educational background and gender. For example, one day in 2012, I was introduced to a group of women in a textile project run by a piquetero organization and funded by the national government. The women were having a break and chatting among themselves. However, as soon as I entered the room, they hurried back to work. A few moments later, they explained among laughter that they had thought I was a state official in charge of checking their work.

Markers of privilege are a deeply ingrained component of social stratification, and thus, their influence in my fieldwork was impossible to overcome entirely. However, the very consistency of my research, the fact that I always returned to the same organizations and shared the daily routines of their members, served to place me in a more horizontal relationship with them. I did not become a complete insider (something that was never my goal), but it was harder for my respondents to see me as a total outsider after me repeatedly working, having meals, and blocking roads with them.

The second dimension was my role as a researcher. My status as a young sociologist from a foreign university (who needed to obtain information in order to finish his degree) affected my work. Not only did it determine my priorities and shape the way I conducted research, but it also placed me in a given position vis-à-vis my respondents. For instance, when I first met activists and told them who I was, a frequent reply was, "[O]h, like the German/French/American/Italian that came here not long ago." That is, people in these organizations are used to scholars who come from developed countries and study them. As a result, I was automatically inserted from day one into a set of expectations about my work.

Even though I did not succeed completely (some people still confused me for an American, especially when they first met me), over time, I did manage to overcome some of the stereotypes associated with foreign scholars. The fact that I am Argentinean meant that I shared aspects of a common culture with respondents. As a result, not only did I know about my country's history and politics, but I was also able to have conversations on other topics. For instance, my knowledge of local soccer clubs (mostly from lesser-known second and third division leagues) helped me connect with participants and show that I could talk about more than sociology. In addition, some aspects of my personal history intersected with those of my respondents. For example, my mother worked for decades as a kindergarten teacher in some of the same neighborhoods I did research on, and even though I never joined any political group, I have participated in events closely associated with the piqueteros since I was a teenager. Coupled with the consistency of my fieldwork, these personal characteristics undermined some of the respondents' original preconceptions about my work.

The third dimension is what Loïc Wacquant calls the "intellectualist bias," the tendency to "see the world as a spectacle, as a set of significations to be interpreted rather than concrete problems to be solved practically" (1992: 41). Events that I saw as interesting social phenomena were, for my subjects, just a portion of their lives. This situation frequently caused a gap between me and my respondents with regard to what was important about their experiences. Some of the most fascinating interviews I had began with the interviewee apologizing for "not having anything interesting to say."

Reflexivity also entails honesty regarding the ethics of social research. I received IRB approval for my fieldwork and followed its directives. However, as is frequently the case for social researchers, some of the main dilemmas I faced exceeded the requirements of this office (see Blee and Currier 2011). Three of them were particularly important.

The first one refers to voluntariness. Prior to all my interviews, I made clear that participation was in no way mandatory. However, since many times local leaders encouraged people to talk to me, I wonder whether some did so only because they wanted to please my sponsor. I tried to counterbalance this issue by emphasizing that the respondent could refuse to participate at any moment, but it is hard to know how effective this was.

The second dilemma relates to my results. What if I found something that could be held against the organizations I study? More in general, what if my conclusions are used to delegitimize the piquetero movement? For example, one of my findings is that residents frequently perceive these organizations as part of traditional patronage networks linked to local political parties (see Auyero 2001; Quirós 2006). Although I interpret this as a positive thing (it is a sign that the piqueteros are effective problem-solvers), someone might use it to reinforce negative media stereotypes of the movement.

The third dilemma is what Gloria González-López (2011) calls "the maquiladora syndrome," that is, the dynamic by which researchers from developed nations visit a country in the Global South, extract information about the experiences of poor people, return to their universities, and use that evidence to advance their academic careers. Most activists said they were happy to tell their stories if it helped me obtain my degree. After I graduated, I shared my results with them, visiting organizations in 2016, 2017, and 2019 and distributing Spanish translations of each of my articles among activists. However, these measures can only ameliorate a structurally unequal relationship between researcher and subject.

Finally, I confronted many logistical challenges associated with doing international research. As a foreign graduate student at an American public university, these difficulties were compounded by limited funding options and recurrent budget cuts. Consequently, like innumerable other PhD students, I was unable to follow the traditional structure of doctoral programs involving ethnography (a few years of courses, followed by comprehensive exams, then a dissertation proposal, then a long period of data collection, and finally the writing of a thesis). Instead, I took advantage of summers to gather valuable ethnographic evidence. By the time I defended my proposal, I had already spent a total of five months in the field. This not only allowed me to improve my research design and strengthen applications for fellowships, it also offered flexibility in case lack of funding forced me to shorten my dissertation fieldwork.

Some personal characteristics, however, played in my favor. As a native of Greater Buenos Aires, I did not need to spend as much time familiarizing myself with the field site as I would if I had studied another location. My knowledge of local language, culture, and geography increased the efficiency of data collection and analysis at each stage. The fact that most of my relatives live in the area allowed me to save money on housing, at least for short periods of time.

Still, the financial costs of research were significant. Thankfully, I was able to cover them using several different fellowships. I received three summer scholarships from the Department of Latin American Studies at University of Texas at Austin: a Tinker Fellowship, a Lozano Long Field Research Grant, and an Argentinean Studies Program Award. The Department of Sociology at that same institution granted me an Urban Ethnography Lab Summer Grant and a Graduate Excellence Award. Two faculty, Javier Auyero and Sheldon Ekland-Olson, generously donated part of their research funds to cover some expenses. Finally, in early 2014, I received a Doctoral Dissertation Research Improvement Grant from the National Science Foundation (Award ID: 1406244). Together, these resources permitted me to spend more time in the field than I originally expected.

Beyond logistical issues, none of this research would have been possible without the help of hundreds of activists in the piquetero movement, who from the very beginning of my project were exceedingly supportive. They told me their personal histories, shared powerful memories, and invited me into their homes, their work, and their struggle. My gratitude to them, as well as my admiration for their efforts, knows no limits.

APPENDIX B

List of Recorded Interviewees

	Name (pseudonym)	Gender	Age [a]	District [b]	National origin	Beginning of participation	Organization (pseudonym)	Dropout? [a]	Date(s) of interview(s)
1	Julia	F	70s	Autonomous City of Buenos Aires	Paraguay	1994	ATDA	No	July 13, 2011
2	Luciano	M	50s	Lomas de Zamora	Argentina	1995	ATDA	No	July 13, 2011
3	Gustavo	M	40s	Lomas de Zamora	Argentina	1990s	MSP	No	July 16, 2011
4	Laura	F	40s	Florencio Varela	Argentina	1990s	FLS	No	July 18, 2011
5	Julio	M	40s	Florencio Varela	Argentina	1990s	FLS	No	July 18, 2011
6	Alberto	M	70s	Autonomous City of Buenos Aires	Argentina	2005	ATDA	No	July 20, 2011
7	Aarón	M	60s	Lomas de Zamora	Argentina	1990s	ATDA	No	July 20, 2011
8	Graciela	F	50s	Autonomous City of Buenos Aires	Argentina	2000	MOEL	No	July 20, 2011
9	Abelardo	M	60s	Autonomous City of Buenos Aires	Argentina	1990s	MOEL	No	July 20, 2011
10	Carlos	M	30s	Autonomous City of Buenos Aires	Argentina	1990s	MND	No	July 20, 2011
11	Cristian	M	20s	Autonomous City of Buenos Aires	Argentina	Unknown	FTEO	No	July 21, 2011
12	Patricio	M	50s	Autonomous City of Buenos Aires	Argentina	1990s	FTEO	No	July 21, 2011

(continued)

	Name (pseudonym)	Gender	Age [a]	District [b]	National origin	Beginning of participation	Organization (pseudonym)	Dropout? [a]	Date(s) of interview(s)
13	Humberto	M	50s	Autonomous City of Buenos Aires	Argentina	1990s	TVD	No	July 21, 2011
14	Tito	M	60s	Florencio Varela	Argentina	2000s	FLS	No	July 25, 2011, May 14, 2012, May 25, 2012
15	Clarisa	F	20s	Florencio Varela	Argentina	2004	FLS	No	July 25, 2011
16	Ciro	M	60s	Autonomous City of Buenos Aires	Argentina	2002	MOEL	No	July 26, 2011
17	Damián	M	50s	Autonomous City of Buenos Aires	Uruguay	2004	MOEL	No	July 26, 2011
18	Mario	M	40s	Lomas de Zamora	Argentina	1990s	MSP	No	July 28, 2011
19	Silvio	M	30s	Lomas de Zamora	Argentina	2010s	MSP	No	July 28, 2011
20	Anabella	F	40s	Lomas de Zamora	Argentina	2000s	MSP	No	July 28, 2011
21	Constanza	F	50s	Lomas de Zamora	Argentina	1990s	MSP	No	July 28, 2011, May 17, 2012
22	Alan	M	20s	Lomas de Zamora	Argentina	2008	MSP	No	July 28, 2011, April 11, 2014
23	Patricia	F	20s	La Matanza	Argentina	2005–2006	MND	No	July 28, 2011
24	Claudia	F	40s	La Matanza	Argentina	2010	MND	No	July 30, 2011, January 22, 2014, January 27, 2014

#	Name	Sex	Age	Location	Country	Year			Interview dates
25	Angelina	F	50s	La Matanza	Argentina	2005–2006	MND	No	July 30, 2011, February 19, 2014, February 21, 2014
26	Tita	F	70s	La Matanza	Paraguay	2003	MND	Yes	July 30, 2011, March 11, 2014
27	Josefa	F	60s	La Matanza	Argentina	2007	MND	No	July 30, 2011
28	Analía	F	50s	La Matanza	Argentina	2005	MND	No	July 30, 2011, August 5, 2011, January 9, 2014, July 15, 2014
29	Mariana	F	30s	La Matanza	Argentina	2001	MND	No	July 30, 2011
30	Leila	F	20s	La Matanza	Argentina	2003	MND	No	July 30, 2011
31	Bautista	M	50s	La Matanza	Argentina	2004	MND	No	August 5, 2011, June 14, 2013
32	Lourdes	F	50s	La Matanza	Argentina	2000	MND	No	August 6, 2011, April 24, 2014
33	Osvaldo	M	50s	Autonomous City of Buenos Aires	Argentina	2000	MOEL	No	August 9, 2011
34	Arnaldo	M	50s	Autonomous City of Buenos Aires	Argentina	1995	MOEL	No	August 9, 2011
35	Facundo	M	40s	La Matanza	Argentina	2001	MND	No	May 15, 2012

(*continued*)

	Name (pseudonym)	Gender	Age [a]	District [b]	National origin	Beginning of participation	Organization (pseudonym)	Dropout? [a]	Date(s) of interview(s)
36	Salvador	M	20s	Lanús	Argentina	2002	CEP	No	May 16, 2012
37	Brian	M	20s	Lanús	Argentina	2002	CEP	No	May 16, 2012
38	Paula	F	20s	Lomas de Zamora	Argentina	2011	MSP	No	May 17, 2012
39	Samuel	M	20s	Lomas de Zamora	Argentina	2012	MSP	No	May 17, 2012
40	Gisela	F	30s	Lomas de Zamora	Argentina	2001	MSP	No	May 17, 2012, June 9, 2013
41	Juliana	F	40s	La Matanza	Argentina	2010	MND	No	May 18, 2012
42	Lucía	F	20s	La Matanza	Argentina	2007	MND	No	May 18, 2012
43	Hortencia	F	60s	Lomas de Zamora	Argentina	1990s	MSP	No	May 19, 2012
44	Pablo	M	70s	Lomas de Zamora	Argentina	Unknown	MSP	No	May 19, 2012
45	Aurora	F	50s	Lomas de Zamora	Argentina	2004	MSP	No	May 19, 2012, May 29, 2012
46	Paola	F	40s	La Matanza	Argentina	2003	MND	No	May 22, 2012
47	Ernestina	F	60s	Florencio Varela	Argentina	2003	FLS	No	May 25, 2012
48	Eugenio	M	70s	Florencio Varela	Argentina	2000s	FLS	No	May 25, 2012
49	Belén	F	50s	La Matanza	Argentina	1990s	MOEL	No	May 28, 2012
50	Evangelina	F	20s	Lomas de Zamora	Argentina	2010	MSP	No	May 28, 2012
51	Luciana	F	30s	Lomas de Zamora	Argentina	2010	MSP	No	May 28, 2012

	Name	Sex	Age	Location	Country	Year	Org	Leader	Date
52	Sergio	M	40s	La Matanza	Argentina	2008	MLJ	No	June 1, 2012
53	Inés	F	50s	La Matanza	Argentina	1999	MLJ	No	June 1, 2012
54	Jonathan	M	30s	La Matanza	Argentina	2000s	MLJ	No	June 1, 2012
55	Fernanda	F	50s	La Matanza	Bolivia	2002	MLJ	No	June 1, 2012, June 6, 2013
56	Norma	F	60s	La Matanza	Argentina	1993	MLJ	No	June 1, 2012, January 15, 2014, April 1, 2014
57	Antonio	M	20s	Florencio Varela	Argentina	2011	FLS	No	June 4, 2012
58	Federica	F	50s	Lomas de Zamora	Argentina	1998	MSP	No	June 6, 2012
59	Simón	M	40s	Lomas de Zamora	Argentina	2007	ATDA	No	June 6, 2012
60	Lía	F	50s	Lomas de Zamora	Argentina	2001	ATDA	No	June 6, 2012
61	Diego	M	50s	La Matanza	Uruguay	1990s	MLJ	No	June 9, 2012
62	Iván	F	20s	La Matanza	Argentina	2005	MLJ	No	June 9, 2012
63	Néstor	M	30s	La Matanza	Argentina	2009	MND	Yes	June 11, 2012
64	Luisa	M	70s	Esteban Echeverría	Argentina	2000s	TVD	No	June 12, 2012
65	Virginia	F	40s	Lanús	Argentina	1999	CEP	No	June 14, 2012
66	Iliana	F	40s	Lanús	Argentina	2009	CEP	No	June 14, 2012
67	Gloria	F	50s	Lanús	Paraguay	1999	CEP	No	June 14, 2012
68	Estela	F	40s	Lanús	Argentina	2001	CEP	No	June 26, 2012

(continued)

	Name (pseudonym)	Gender	Age [a]	District [b]	National origin	Beginning of participation	Organization (pseudonym)	Dropout? [a]	Date(s) of interview(s)
69	Carmen	F	50s	Lanús	Argentina	2000	CEP	No	June 26, 2012
70	Andrés	M	60s	Lanús	Argentina	2000	CEP	No	June 26, 2012
71	Luis	M	40s	Lomas de Zamora	Argentina	2009	MSP	Yes	May 13, 2013, June 27, 2013
72	Ernesto	M	40s	La Matanza	Argentina	2010	MND	Yes	May 17, 2013, June 20, 2013, June 6, 2014
73	Víctor	M	20s	Lomas de Zamora	Argentina	2009	MSP	No	May 21, 2013
74	Fabián	M	30s	Florencio Varela	Argentina	2003	FLS	No	May 23, 2013, June 5, 2013, June 25, 2013
75	Carolina	F	20s	La Matanza	Argentina	1990s	MLJ	No	May 24, 2013
76	Lucila	F	20s	La Matanza	Argentina	2005	MLJ	No	May 24, 2013, June 3, 2013
77	Maitén	F	20s	Lomas de Zamora	Argentina	2010	MSP	No	June 9, 2013, June 27, 2013
78	Guadalupe	F	50s	La Matanza	Uruguay	1994	MLJ	No	June 13, 2013
79	Aníbal	M	50s	La Matanza	Argentina	2000s	MLJ	No	June 13, 2013
80	David	M	30s	La Matanza	Argentina	2007	MLJ	Yes	June 13, 2013

	Name	Sex	Age	Location	Country	Year	Interviewer	Consent	Dates
81	Lionel	M	20s	Florencio Varela	Argentina	2006	FLS	No	June 19, 2013, June 21, 2013
82	Kevin	M	20s	Florencio Varela	Argentina	2008	FLS	No	June 19, 2013, June 27, 2013
83	Melina	F	30s	La Matanza	Argentina	2010	MND	No	June 20, 2013
84	Celeste	F	30s	Florencio Varela	Argentina	2001	FLS	No	June 26, 2013
85	Milagros	F	50s	La Matanza	Argentina	2000	MLJ	No	January 2, 2014, March 10, 2014
86	Paloma	F	20s	La Matanza	Argentina	2010	MND	No	January 13, 2014, March 14, 2014
87	Olivia	F	50s	La Matanza	Argentina	1999	MLJ	No	January 15, 2014
88	Renata	F	60s	La Matanza	Argentina	1994	MLJ	No	January 20, 2014
89	Violeta	F	40s	La Matanza	Argentina	2012	MLJ	No	January 23, 2014, January 30, 2014
90	Aldana	F	60s	La Matanza	Argentina	2000	MLJ	No	February 12, 2014
91	Brisa	F	50s	Florencio Varela	Argentina	1997	FLS	No	February 13, 2014
92	Vanesa	F	50s	Florencio Varela	Argentina	1990s	FLS	No	February 13, 2014, February 18, 2014
93	Valentina	F	60s	La Matanza	Argentina	2001	MLJ	No	February 14, 2014
94	Sol	F	20s	La Matanza	Argentina	2012–2013	MND	Yes	February 21, 2014
95	Jazmín	F	50s	La Matanza	Argentina	2010	MND	No	February 25, 2014, May 26, 2014

(continued)

	Name (pseudonym)	Gender	Age[a]	District[b]	National origin	Beginning of participation	Organization (pseudonym)	Dropout?[a]	Date(s) of interview(s)
96	Alejandro	M	50s	La Matanza	Argentina	1990s	MND	No	February 26, 2014, July 15, 2014
97	Giugliana	F	30s	La Matanza	Argentina	2000s	MND	No	February 26, 2014
98	Tatiana	F	40s	La Matanza	Argentina	2000s	MLJ	No	February 27, 2014, March 10, 2014
99	Pilar	F	60s	La Matanza	Argentina	2001	MND	Yes	March 12, 2014
100	Axel	M	30s	Florencio Varela	Argentina	2004	FLS	Yes	March 26, 2014, March 31, 2014
101	Ezequiel	M	40s	Lomas de Zamora	Argentina	1990s	MSP	No	March 28, 2014
102	Malena	F	60s	La Matanza	Argentina	2013	MND	No	April 3, 2014
103	Mauro	M	50s	La Matanza	Argentina	2000s	MLJ	No	April 21, 2014, May 5, 2014
104	Camila	F	60s	La Matanza	Argentina	2009	MND	Yes	April 24, 2014, April 25, 2014
105	Mabel	F	60s	La Matanza	Argentina	2014	MND	Yes	April 25, 2014
106	Fabricio	M	20s	Florencio Varela	Argentina	2006	MND	Yes	April 29, 2014
107	Macarena	F	50s	La Matanza	Argentina	1997	MLJ	No	May 5, 2014
108	Catalina	F	40s	La Matanza	Argentina	1996	MLJ	No	May 6, 2014

	Name	Sex	Age	Location	Country	Year	Code	Interviewed	Date
109	Isabel	F	70s	La Matanza	Argentina	2003	MLJ	No	May 6, 2014, June 9, 2014
110	Priscila	F	60s	La Matanza	Paraguay	2000s	MLJ	No	May 19, 2014
111	Jessica	F	20s	La Matanza	Argentina	2000s	MLJ	No	May 19, 2014
112	Mora	F	50s	La Matanza	Argentina	2000s	MND	No	May 22, 2014
113	Miranda	F	50s	La Matanza	Argentina	2006	MND	No	May 22, 2014, July 15, 2014
114	Brenda	F	40s	La Matanza	Peru	2011	MND	No	May 22, 2014
115	Sofía	F	50s	La Matanza	Argentina	2011	MND	No	May 26, 2014
116	Victoria	F	50s	Florencio Varela	Argentina	1999	FLS	No	May 27, 2014, June 10, 2014
117	Sabrina	F	50s	La Matanza	Argentina	2003	MLJ	No	June 2, 2014
118	Horacio	M	50s	La Matanza	Paraguay	2013	MND	No	June 6, 2014
119	Juan Pablo	M	40s	La Matanza	Paraguay	2000	MLJ	Yes	June 7, 2014
120	Clara	F	40s	Florencio Varela	Paraguay	2013	FLS	No	June 10, 2014
121	Enzo	M	40s	La Matanza	Argentina	Unknown	MLJ	No	June 16, 2014
122	Candela	F	40s	La Matanza	Argentina	2000	MLJ	No	June 16, 2014
123	Elías	M	60s	La Matanza	Argentina	1990s	MLJ	No	June 18, 2014
124	Pedro	M	40s	Florencio Varela	Argentina	2002	FLS	Yes	June 22, 2014
125	Rocío	F	50s	La Matanza	Argentina	2011	MND	No	June 24, 2014
126	Ornella	O	40s	La Matanza	Argentina	2012	MND	No	June 24, 2014, July 8, 2014

(continued)

	Name (pseudonym)	Gender	Age [a]	District [b]	National origin	Beginning of participation	Organization (pseudonym)	Dropout? [a]	Date(s) of interview(s)
127	Lázaro	M	50s	La Matanza	Argentina	2001	MLJ	No	June 27, 2014
128	Nahuel	M	40s	La Matanza	Argentina	1990s	MLJ	No	July 6, 2014
129	Bianca	O	50s	La Matanza	Argentina	2011–2012	MND	No	July 8, 2014
130	Antonella	F	60s	La Matanza	Argentina	1999	MLJ	No	July 23, 2014
131	Gabriel	M	60s	La Matanza	Argentina	2001	MLJ	No	July 23, 2014
132	Dante	M	50s	La Matanza	Argentina	1990s	MND	Yes	July 24, 2014
133	Soledad	F	60s	La Matanza	Argentina	1996	MLJ	Yes	July 25, 2014

Notes
[a] At the time of the last interview with the respondent.
[b] Refers to the district where the interview was performed.

List of Organizations

Organization (pseudonym)	Overall position with regard to the national government [c]
ATDA	Anti-government
MSP	Pro-government
FLS	Anti-government
MOEL	Pro-government
MND	Anti-government
FTEO	Anti-government
TVD	Anti-government
CEP	Anti-government
MLJ	Anti-government

Notes
[c] During the duration of the fieldwork (2011–2014).

References

Almeida, Paul. 2007. "Defensive Mobilization: Popular Movements against Economic Adjustment Policies in Latin America." *Latin American Perspectives* 34(3): 123–139.

Alvaredo, Facundo, Guillermo Cruces, and Leonardo Gasparini. 2018. "A Short Episodic History of Income Distribution in Argentina." *Latin American Economic Review* 27(7): 1–45.

Alvarez, Sonia. 1999. "Advocating Feminism: The Latin American Feminist NGO 'Boom'." *International Feminist Journal of Politics* 1(2): 181–209.

Alvarez, Sonia. 2009. "Beyond NGO-ization?: Reflections from Latin America." *Development* 52: 175.

Amnesty International. 2017. "Urgent Action: Arbitrarily Detained for Over a Year." Retrieved February 28, 2018, from www.amnesty.org/download/Documents/AMR1356122017ENGLISH.pdf.

Amnesty International. 2018. "Argentina: Amnesty International Calls on President Macri to Address Key Human Rights Issues." Press Release, in April 12, 2018, https://www.refworld.org/docid/5b323264a.html.

Andrews, Molly. 1991. *Lifetimes of Commitment*. Cambridge: Cambridge University Press.

Assusa, Gonzalo. 2018. "Ni jóvenes, ni desempleados, ni peligrosos, ni novedosos. Una crítica sociológica del concepto de 'jóvenes nini' en torno los casos de España, México y Argentina." *Cuadernos de Relaciones Laborales* 37 (1): 91–111.

Atkinson, Robert. 1998. *The Life Story Interview*. Thousand Oaks: SAGE.

Auyero, Javier. 2001. *Poor People's Politics*. Durham: Duke University Press.

Auyero, Javier. 2002. *La Protesta*. Buenos Aires: Libros del Rojas.

Auyero, Javier. 2003. *Contentious Lives: Two Argentine Women, Two Protests, and the Quest for Recognition*. Durham: Duke University Press.

Auyero, Javier. 2012. *Patients of the State: The Politics of Waiting in Argentina*. Durham: Duke University Press.

Auyero, Javier and Débora Swistun. 2009. *Flammable. Environmental Suffering in an Argentinean Shantytown*. New York: Oxford University Press.

Auyero, Javier and Kristine Kilanski. 2015. "From 'Making Toast' to 'Splitting Apples': Dissecting 'Care' in the Midst of Chronic Violence." *Theory and Society* 44(5): 393–414.

Auyero, Javier and María Fernanda Berti. 2015. *In Harm's Way. The Dynamics of Urban Violence*. Princeton: Princeton University Press.

Baiocchi, Gianpaolo. 2005. *Militants and Citizens: The Politics of Participatory Democracy in Porto Alegre*. Stanford: Stanford University Press.

Baker, Andy and Kenneth F. Greene. 2011. "The Latin American Left's Mandate: Free Market Policies and Issue Voting in New Democracies." *World Politics* 63 (1): 43–77.

Barbetta, Pablo and Pablo Lapegna. 2001. "Cuando la protesta toma forma: los cortes de ruta en el norte salteño." Pp. 231–257 in *La protesta social en la Argentina: transformaciones económicas y crisis social en el interior del país*, edited by Norma Giarraca. Buenos Aires: Alianza Editorial.

Barrientos, Armando and Claudio Santibañez. 2009. "New Forms of Social Assistance and the Evolution of Social Protection in Latin America." *Journal of Latin American Studies* 41: 1–26.

Battezzati, Santiago. 2012. "La Tupac Amaru: Intermediación De Intereses De Los Sectores Populares Informales En La Provincia De Jujuy." *Desarrollo Económico* 52(205): 147–171.

Battistini, Osvaldo. 2007. "Luchas sociales en crisis y estabilidad." Pp. 95–103 in *Movimientos sociales y acción colectiva en la Argentina de hoy*, edited by E. Villanueva and A. Massetti. Buenos Aires: Prometeo.

Becker, Howard. 1963. *Outsiders. Studies in the Sociology of Deviance*. New York: Free Press.

Becker, Howard. 2002. "The Life History and the Scientific Mosaic." Pp. 63–74 in *Qualitative Research Methods*, edited by Darin Weinberg. Oxford: Blackwell

Benclowicz, José Daniel. 2011. "Repensando los orígenes del movimiento piquetero: Miseria y experiencias de lucha antes de las contrarreformas de la decada de 1990 en el norte argentino." *Latin American Research Review* 46(2): 79–103.

Benclowicz, José Daniel. 2013. *Estado de malestar y tradiciones de lucha: genealogía del movimiento piquetero de Tartagal-Mosconi (1930–2001)*. Buenos Aires: Biblos.

Benford, Robert and David Snow. 2000. "Framing Processes and Social Movements: An Overview and Assessment." *Annual Review of Sociology* 26: 611–639.

Benzecry, Claudio. 2011. *The Opera Fanatic: Ethnography of an Obsession*. Chicago: University of Chicago Press.

Bertranou, Fabio and Luis Casanova. 2014. *Informalidad laboral en Argentina. Segmentos críticos y políticas para la formalización*. Buenos Aires: Organización Internacional del Trabajo.

Bidaseca, Karina. 2006. "Piqueteras: Identidad, política y resistencia." *Realidad Económica* 296.

Bird, Caroline. 1966. *The Invisible Scar: The Great Depression, and What It Did to American Life, from Then Until Now.* London: Longman.

Blee, Kathleen. 2012. *Democracy in the Making. How Activists Group Form.* New York: Oxford University Press.

Blee, Kathleen and Ashley Currier. 2011. "Ethics Beyond the IRB: An Introductory Essay." *Qualitative Sociology* 34(3): 401–413.

Bourdieu, Pierre. 1977. *Outline of a Theory of Practice.* New York: Cambridge University Press.

Bourdieu, Pierre. 1988. "Vive la crise! For Heterodoxy in Social Science." *Theory and Society* 17: 773–787.

Bourdieu, Pierre. 1997. *Pascalian Meditations.* Stanford: Stanford University Press.

Bourgois, Philippe. 1996. *In Search of Respect. Selling Crack in El Barrio.* New York: Cambridge University Press.

Boyanovsky Bazán, Christian. 2010. *El Aluvión. Del piquete al gobierno. Los movimientos sociales y el kirchnerismo.* Buenos Aires: Sudamericana.

Bromley-Davenport, Harry, Julie MacLeavy, and David Manley. 2018. "Brexit in Sunderland: The Production of Difference and Division in the UK Referendum on European Union Membership." *Environment and Planning C: Politics and Space* 37(5): 795–812.

Burbach, Roger, Michael Fox, and Federico Fuentes. 2013. *Latin America's Turbulent Transitions: The Future of Twenty-First Century Socialism.* New York: Zed Books.

CAC (Cámara Argentina de Comercio). 2013. "Empleo No Registrado: Evolución, características y disparidades regionales." Retrieved April 17, 2020, from www.ucaece.edu.ar/wp-content/uploads/2016/04/CAC-Informe-Empleo-No-Registrado-Nov2013.pdf.

Cárdenas, Mauricio, Rafael De Hoyos, and Miguel Székely. 2015. "Out-of-School and Out-of-Work Youth in Latin America: A Persistent Problem in a Decade of Prosperity." *Economía* 16(1): 1–40.

CELS (Centro de Estudios Legales y Sociales). 2003. "El Estado frente a la protesta social 1996–2002." Retrieved November 4, 2016, from www.cels.org.ar/common/documentos/protesta_social.pdf.

CELS (Centro de Estudios Legales y Sociales). 2017. "El Derecho a la Protesta Social en Argentina." Retrieved April 15, 2020, from www.cels.org.ar/web/wp-content/uploads/2017/06/Protesta_Arg.pdf.

CEPAL (Comisión Económica para América Latina y el Caribe). 2015. "Bases de datos y publicaciones estadísticas." Retrieved April 21, 2017, from http://estadisticas.cepal.org/cepalstat/WEB_CEPALSTAT/Portada.asp.

Charlesworth, Simon. 2000. *A Phenomenology of Working Class Experience.* Cambridge: Cambridge University Press.

Colabella, Laura. 2012. "La casa, el comedor y la copa de leche. Los espacios de la comensalía en los sectores populares." *Apuntes de Investigación del CECYP* 22: 59–78.

Colectivo Situaciones and MTD Solano. 2002. *La Hipótesis 891. Más Allá de los Piquetes.* Buenos Aires: Editorial El Colectivo.

Cooley, Charles Horton. 1902. *Human Nature and the Social Order*. New York: Schocken Books

Coontz, Stephanie. 1992. *The Way We Never Were: American Families and the Nostalgia Trap*. New York: Basic Books.

Corrigall-Brown, Catherine. 2011. *Patterns of Protest: Trajectories of Participation in Social Movements*. Stanford: Stanford University Press.

Corsiglia, Lucía. 2012. *Jóvenes piqueteros y encapuchados: Algunas preguntas sobre las marcas de lo plebeyo en las formas de la acción colectiva*. La Plata: Universidad Nacional de La Plata, Facultad de Periodismo y Comunicación Social.

Cross, Cecilia and Ada Cora Freytes Frey. 2007. "Movimientos Piqueteros: tensiones de género en la definición del liderazgo." *Argumentos* 20(55): 77–94.

Crossley, Nick. 2003. "From Reproduction to Transformation. Social Movement Fields and the Radical Habitus." *Theory, Culture and Society* 20(6): 43–68.

D'Alessandre, Vanesa. 2013. "Soy lo que ves y no es. Adolescentes y jóvenes que no estudian ni trabajan en América Latina." *Cuaderno SITEAL, UNESCO* 17: 1-44.

D'Alimonte, Roberto. 2019. "How the Populists Won in Italy." *Journal of Democracy* 30(1): 114–127.

Delamata, Gabriela. 2004. *Los Barrios Desbordados. Las Organizaciones de Desocupados del Gran Buenos Aires*. Buenos Aires: Eudeba.

Delamata, Gabriela (ed.). 2009a. *Movilizaciones Sociales: ¿Nuevas Ciudadanías?*. Buenos Aires: Biblos.

Delamata, Gabriela. 2009b. "Movilización colectiva y transformaciones de la ciudadanía en la Argentina reciente (1980–2007)." *Ayer* 73(1):73–102.

Denzin, Norman. 1978. *Sociological Methods: A Sourcebook*. Hawthorne: Aldine De Gruyter

Desmond, Matthew. 2007. *On the Fireline: Living and Dying with Wildland Firefighters*. Chicago: University of Chicago Press.

Diani, Mario. 2004. "Networks and Participation." Pp. 339–359 in *The Blackwell Companion to Social Movements*, edited by D. Snow, S. Soule and H. Kriesi. Oxford: Blackwell.

Donza. Eduardo (ed.). 2019. *Heterogeneidad y fragmentación del mercado de trabajo (2010–2018)*. Buenos Aires: Editorial de la Universidad Católica Argentina.

Dorling, Danny and Sally Tomlinson. 2019. *Rule Britannia: Brexit and the End of Empire*. London: Biteback Publishing.

Ellner, Steve. 2013. "Latin America's Radical Left in Power. Complexities and Challenges in the Twenty-first Century." *Latin American Perspectives* 40(3): 5-25.

Ellner, Steve. 2020. *Latin America's Pink Tide. Breakthroughs and Shortcomings*. London: Rowman and Littlefield.

Emerson, Robert, Rachel Fretz, and Linda Shaw. 1995. *Writing Ethnographic Fieldnotes*. Chicago: University of Chicago Press.

Epstein, Edward. 2006. "The Piquetero Movement in Greater Buenos Aires: Political Protests by the Unemployed Poor during the Crisis." Pp. 95–115 in

Broken Promises? The Argentine Crisis and Argentine Democracy, edited by Edward. Epstein, and David Pion-Berlin. Lanham: Lexington Books.

Epstein, Edward. 2009. "Perpetuating Social Movements amid Declining Opportunity: the Survival Strategies of Two Argentine Piquetero Groups." *European Review of Latin American and Caribbean Studies* 86: 3–19.

Ferraudi Curto, Maria Cecilia. 2009. "Hoy a las 2, Cabildo. Etnografía en una organización piquetera." Pp. 153–177 in *La vida política en los barrios populares de Buenos Aires*, edited by A. Grimson, M. C. Ferraudi Curto, and R. Segura. Buenos Aires: Prometeo.

Ferree, Myra Marx and Carol McClurg Mueller. 2004. "Feminism and the Women's Movement: A Global Perspective." Pp. 576–604 in *The Blackwell Companion to Social Movements*, edited by D. Snow, S. Soule, and H. Kriesi. Oxford: Blackwell.

Ferrero, Juan Pablo, Ana Natalucci, and Luciana Tatagiba (eds.). 2019. *Socio-Political Dynamics Within the Crisis of the Left: Argentina and Brazil*. London: Rowman & Littlefield.

Fillieule, Olivier. 2010. "Some Elements of an Interactionist Approach to Political Disengagement." *Social Movement Studies* 9(1): 1–15.

Fisher, Dana and Paul-Brian McInerney. 2012. "The Limits of Networks in Social Movement Retention: On Canvassers and Their Careers." *Mobilization* 17(2): 102–128.

Flores, Toty (ed.). 2005. *De la culpa a la autogestión: un recorrido del Movimiento de Trabajadores Desocupados de La Matanza*. Buenos Aires: Peña Lillo

Flores, Toty (ed.). 2007. *Cuando con otros somos nosotros: la experiencia asociativa del Movimiento de Trabajadores Desocupados de La Matanza*. Buenos Aires: Continente.

Fougère, Denis, Julien Pouget and Francis Kramarz. 2009. "Youth Unemployment and Crime in France." *Journal of the European Economic Association* 7(5): 909–938.

FPDS (Frente Popular Darío Santillán). 2003. *Darío y Maxi: Dignidad piquetera*. Buenos Aires: Editorial El Colectivo

Frank, Thomas. 2004. *What's the Matter with Kansas?*. New York: Henry Holt.

Feijoó, Maria del Carmen. 2015. "Los ni-ni: una visión mitológica de los jóvenes latinoamericanos." *Voces en el Fenix* 6(51): 22–31.

Festinger, Leon. 1957. *A Theory of Cognitive Dissonance*. Stanford: Stanford University Press

Forni, Pablo. 2020. "The missionaries of Francis. The Theology of the People and the Unification of the Argentina Piquetero Movement." *Latin American Perspectives* 47(5): 35–48.

Fornillo, Bruno, Analía García and Melina Vazquez. 2008. "Las organizaciones de desocupados autónomas en la Argentina reciente. Redefiniciones Político-ideologicas e identitarias en el Frente Popular Darío Santillán." Pp. 367–394 in *La huella piquetera: avatares de las organizaciones de desocupados después de 2001*, edited by S. Pereyra, G. Pérez and F. Schuster. La Plata: Ediciones Al Margen.

Frederic, Sabina. 2009. "Trabajo barrial, reconocimiento y desigualdad en Lomas de Zamora, 1990–2005." Pp. 249–266 in *La vida política en los barrios populares de Buenos Aires*, edited by A. Grimson, M. C. Ferraudi Curto, and R. Segura. Buenos Aires: Prometeo.

Fridman, Daniel. 2016. *Freedom from Work. Embracing Financial Self-Help in the United States and Argentina*. Stanford: Stanford University Press.

Garay, Candelaria. 2007. "Social Policy and Collective Action: Unemployed Workers, Community Associations and Protest in Argentina." *Politics & Society* 35(2): 301–328.

Geertz, Clifford. 1973. *The Interpretation of Cultures*. New York: Basic Books.

Gerchunoff, Pablo and Lucas Llach. 2003. *El Ciclo de la Ilusión y el Desencanto*. Buenos Aires: Ariel.

Gerchunoff, Pablo and Lucas Llach. 2004. *Entre la Equidad y el Crecimiento*. Buenos Aires: Siglo XXI.

Gerchunoff, Pablo and Pablo Fajgelbaum. 2006. *¿Por qué la Argentina no fue Australia?* Buenos Aires: Siglo XXI.

Gerschick, Thomas. 2000. "Toward a Theory of Disability and Gender." *Signs* 25 (4): 1263–1268.

Gethin, Amory and Marc Morgan. 2018. "Brazil Divided: Hindsights on the Growing Politicisation of Inequality." *World Inequality Database, World Issue Brief* 2018/3.

Giddens, Anthony. 1979. *Central Problems in Social Theory*. Berkeley: University of California Press.

Giugni, Marco. 2007. "Personal and Biographical Consequences." Pp. 489–507 in *The Blackwell Companion to Social Movements*, edited by David Snow, Sarah Soule, y Hanspeter Kriesi. Oxford: Blackwell.

Giusto, Patricio. 2016. "Por segundo año consecutivo hubo más de 6.000 piquetes." Informe de Monitoreo. Buenos Aires: Diagnóstico Político.

Goffman, Erving. 1959. *The Presentation of Self in Everyday Life*. New York: Anchor Books.

Gómez, Marcelo. 2009. "Las políticas de empleo como respuesta estatal a la acción colectiva de los movimientos de desocupados. Entre el clientelismo, el 'empowerment' y la lucha política." Pp. 117–152 in *Los Movimientos Sociales Dicen*, edited by M. Gómez and A. Massetti. Buenos Aires: Nueva Trilce.

Gómez, Marcelo and Astor Massetti. 2009. *Los Movimientos Sociales Dicen*. Buenos Aires: Nueva Trilce.

González de la Rocha, Mercedes. 1986. *Los Recursos de la Pobreza. Familias de bajos ingresos en Guadalajara*. Guadalajara: El Colegio de Jalisco.

González de la Rocha, Mercedes. 2006. "Vanishing Assets: Cumulative Disadvantage among the Urban Poor." *The Annals of the American Academy of Political and Social Science* 606: 68–94.

González-López, Gloria. 2011. "Mindful Ethics: Comments on Informant-centered Practices in Sociological Research." *Qualitative Sociology* 34: 447–461.

Goodwin, Jeff. 1997. "The Libidinal Constitution of a High-Risk Social Movement: Affectual Ties and Solidarity in the Huk Rebellion, 1946 to 1954." *American Sociological Review* 62(1): 53–69.

Goodwin, Jeff and James Jasper. 1999. "Caught in a Winding, Snarling Vine: The Structural Bias of Political Process Theory." *Sociological Forum* 14(1): 27–54.

Goodwin, Jeff, James Jasper and Francesca Polletta (eds.). 2001. *Passionate Politics. Emotions and Social Movements.* Chicago: University of Chicago Press.

Gould, Deborah. 2009. *Moving Politics: Emotions and ACT-UP's Fight Against AIDS.* Chicago: University of Chicago Press.

Grabia, Gustavo. 2015. *La Doce. La Verdadera Historia De La Barra Brava De Boca.* Buenos Aires: Sudamericana.

Grimson, Alejandro. 2007. "Ethnic (In)Visibility in Neoliberal Argentina." *NACLA*, September 25, 2007, https://nacla.org/article/ethnic-invisibility-neoliberal-argentina.

Grimson, Alejandro. 2009. "Introducción: clasificaciones espaciales y territorialización de la política en Buenos Aires." Pp. 11–38 in *La Vida Política en los Barrios Populares de Buenos Aires*, edited by Grimson, Alejandro, Maria Cecilia Ferraudi Curto and Ramiro Segura, Buenos Aires: Prometeo.

Grimson, Alejandro, Maria Cecilia Ferraudi Curto and Ramiro Segura (eds.). 2009. *La Vida Política en los Barrios Populares de Buenos Aires.* Buenos Aires: Prometeo.

Grimson, Alejandro. 2018. *Mitomanías Argentinas. Como Hablamos de Nosotros Mismos.* Buenos Aires: Siglo XXI.

Groisman, Fernando. 2013. "Gran Buenos Aires: Polarización de ingresos, clase media e informalidad laboral, 1974–2010." *Revista CEPAL* 109: 85–105.

Gross, Steven Jay and C. Michael Niman. 1975. "Attitude Behavior Consistency: A Review." *Public Opinion Quarterly* 39(3): 358–368.

Hale, Charles. 2011. "Resistencia Para Que? Territory, Autonomy and Neoliberal Entanglements in the 'Empty Spaces' of Central America." *Economy and Society* 40: 184–210.

Harvey, David. 2005. *A Brief History of Neoliberalism.* New York: Oxford University Press.

Hendler, Ariel, Mariano Pacheco, and Juan Rey. 2012. *Darío Santillán. El militante que puso el cuerpo.* Buenos Aires: Planeta.

Hintze, Susana. 1989. *Estrategias Alimentarias de Supervivencia. Un estudio de caso en el Gran Buenos Aires.* Buenos Aires: Centro Editor de América Latina.

Hirschman, Albert O. 1982. *Shifting Involvements. Private Interest and Public Action.* Princeton: Princeton University Press.

Hobsbawm, Eric. 1994. *The Age of Extremes: A History of the World, 1914–1991.* New York: Vintage.

Hochschild, Arlie. 2016. *Strangers in Their Own Land: Anger and Mourning on the American Right.* New York: The New Press.

Hoggart, Richard. 1963. *The Uses of Literacy.* Harmondsworth: Penguin.

HRW (Human Rights Watch). 2016. "Letter to President Macri on the Sala Case." Retrieved February 28, 2018, from www.hrw.org/news/2016/12/22/letter-president-macri-sala-case#.

Hunter, Wendy and Timothy Power. "Bolsonaro and Brazil's Illiberal Backlash." *Journal of Democracy* 30(1): 68–82.

Ihlanfeldt, Kevin. 2007. "Neighborhood Drug Crime and Young Males' Job Accessibility." *The Review of Economics and Statistics* 89(1): 151–164.

Inzlicht Michael, Amitai Shenhav, Christopher Olivola. 2018. "The Effort Paradox: Effort Is Both Costly and Valued." *Trends in Cognitive Science* 22 (4): 337–349.

Jahoda, Marie, Paul Lazarsfeld and Hans Zeisel. 1977. *Marienthal. The Sociography of an Unemployed Community*. Piscataway: Transaction Publishers.

James, Daniel. 1988. *Resistance and Integration. Peronism and the Argentine Working Class. 1946–1976*. New York: Cambridge University Press.

Jasper, James M. 1997. *The Art of Moral Protest*. Chicago: Chicago University Press.

Jasper, James M. 2011. "Emotions and Social Movements: Twenty Years of Theory and Research." *Annual Review of Sociology* 37: 285–303.

Jerolmack, Colin and Shamus Khan. 2014. "Talk is Cheap: Ethnography and the Attitudinal Fallacy." *Sociological Methods and Research* 43(2): 178–209.

Johnston, Hank and Paul Almeida (eds.). 2006. *Latin American Social Movements: Globalization, Democratization, and Transnational Networks*. Lanham: Rowman & Littlefield.

Katz, Jack. 1988. *Seductions of Crime: Moral and Sensual Attractions in Doing Evil*. New York: Basic Books.

Katz, Jack. 2001. "From How to Why. On Luminous Description and Causal Inference in Ethnography (Part 1)." *Ethnography* 2(4): 443–473.

Katz, Jack. 2002. "From How to Why. On Luminous Description and Causal Inference in Ethnography (Part 2)." *Ethnography* 3(1): 63–90.

Kessler, Gabriel. 1997. "Algunas implicancias de la experiencia de desocupación para el individuo y su familia." Pp. 111–160 in *Sin Trabajo. Las características del desempleo y sus efectos en la sociedad argentina*, edited by Luis Beccaria and Néstor López, Buenos Aires: Losada.

Kaese, Fynn and Jonas Wolff. 2016. "Piqueteros after the Hype: Unemployed Movements in Argentina, 2008–2015." *European Review of Latin American and Caribbean Studies* 102: 47–68.

Klandermans, Bert. 1997. *The Social Psychology of Protest*. Oxford: Blackwell.

Klatch, Rebecca. 2004. "The Underside of Social Movements: The Effects of Destructive Affective Ties." *Qualitative Sociology* 27(4): 487–509.

Kohan, Aníbal. 2002. *A las calles!: una historia de los movimientos piqueteros y caceroleros de los '90 al 2002*. Buenos Aires: Colihue.

Kruger, Justin, Derrick Wirtz, Leaf Van Boven, and William Altermatt. 2004. "The Effort Heuristic." *Journal of Experimental Social Psychology* 40: 91–98.

Laing, Ronald. 1961. *The Self and Others*. London: Tavistock.

Lamont, Michelle. 2000. *The Dignity of Working Men*. Cambridge: Harvard University Press.

Lapegna, Pablo. 2013. "Social Movements and Patronage Politics: Processes of Demobilization and Dual Pressure." *Sociological Forum* 28(4): 842–863.

Lapegna, Pablo. 2016. *Soybeans and Power. Genetically Modified Crops, Environmental Politics, and Social Movements in Argentina*. New York: Oxford University Press.

Latinobarómetro. 2018. "Informe 2018." Retrieved April 14, 2020, from www.latinobarometro.org/latdocs/INFORME_2018_LATINOBAROMETRO .pdf

Levitsky, Steven. 2003. *Transforming Labor-Based Parties in Latin America. Argentine Peronism in Comparative Perspective.* New York: Cambridge University Press.

Levitsky, Steven and Kenneth M. Roberts (eds.). 2011. *The Resurgence of the Latin American Left.* Baltimore: Johns Hopkins University Press.

Litcherman, Paul and Nina Eliasoph. 2015. "Civic Action." *American Journal of Sociology.* 120(3): 798–863.

Lo Vuolo, Ruben, Alberto Barbeito, Laura Pautassi, and Corina Rodriguez. 2004. *La pobreza … de la política contra la pobreza.* Buenos Aires: Miño y Dávila.

Lobato, Mirta Zaida and Juan Suriano. 2003. *La protesta social en la Argentina.* Buenos Aires: Fondo de Cultura Económica.

Lofland, John and Rodney Stark. 1965. "Becoming a World-Saver: A Theory of Conversion to a Deviant Perspective." *American Sociological Review* 30(6): 862–874.

Lomnitz, Larissa. 1975. *Cómo Sobreviven los Marginados.* Ciudad de México: Siglo XXI.

Lozano, Claudio. 2002. "Catástrofe Social en Argentina" CTA. Retrieved July 7, 2016, from www.bibliotecacta.org.ar/bases/pdf/IDE00384.pdf

Maneiro, María. 2012. *De Encuentros y Desencuentros. Estado, Gobierno, y Movimientos de Trabajadores Desocupados.* Buenos Aires: Biblos.

Manzano, Virginia. 2013. *La Política en Movimiento. Movilizaciones Colectivas y Políticas Estatales en la Vida del Gran Buenos Aires.* Buenos Aires: Prohistoria.

Massetti, Astor. 2004. *Piqueteros. Protesta Social e Identidad Colectiva.* Buenos Aires: Editorial de las Ciencias.

Massetti, Astor. 2006. "'Piqueteros eran los de antes': Sobre las transformaciones en la Protesta Piquetera." *Labvoratorio. Estudios sobre Cambio Estructural y Desigualdad Social* 8(19): 29–36.

Massetti, Astor. 2009. "¿A dónde van los Piqueteros K?" Pp. 153–180 in *Los Movimientos Sociales Dicen*, edited by Marcelo Gómez and Astor Massetti, Buenos Aires: Nueva Trilce.

Mazzeo, Miguel. 2004. *Piqueteros: Notas para una Tipología.* Buenos Aires: Fundación de Investigaciones Sociales y Políticas.

McAdam, Doug. 1982. *Political Process and the Development of Black Insurgency.* Chicago: University of Chicago Press.

McAdam, Doug. 1988. *Freedom Summer.* Oxford: Oxford University Press.

McAdam, Doug and Hillary Boudet. 2012. *Putting Social Movements in their Place.* New York: Cambridge University Press.

Mead, George Herbert. 1934. *Mind, Self, and Society.* Chicago: University of Chicago Press.

Meekosha, Helen. 2006. "What the Hell are You? An Intercategorical Analysis of Race, Ethnicity, Gender and Disability in the Australian Body Politic." *Scandinavian Journal of Disability Research* 8(2–3): 161–176.

Melucci, Alberto. 1989. *Nomads of the Present: Social Movements and Individual Needs in Contemporary Society*. Philadelphia: Temple University Press.

Merklen, Denis. 2005. *Pobres ciudadanos: las clases populares en la era democrática (Argentina, 1983–2003)*. Buenos Aires: Editorial Gorla.

Mische, Ann. 2008. *Partisan Publics: Communication and Contention across Brazilian Youth Activist Networks*. Princeton: Princeton University Press.

MTEYSS (Ministerio de Trabajo, Empleo y Seguridad Social). 2010. "Trabajo y Empleo en el Bicentenario." Retrieved September 24, 2015, from www .trabajo.gov.ar/left/estadisticas/bicentenario/Texto_Publicacion_TRABAJO_ Y_EMPLEO_EN_EL_BICENTENARIO.pdf

MTEYSS (Ministerio de Trabajo, Empleo y Seguridad Social). 2013. "Trabajo no registrado: Avances y Desafíos para una Argentina inclusiva." Retrieved April 14, 2020, from www.cta.org.ar/IMG/pdf/trabajo_no_registrado.pdf

MTEYSS (Ministerio de Trabajo, Empleo y Seguridad Social). 2017. "Jóvenes y Empleo." Retrieved April 15, 2020, from www.trabajo.gov.ar/downloads/es tadisticas/genero/Jovenes_y_trabajo_2017.pdf

Munson, Ziad. 2008. *The Making of Pro-Life Activists: How Social Mobilization Works*. Chicago: University of Chicago Press.

Neffa, Julio Cesar, Maria Laura Oliveri and Juliana Persia. 2010. "Transformaciones del mercado de trabajo en Argentina: 1974–2009." *Revista Atlántida* 2: 19–48.

Nepstad, Sharon. 2004. "Persistant Resistance: Commitment and Community in the Plowshares Movement." *Social Problems* 51(1):43–60.

Newman, Katherine. 1999. *No Shame in My Game: The Working Poor in the Inner City*. New York: Vintage.

Nueva Mayoría. 2008. "Los riesgos del contrapiquete." Retrieved February 15, 2016, from www.nuevamayoria.com/index.php?option= com_content&task=view&id=414&Itemid=1

Nueva Mayoría. 2009. "Con 5608 cortes de rutas y vías públicas, el 2008 registró la mayor cantidad de cortes desde 1997." Retrieved February 09, 2016, from www .nuevamayoria.com/index.php?option=com_content&task=view&id=1192& Itemid=30

Nueva Mayoría. 2016. "Los Cortes de Rutas y Vías Públicas (1997–2016)." Retrieved November 04, 2016, from www.nuevamayoria.com/index.php? option=com_content&task=view&id=5037&Itemid=30

OAS (Organization of American States). 2017. "IACHR Finds Failure to Comply with Precautionary Measures for Milagro Sala in Argentina and Sends Request to Inter-American Court." Press Release, November 3, 2017.

OIT (Organización Internacional del Trabajo). 2013. *Trabajo Decente y Juventud en América Latina*. Lima: OIT, Oficina Regional para América Latina y el Caribe.

Olson, Mancur. 1965. *The Logic of Collective Action*. Cambridge: Harvard University Press.

ODSA (Observatorio de la Deuda Social Argentina). 2011. *El problema de la inseguridad en la Argentina*. Buenos Aires: UCA.

Oslender, Ulrich. 2016. *The Geographies of Social Movements: Afro-Colombian Mobilization and the Aquatic Space*. Durham: Duke University Press.

Oviedo, Luis. 2004. *Una Historia del Movimiento Piquetero: De las primeras coordinadoras al Argentinazo.* Buenos Aires: Ediciones Rumbos.

Owens, Lynn. 2009. *Cracking Under Pressure. Narrating the Decline of the Amsterdam Squatters' Movement.* University Park: The Pennsylvania State University Press.

Pacheco, Mariano. 2010. *De Cutral-Co a Puente Pueyrredón. Una genealogía de los Movimientos de Trabajadores Desocupados.* Buenos Aires: Editorial El Colectivo.

Park, Yun-Joo and Patricia Richards. 2007. "Negotiating Neoliberal Multiculturalism: Mapuche Workers in the Chilean State." *Social Forces* 85 (3): 1319–1339.

Partenio, Florencia. 2008. "Género y participación política: Los desafíos de la organización de las mujeres dentro de los movimientos piqueteros en Argentina." *CLACSO.* Retrieved December 28, 2019, from http://bibliotecavir tual.clacso.org.ar/ar/libros/becas/2008/deuda/partenio.pdf.

Passy, Florence and Marco Giugni. 2000. "Life Spheres, Networks and Sustained Participation in Social Movements: A Phenomenological Approach to Political Commitment." *Sociological Forum* 15(1): 117–144.

Perelmiter, Luisina. 2012. "Fronteras inestables y eficaces. El ingreso de organizaciones de desocupados a la burocracia asistencial del Estado. Argentina (2003–2008)." *Estudios Sociológicos* 30(89): 431–458.

Pereyra, Sebastián. 2008. *¿La lucha es una sola?: la movilización social entre la democratización y el neoliberalismo.* Buenos Aires: UNGS y Biblioteca Nacional.

Pereyra, Sebastián, Germán Pérez and Federico Schuster (eds.). 2008. *La huella piquetera: avatares de las organizaciones de desocupados después de 2001.* La Plata: Ediciones Al Margen.

Pérez, Marcos. 2018. "Institutional Strengthening in a Receding Movement: The Trajectory of Piquetero Organizations between 2003 and 2015." *Latin American Research Review* 53(2): 287–302.

Piketty, Thomas. 2014. *Capital in the Twenty-First Century.* Cambridge: Harvard University Press.

Poletta, Francesca and James Jasper. 2001. "Collective Identity and Social Movements." *Annual Review of Sociology* 27: 283–305.

Pozzi, Pablo and Fabio Nigra. 2015. "Argentina a Decade after the Collapse: The Causes of the Crisis and Structural Changes." *Latin American Perspectives* 42: 3–10.

Prevost, Gary, Carlos Oliva Campos, and Harry Vanden (eds.). 2012. *Social Movements and Leftist Governments in Latin America: Confrontation or Co-optation?* New York: Zed Books.

Quirós, Julieta. 2006. *Cruzando la Sarmiento: Una etnografía sobre piqueteros en la trama social del sur del Gran Buenos Aires.* Buenos Aires: IDES.

Quirós, Julieta. 2011. *El Porqué de los Que Van. Peronistas y Piqueteros en el Gran Buenos Aires. (Una Antropología de la Política Vivida).* Buenos Aires: Antropofagia.

Ramos, Marcelo (ed.). 2009. *Jujuy bajo el signo neoliberal. Política, sociedad y cultura en la década del noventa.* San Salvador de Jujuy: EdiUNJu.

Ramos Ávila, Isabel. 2003. "Cultura, feminismo y representación política en las prácticas de organización de las piqueteras argentinas." *INTI* 57/58: 51–79.

Roberts, Bryan and Alejandro Portes. 2006. "Coping With the Free Market City." *Latin American Research Review* 41: 57–83.

Roberts, Kenneth. 2008. "The Mobilization of Opposition to Economic Liberalization." *Annual Review of Political Science* 11: 327–349.

Robnett, Belinda. 1997. *How Long? How Long?*. New York, NY: Oxford University Press.

Romei, Valentina. 2018. "Italy's Election: Charts Show How Economic Woes Fueled Five Star." *The Financial Times*, July 03, 2018, https://www.ft.com/content/175d55b8-20a0-11e8-a895-1ba1f72c2c11.

Rossi, Federico. 2015. "The Second Wave of Incorporation in Latin America: A Conceptualization of the Quest for Inclusion Applied to Argentina." *Latin American Politics and Society* 57(1): 1–28.

Rossi, Federico. 2017. *The Poor's Struggle for Political Incorporation. The Piquetero Movement in Argentina*. New York: Cambridge University Press.

Rubio, María Berenice and Agustín Salvia. 2018. "Los jóvenes en el mercado laboral argentino bajo regímenes macroeconómicos diferentes: neoliberalismo y neodesarrollismo (1992–2014)." *Revista Colombiana de Ciencias Sociales 9* (1): 176–209.

Rupp, Leila and Verta Taylor. 1987. *Survival in the Doldrums: The American Women's Rights Movement, 1945 to the 1960s*. New York: Oxford University Press.

Salvia Agustín, Santiago Poy y Julieta Vera. 2015. "La política social y sus efectos sobre la pobreza y la desigualdad durante distintos regímenes socioeconómicos en la Argentina (1992–2012)." *Seminario Internacional: Temas de la política social en Argentina, México y Uruguay*. México, DF: El Colegio de México.

Savoia, Claudia, Pablo Calvo and Alberto Amato. 2004. "Jaque a los piqueteros. El desafío de la convivencia social." *Clarín*, 08–08–2004. Retrieved November 2, 2011, from http://edant.clarin.com/suplementos/zona/2004/08/0 8/z-03015.htm

Schneider Mansilla, Iván and Ramiro Conti. 2003. *Piqueteros: una mirada histórica*. Buenos Aires: Astralib.

Schuman, Howard and Michael Johnson. 1976. "Attitudes and Behaviors." *Annual Review of Sociology* 2: 161–207.

Schuster, Federico, Germán Pérez, Sebastián Pereyra, Melchor Armesto, Martín Armelino, Analía García, Ana Natalucci, Melina Vázquez, and Patricia Zipcioglu. 2006. "Transformaciones de la protesta social en Argentina (1989–2003)." Documento de Trabajo 48; Instituto de Investigaciones Gino Germani, University of Buenos Aires.

Shapira, Harel. 2013. *Waiting for Jose. The Minutemen's Pursuit of America*. Princeton: Princeton University Press.

Sherman, Jennifer. 2009. *Those Who Work, Those Who Don't: Poverty, Morality and Family in Rural America*. Minneapolis: University of Minnesota Press.

SIEMPRO (Sistema de Información, Evaluación y Monitoreo de Programas Sociales). 2018. "Boletín de Trabajo." May 1 2018.

Silva, Eduardo. 2009. *Challenging Neoliberalism in Latin America.* New York: Cambridge University Press.

Silva, Eduardo (ed.). 2013. *Transnational Activism and National Movements in Latin America.* New York: Routledge.

Silva, Eduardo and Federico Rossi (eds.). 2018. *Reshaping the Political Arena in Latin America: From Resisting Neoliberalism to the Second Incorporation.* Pittsburgh: University of Pittsburgh Press.

Skocpol, Theda and Vanessa Williamson. 2012. *The Tea Party and the Remaking of Republican Conservatism.* New York: Oxford University Press.

Snow, David and Cynthia Phillips. 1980. "The Lofland-Stark Conversion Model: A Critical Reassessment." *Social Problems* 27(4): 430–447.

Snow, David, Daniel Cress, Liam Downey, and Andrew Jones. 1998. "Disrupting the 'Quotidian': Reconceptualizing the Relationship between Breakdown and the Emergence of Collective Action." *Mobilization* 3(1): 1–22.

Staggenborg, Suzanne. 1998. "Social Movement Communities and Cycles of Protest: The Emergence and Maintenance of a Local Women's Movement." *Social Problems* 45(2): 180–204.

Stahler-Sholk, Richard, Harry E. Vanden, and Glen David Kuecker (eds.). 2008. *Latin American Social Movements in the Twenty-First Century. Resistance, Power and Democracy.* Lanham: Rowman and Littlefield.

Summers-Effler, Erika. 2010. *Laughing Saints and Righteous Heroes: Emotional Rhythms in Social Movement Groups.* Chicago: University of Chicago Press

Sutton, Barbara. 2008. "Contesting Racism: Democratic Citizenship, Human Rights, and Antiracist Politics in Argentina." *Latin American Perspectives* 35 (6): 106–121.

Svampa, Maristella. 2005. *La sociedad excluyente: La Argentina bajo el signo del neoliberalismo.* Buenos Aires: Taurus.

Svampa, Maristella. 2008. *Cambio de época: movimientos sociales y poder político.* Buenos Aires: Siglo XXI

Svampa, Maristella and Sebastián Pereyra. 2003. *Entre la Ruta y el Barrio: la experiencia de las organizaciones piqueteras.* Buenos Aires: Biblios.

Swidler, Ann. 2001. *Talk of Love. How Culture Matters.* Chicago: University of Chicago Press.

Tavory, Iddo. 2016. *Summoned. Identification and Religious Life in a Jewish Neighborhood.* Chicago: University of Chicago Press.

Taylor, Verta and Nancy Whittier. 1992. "Collective Identity in Social Movement Communities: Lesbian Feminist Mobilization." Pp. 104–129 in *Frontiers in Social Movement Theory*, edited by A. Morris and C. Mueller. New Haven: Yale University Press.

Taylor, Verta, Katrina Kimport, Nella Van Dyke, and Ellen Ann Andersen. 2009. "Culture and Mobilization: Tactical Repertoires, Same-Sex Weddings, and the Impact on Gay Activism." *American Sociological Review* 74(6): 865–890.

The Economist. 2014. "The Parable of Argentina. What Other Countries Can Learn from a Century of Decline." *The Economist*, February 15th–21st 2014 edition.

Thompson, Edward Palmer. 1971. "The Moral Economy of the English Crowd in the Eighteenth Century." *Past and Present* 50: 76–136.

Tillin, Louise. 2015. "Indian Elections 2014: Explaining the Landslide." *Contemporary South Asia* 23(2): 117–122.

Torres, Florencia. 2006. *Todavía Piqueteros: la CTD Aníbal Verón*. La Plata: UNLP.

UTDT (Universidad Torcuato Di Tella). 2011. "Índice de Confianza en el Gobierno (Febrero 2011)." Retrieved March 05, 2011, from www.utdt.edu/d ownload.php?fname=_129892560455381800.pdf

Vaishnav, Milan (ed.). 2019. "The BJP in Power: Indian Democracy and Religious Nationalism." Carnegie Endowment for International Peace. Retrieved April 16, 2020, from https://carnegieendowment.org/files/BJP_In_Power_final .pdf

Vaughan, Dianne. 2004. "Theorizing Disaster. Analogy, Historical Ethnography and the Challenger Disaster." *Ethnography* 5(3): 315–347.

Vaughan, Dianne. 2014. "Analogy, Cases, and Comparative Social Organization." Pp. 61–84 in *Theorizing in Social Science: The Context of Discovery*, edited by R. Swedberg, Stanford: Stanford University Press.

Veiga, Gustavo. 1998. *Donde manda la patota: barrabravas, poder y política*. Buenos Aires: Agora.

Viterna, Jocelyn. 2013. *Women in War. The Micro-Processes of Mobilization in El Salvador*. New York: Oxford University Press.

Wacquant, Loïc. 1992. "Toward a Social Praxeology: The Structure and Logic of Bourdieu's Sociology." Pp. 1–59 in *An Invitation to Reflexive Sociology*, edited by Pierre Bourdieu and Loïc Wacquant, Chicago: University of Chicago Press.

Wacquant, Loïc. 2004. *Body & Soul. Notebooks of an Apprentice Boxer*. New York: Oxford University Press.

Wainfeld, Mario. 2019. *Estallidos Argentinos. Cuando se desbarata el vago orden en que vivimos*. Buenos Aires: Siglo XXI.

Walder, Andrew. 2009. "Political Sociology and Social Movements." *Annual Review of Sociology* 35: 393–412.

Weiss, Robert. 1994. *Learning From Strangers: The Art and Method of Qualitative Interview Studies*. New York: Free Press.

White, Robert. 2010. "Structural Identity Theory and the Post-Recruitment of Irish Republicans: Persistence, Disengagement, Splits, and Dissidents in Social Movement Organizations." *Social Problems* 57(3): 341–370.

Wilkis, Ariel. 2018. *The Moral Power of Money. Morality and Economy in the Life of the Poor*. Stanford: Stanford University Press.

Willis, Paul. 1977. *Learning to Labor: How Working Class Kids Get Working Class Jobs*. New York: Columbia University Press.

Wilson, William. 1996. *When Work Disappears. The World of the New Urban Poor*. New York: Knopf,

Winchester, Daniel. 2008. "Embodying the Faith: Religious Practice and the Making of a Muslim Moral Habitus." *Social Problems* 86(4): 1753–1780.

Wolff, Jonas. 2007. "(De-)mobilizing the Marginalized: A Comparison of the Argentine Piqueteros and Ecuador's Indigenous Movement." *Journal of Latin American Studies* 39: 1–29.

Wolford, Wendy. 2010. *This Land is Ours Now. Social Mobilization and the Meanings of Land in Brazil*. Durham: Duke University Press.

Wood, Elisabeth. 2003. *Insurgent Collective Action and Civil War in El Salvador.* Cambridge: Cambridge University Press.

Young, Gerardo. 2008. *Negro contra Blanco. Luis D'Elía y el Recurso del Odio.* Buenos Aires: Planeta.

Zelizer, Viviana. 1994. *The Social Meaning of Money. Pin Money, Paychecks, Poor Relief, and Other Currencies.* New York: Basic Books.

Index

Political parties. *See also* Peronism
  Connections with piquetero
    organizations, 49, 51, 52, 56, 67, 127,
    173, 174
  In the experience of respondents, 12, 84,
    164, 165–166, 171
Poverty, 33, 38–45, 60
Practices, appeal of, 6, 7–10, 12, 16–17,
  19–21, 53, 70, 182, 185, 201
Predictability, 5, 9, 16, 75, 86, 97, 117, 125,
  133, 187
Problem-solving networks, 68, 138–139
Proceso de Reorganizacion Nacional
  (*Proceso*). *See* Dictatorship
  (1976–1983)
Productive projects, 10, 54, 62, 66, 89, 99,
  116, 122, 140, 172, 173
Province. *See* Government; state level

Race, 122, 210–211
Reincorporation struggles, 16, 68–69, 192
Resistance to quitting, 12, 163, 181–183,
  210
Respectability, 5, 14–15, 97
  Consumption and, 118–119, 185–188
  Moral boundaries and, 8–9, 50, 75, 93,
    96–97, 107–108, 118–119, 124–125,
    140–141, 149, 154–157, 187
  Work and, 9, 29, 75, 91, 117–118, 125,
    170
Retirees, 2, 16, 175, 178
Roadblocks. *See* Piquetero organizations;
  repertoire of protest
Routines
  Development of, 5, 17, 108, 115–119,
    122–123
  Gender and. *See* Gender
  Interaction with personal backgrounds,
    7–8, 9, 163, 182, 185, 189–190, 197
  Protection of, 5, 17, 129–132, 135–141,
    157–159
  Reconstruction of, 5, 17, 73–75, 83–86,
    94–98
Ruta 3 (Greater Buenos Aires location), 58

Security teams, 74, 150–157, 170, 177, 181
Self-defense. *See* Security teams
Small businesses, 42, 142, 143, 166, 176,
  178
Soccer
  As cultural repertoire, 51, 211

As pastime, 30, 44, 45, 113, 130, 150
  Gangs and, 83–84, 153
Social movement theory
  Activist trajectories and, 18–19, 70, 158,
    182–183, 189
  Biographical factors and, 18, 182–183
  Emphasis on early participation in, 6, 19,
    189
  Emphasis on extraordinary events in,
    188, 190–191, 201
  Emphasis on ideological processes in, 6,
    19–20, 189
  Relation between beliefs and actions in, 6,
    18, 19–21, 189
Social policy, 62–64
Sociedades de Fomento (neighborhood
  associations). *See* Neighborhood
  associations
Soup kitchens. *See* Milk cups
Space
  Public, 17, 37, 43–44, 57, 133–135, 141,
    See also Esquina (street corner)
  Strategic use by piquetero organizations,
    57, 68
Sports. *See also* Soccer
  In the experience of respondents, 118, 156
Stigmatization, 36, 73, 84, 92, 114, 149
Survival strategies, 40, 58, 73, 90, 113, 159,
  168–169, 170, 175–176

Thick description, 25
Trabajo genuino (Genuine jobs). *See*
  Genuine jobs
Tradition, progressive mobilization and,
  6–7, 22, 191–192, *See also* culture
Trust, interpersonal, 32, 37, 46, 125,
  133–134, 157–159

Unemployment
  Causes of, 3–4, 10, 31, 33, 39, 57, 58, 65,
    109
  Community effects of, 15, 37–38, 43–47,
    129, 133–135, 166, 184
  Individual effects of, 9, 35–37, 39–43, 72,
    75–79, 80–81, 112–114
  Youth, 40, 109–114
Unions, 31, 33, 76, 134
  Connections with piquetero organizations,
    49, 51, 52, 56, 57, 63, 67
  In the experience of respondents, 76–77,
    79

Books in the Series *(continued from p. iii)*

Milton Keynes UK
Ingram Content Group UK Ltd.
UKHW011520060823
426405UK00015B/657